Academic Freedom and the *Telos*
of the Catholic University

ACADEMIC FREEDOM AND THE *TELOS* OF THE CATHOLIC UNIVERSITY

KENNETH GARCIA

ACADEMIC FREEDOM AND THE *TELOS* OF THE CATHOLIC UNIVERSITY

First published in 2012 by
PALGRAVE MACMILLAN®
in the United States—a division of St. Martin's Press LLC,
175 Fifth Avenue, New York, NY 10010.

Where this book is distributed in the UK, Europe and the rest of the world,
this is by Palgrave Macmillan, a division of Macmillan Publishers Limited,
registered in England, company number 785998, of Houndmills,
Basingstoke, Hampshire RG21 6XS.

Palgrave Macmillan is the global academic imprint of the above companies
and has companies and representatives throughout the world.

Palgrave® and Macmillan® are registered trademarks in the United States,
the United Kingdom, Europe and other countries.

ISBN: 978–1–137–03191–4

Library of Congress Cataloging-in-Publication Data

Garcia, Kenneth N.
    Academic freedom and the telos of the Catholic university /
Kenneth Garcia.
        p. cm.
    ISBN 978–1–137–03191–4 (hardback)
        1. Academic freedom. 2. Catholic universities and colleges.
    3. Scholars—Religious life. I. Title.

LC72.G35 2012
378.1'213—dc23   2012011142

A catalogue record of the book is available from the British Library.

Design by Newgen Imaging Systems (P) Ltd., Chennai, India.

First edition: September 2012

10 9 8 7 6 5 4 3 2 1

Printed in the United States of America.

To my wife Elizabeth, and my children Meghan, Katie, Gabriel, Mary, and Michael, for their patience and support over the years.

Contents

Preface

Following the Second Vatican Council (1961–1965), Catholic colleges and universities went through extensive academic and administrative changes that provoked heated debates over the nature and mission of the Catholic university. The debates covered numerous questions. What is the purpose of Catholic higher education and how does it differ from secular higher education? What is the relation of Catholic theology to modern thought and culture? How should the Catholic university relate to the Church's Magisterium (is it autonomous or beholden to the local bishop)? Are theologians free to dissent from Magisterial teachings? Should speakers hostile to Catholic teachings be given a forum to speak at Catholic universities? And a question central to this book, should academic freedom as understood in the modern American university prevail also in Catholic universities? Many of these questions are still unsettled.

This book presents a theologically grounded understanding of academic freedom that builds on, completes, and *transforms* the prevailing secular understanding. Academic freedom in the secular university, while rightly protecting scholars from external interference by ecclesiastical and political authorities, is constricting in practice because it tends to prohibit most scholars from exploring the relationship between the finite world and the infinite, or God. This constricted understanding contrasts starkly with the ideal of academic freedom at the time of its birth in early nineteenth-century Germany, where it meant *both* the freedom of the scholar to pursue studies unencumbered by external interference, *and* the freedom to pursue knowledge beyond the boundaries of specific academic disciplines to an ultimate horizon. Even more, it conflicts with the traditional Christian understanding of the mind's natural desire for knowledge of God, a desire that cannot come to rest in knowledge of finite things in themselves. The mind must continually move forward to ever-greater knowledge of both the finite world and the divine reality that generates, founds, and completes finite understanding.

Unfortunately, the concept of academic freedom became restricted in the early twentieth century, at least in the American context. Since the Second Vatican Council, most Catholic colleges and universities have rightly adopted the principle of academic freedom. Ironically, though, the version they adopted was a secular one, with the result that it has become difficult to relate theological knowledge to knowledge in other disciplines, in spite of earnest efforts by Catholic university educators to do so. Whenever discussions arise about the need to integrate theological insight into the framework of other academic disciplines, they inevitably become mired in fruitless debates between the *autonomy* of the scholar, on the one hand, and the threat of *heteronomous* church interference in academic life, on the other, as if these were the only alternatives. As a result, theology and other academic disciplines remain isolated from one another, inhabiting separate disciplinary islands. Theology, rather than being an integral part of all knowing and learning, resides at the margins of university life.

I propose a *theonomous* alternative to these fruitless debates. This theonomous alternative can be stated as follows: there is at the heart of all inquiry, whether the inquirer is explicitly aware of it or not, a dynamism (an intellectual and spiritual *eros,* in the words of many church fathers) whose source and goal is the divine. To claim that scholars should remain within their specialized domains, in the realm of the finite, is to make a philosophical and epistemological claim about the human mind. I challenge that claim from a Christian perspective. There is an inner teleology driving us toward ever-greater understanding, toward completeness of understanding within an ultimate horizon. Although scholars in non-theological academic disciplines cannot discover divine reality through their methods of inquiry, their inquiries, if not truncated, lead up to the limits of scientific and humanistic knowledge and to larger questions about purpose, meaning, and ultimately, God. These inquiries lead to the edge of disciplinary islands, to the point where the infinite sea of the divine beckons as a horizon that is distant yet luminous and alluring. The fostering of the mind's movement toward that horizon is the true *telos* of the Catholic university. Not all scholars must pursue the trajectory toward ultimate truth, but all must be *free* to do so, and that is the essence of a theologically grounded understanding of academic freedom. Moreover, in the Catholic university there must be scholars in all disciplines who can make connections between disciplinary knowledge and religious truth, and bring insights from the Catholic tradition to bear on some of the courses they teach. It is time, therefore, for Catholic colleges and universities to adopt a properly theological foundation for academic freedom and to incorporate that understanding into their mission statements and, more importantly, into their institutional policies and bylaws.

This foundation advances the mission of the Catholic university by ensuring that faculty and students may progress toward intellectual and spiritual wholeness.

This book is primarily theological, yet I draw on historical perspectives from the broader Catholic liberal arts tradition—ancient, medieval, and modern. I then review the history of how academic freedom developed, first in the nineteenth-century German university, then in the modern American university. The book is not a practical, "how to" book, even though I do suggest, in the final chapter, some practical implications that flow from its theological foundation, and then offer some concrete steps colleges and universities can take to strengthen their Catholic character. These steps are suggestive, not prescriptive, and I invite scholars in the disciplinary trenches and administrative units to ponder how the implications of a theological understanding of academic freedom can best transform the disciplinary cultures and curricula in their own institutions.

There are several audiences for this book. Primary among them are scholars and administrators in Catholic colleges and universities, as well as bishops and clergy who are concerned with strengthening the Catholic character of these institutions. For more than four decades now they have argued among themselves over how to maintain the Catholic ethos of their institutions while still upholding academic freedom and fostering openness to modern, pluralistic thought. The book will also be of interest to educators in other Christian colleges who face the same challenges as those in Catholic universities. Finally, any scholar—religious or secular—wishing to champion the integrity of academic freedom *rightly understood*, will find the book's thesis stimulating, even if controversial.

My sincere hope is that this book will advance the conversation about Catholic higher education beyond customary liberal-conservative disputes and lead to a more holistic understanding of academic inquiry. I do not argue for either liberal or conservative ideological positions. Instead, I offer an alternative that is grounded in the best features of the entire Catholic tradition. I have endeavored to base my arguments on historical developments, to draw on thinkers throughout Christian history (Catholic and non-Catholic), and to offer a solution to the dilemmas facing Catholic higher education today.

This book came about as a result of a long and often desultory intellectual and spiritual journey. Unschooled in things religious while young, I underwent a transformative religious conversion as a young man, one which led me to experience the interconnectedness of all things and their grounding in an all-encompassing spiritual reality. This drew me, eventually, into the Catholic Church and later, into Catholic universities where I hoped to deepen that religious experience. Surely, I reasoned, study in the Catholic university would entail a search for wisdom that was at once spiritual and intellectual. I would gain a grounding in the Great Tradition of philosophers (Christian and non-Christian), mystics, saints, and theologians who had pursued academic life as a quest for Wisdom. I had read Jean LeClerq's *The Love of Learning and the Desire for God*, which describes how medieval monastics engaged both Greco-Roman classics and Christian literature within the context of a life of study, contemplation, and the search for wisdom. I naively hoped to experience a similar engagement, though updated with the study of modern sciences, social sciences, and humanistic learning. I was disappointed. Apart from having departments of theology or religious studies, and sponsoring regular liturgies, I discovered that the curricula in Catholic universities were not much different than those in their secular counterparts. Things spiritual inhabit a sphere severed from the academic and intellectual, including to some extent even theology departments, which have become isolated from the broader circle of sciences. I was puzzled: if the *telos* of Catholic university education is intellectual and spiritual wholeness, why are intellectual attainment and spiritual quest disconnected? Why must we bracket spiritual from intellectual *eros* while engaged in academic inquiry? And can anything be done to remedy this state of affairs? This book is my modest attempt to contribute to the ongoing conversation about the nature and mission of Catholic colleges and universities, and to offer a more holistic understanding of their finality.

Every scholar is indebted to numerous people without whom one's book could never be written. First and foremost, I am grateful for the patience and forbearance of my wife and children who endured many missed weekend outings and summer vacations during the years I labored over this book. I dedicate this book to them.

I am grateful to Larry Cunningham, Cyril O'Regan, Matt Ashley, Melanie Morey, Kent Emery, Mark Roche, and the late Fred Crosson, all of whom read and critiqued some or all the chapters and whose advice and insights were invaluable. Thanks also to Krista Duttenhaver who pointed me to the educational writings of the German idealists, which form the basis of chapter 3, "Berlin: the Prototype of the Modern University."

I have been blessed to work in a unique office at the University of Notre Dame—the Institute for Scholarship in the Liberal Arts (ISLA)—which has placed me in contact with scholars from numerous academic disciplines in the humanities, social sciences, and fine arts, and whose engaging scholarship has enhanced my own. Most importantly, I am grateful to the various directors of ISLA who over the years have allowed me the time and provided me the resources to carry out the research for this book. Special thanks go to Christopher Fox, Julia Douthwaite, Cindy Bergeman,

Julie Braungart-Rieker, Gretchen Reydams-Schils, Ruth Abbey, Agustin Fuentes, and Tom Merluzzi for their encouragement and support. Greg Sterling, Maura Ryan, and Dan Myers in the dean's office of the College of Arts and Letters generously approved summer research leaves so that I could begin and finish this manuscript. Thanks also to Liz Rulli and Heather Boyd in Notre Dame's Office of Research for funding portions of the research through the Kobayashi Research Travel Fund.

I am grateful to many archivists at Catholic colleges and universities for their generous assistance over the years: to Kevin Cawley of the University of Notre Dame; the late Nicholas Varga at Loyola College of Baltimore; J. Leon Hooper at the John Courtney Murray Archives at the Woodstock Theological Center; and to archivists at Fairfield University, Mount St. Mary's University, the College of Notre Dame in Baltimore, and the University of St. Thomas in St. Paul, whose names I have forgotten but whose helpfulness and generosity I remember well.

Portions of chapter 1 and chapter 7 first appeared as "Academic Freedom and the Service Theologians Must Render the Academy" in *Horizons: The Journal of the Catholic Theology Society* (Spring 2011), 75–103. I am grateful to Anthony Godzieba for permission to use that material here.

Without the support of John Cavadini, Joseph Wawrykow, and Don Pope-Davis, who helped facilitate my entrance into the theology doctoral program at the University of Notre Dame, the dissertation on which this book is based could not have been written. Thank you for your confidence in me. I am also grateful to Burke Gerstenschlager and Kaylan Connally at Palgrave MacMillan for their expert editorial assistance.

John D. Burzynski's photograph of the "Word of Life" mural on the front of Notre Dame's Hesburgh Library adorns the cover of this book. Burzynski's photograph beautifully captures the amber background light emanating from Christ and the scholars in a way other photographs of the mural do not. The mural, created by artist Millard Sheets, depicts Christ surrounded by many generations of great scholars, thinkers, and teachers, both Christian and non-Christian. Christ is the central figure toward whom they all move in procession; he is the great teacher, the "universal pedagogue." The inscription on a marker near the mural reads as follows:

> With [Christ] in spirit are gathered the saints, the scholars, the scribes, and the teachers stretching through time, who have dedicated themselves to the preservation of truth... and the preparation of men's minds to receive that truth. Their knowledge, their thoughts, their written word, which through the ages have illuminated and enriched the understanding of their own and succeeding generations, is the treasure house of knowledge housed within the walls of this [library].

Scholars in Catholic colleges and universities today are the heirs of these great scholars and thinkers. The faithful passing on of the great wisdom tradition we have received from them, and the vigorous engagement of that tradition with the thought of our own time, is the mission we hold in trust.

Chapter 1

The Current State of Catholic
Higher Education

Scholars and administrators in American Catholic colleges and universities have participated in long and serious reflections since the 1960s about the nature and mission of the Catholic university. What distinguishes it from other kinds of universities? Does the adjective "Catholic" mean simply adding something to secular academic discourse, or does it imply something about the way scholars should conduct inquiry and the kind of questions they bring to their subject matter? Is there a telos to the inquiries of the human mind—and therefore a telos to university education—that should inform the mission and curriculum of Catholic universities? Is there a theological basis for academic freedom, or must we rely on secular principles? What is the relation of Catholic spirituality and theology to nontheological academic disciplines? Can academic pursuits be truly competent and satisfactory without the undergirding of a spiritual dimension? These are the questions explored in this book.

Catholic authors across the centuries have acknowledged that scholarly effort and spiritual progress complement one another, and they have pursued both as interrelated endeavors. At the same time, the relationship between them has sometimes been tense. How do we do justice to one without doing a disservice to the other? A settled Catholic principle is the indissoluble unity between the knowledge of reason and the knowledge of faith.[1] Can faith and reason work together successfully? How should Christians relate their faith to the philosophical currents of the surrounding culture? Christians have oscillated between suspicion of secular or worldly knowledge, on the one hand, and an excessive accommodation to the spirit of the age, on the other. Between these, the prudent course has been to maintain a dialectical relationship between Catholic thought and the surrounding culture, between religious knowledge and knowledge gained through analytical reason, carefully discerning in non-Christian thought what is complementary and what is contradictory to Catholic teachings. In spite of the tensions that naturally arise in this process, the dominant rule in Catholic universities has been a mutually informing and challenging engagement. This encounter is not always a comfortable process—for either side—but it is undertaken in the certainty that all truth is one and that truth discovered through reason cannot, in the end, contradict religious truth.

Discussions about the relationship of spirituality and theology to non-theological academic disciplines are not undertaken without some anxiety. Many scholars fear it may lead to heteronomous church intervention in academic matters. Since the Second Vatican Council, Catholic college leaders have endeavored to prevent such intervention. In the 1967 "Land O'Lakes Statement," the presidents of Catholic universities worldwide declared that "the Catholic university must have a true autonomy and academic freedom in the face of authority of whatever kind, lay or clerical, external to the academic community itself."[2] The essential element of this statement is that the Catholic university, like any university, must be free of heteronomous church or state intervention. Scholars must have autonomy to pursue their subject matter to its conclusion, to publish the results of their investigations, and to freely debate the soundness of the conclusions. While this statement rightly rejects heteronomy, it implicitly assumes that autonomy—as understood by academics in the modern university—is the only alternative to heteronomous church control. I will challenge that assumption.

In the years before and after the "Land O'Lakes Statement," scholars at Catholic colleges and universities extensively discussed the nature and role of academic freedom and autonomy within the Catholic university.[3] None of these discussions, however, grounded academic freedom in Catholic theological principles and, specifically, in a theological anthropology that understands the human person as oriented to God. Nor did they base their views in a theological epistemology that seeks to understand the dynamism of the mind as a desire for knowledge of God—a desire that pervades all inquiry. I will attempt to do so in this book.

It is widely recognized that the religious and the academic are *not* well connected in the academy. For a variety of reasons, academic disciplines have become increasingly specialized, fragmented, and secularized over the past two centuries. Theology and philosophy, once integral components of all higher learning, have gradually been severed from other disciplines and have even split within themselves, while efforts to form broad, integrating structures of knowledge have steadily waned.[4] Even so, integrated learning remains the ideal in Catholic institutions, as it was for John Henry Newman over a century ago. Newman believed that all branches of knowledge form part of a whole and, taken together, "form one integral subject for contemplation," with each branch contributing a piece of the whole. Among these branches of knowledge, theology and philosophy should serve as integrative discourses.[5]

This book focuses on the telos of the Catholic university in the modern world, founded on a theological understanding of the telos of the human mind seldom considered by most modern Catholic educators. Theodore Hesburgh's essay "The Challenge and Promise of the Catholic University" articulates what may be the mainstream Catholic vision for a model Catholic university in the modern world. A central principle in Hesburgh's thought is that "a great Catholic university must begin by being a great university that is also Catholic." Hesburgh understands "a great university" in terms of the "modern world of the university" and of the way the modern university is understood and universally recognized.[6] The university may have its roots in the medieval church, but the modern university is an altogether different reality from its medieval ancestor. Only once this modern university is established can we add whatever adjective we like (American, Catholic, British) to it.[7] Hesburgh makes the common assumption that the university in the "modern sense" is characterized by academic freedom, open debate over disputed positions, and a desire to pursue truth wherever it may lead.

Some scholars question whether the modern university is really open to the free pursuit of truth, especially when that pursuit tends toward the religious. Disciplinary communities in the academy, notes Mark U. Edwards, have become largely secular and "set and enforce standards for scholarship and teaching" that tend to "exclude explicitly religious discourse from most scholarship and much teaching."[8] Douglas and Rhonda Jacobsen point out that secularism has become an ideology that is not neutral to religion and actively seeks its exclusion in public life and in the academy.[9] To the extent that individual academic disciplines within Catholic universities mirror the standards of the broader disciplinary communities dominated by secular ideologies, they also exclude religious discourse and are sometimes even hostile to it. David Schindler challenges the assumption that the modern research university is a place of free and neutral scholarship. The modern university, in its assumptions and structures, is not a neutral forum for analyzing, defending, or criticizing the variant and often conflicting lines of debate and inquiry. It has certain assumptions built into its structure that already disadvantage Catholic thought. The modern university as we know it, claims Schindler, is thoroughly secular and already excludes the religious dimension in education and inquiry.[10] The religious dimension may only be *added to* the basic operation of secular rational discourse.

Hesburgh affirms the view that philosophy and theology are needed to complete other studies and that unless theology engages all other disciplines at the highest intellectual level, we will end up with knowledge that detaches moral, intellectual, and spiritual dimensions.[11] Drawing on John Henry Newman, he writes that theology must be more than a peripheral concern in a Catholic university—that it "must be engaged on the highest level of intellectual inquiry so that it may be in living dialogue with all the other disciplines in the university."[12] This remains an ideal in most Catholic institutions, yet few would argue that this engagement occurs to a significant extent today. Most Catholic college and university administrators are aware that educators in Catholic colleges and universities are failing to foster dialogue between Catholic thought and nontheological disciplines. Unfortunately, most of those same administrators lack a clear sense of how to do so and what it is that would make a Catholic university—other than having a theology department—different from its secular counterparts.[13] The modern American research university is secular at its core and is structured—as Edwards, the Jacobsens, and Schindler have argued—to prohibit the very dialogue with theology and philosophy that many Catholic educational leaders advocate.[14]

Some claim that ideals of social justice and service to the poor are what make Catholic colleges unique among institutions of higher education, but as Melanie Morey and John Piderit point out, all universities, secular as well as Catholic, have a concern for instilling a sense of service and social concern in their students.[15] There is nothing uniquely Catholic about concern for social justice and service, even though the motivation for incorporating these ideals may be distinct. Though social justice and service are necessary aspects of being Catholic, they are not sufficient in themselves. Unfortunately, the mutual engagement of theology and other disciplines that many Catholic university leaders advocate rarely takes place nor has there been a coherent theory for how that can be done. In this regard, the goals articulated by Fr. Hesburgh and others, though partially realized, have yet to be fully accomplished. In this book, I hope to contribute to the furtherance of those goals.

Even adding a theological dimension, as Hesburgh advocates, is not acceptable to most scholars in today's academy. Most academics insist that scholars remain within the realm of the empirically knowable and the realm of purely (secular) rational discourse. Using the scientific paradigm that arose during the Enlightenment, which understands truth as that which is verifiable through empirical observation and measurement, the depth dimension of existence is excluded from study. To experience that depth dimension requires a contemplative, spiritual stance toward existence that is different from, though not contradictory to, the objectifying, analytical stance employed by scientific reason. To exclude such a contemplative stance from academic inquiry is to restrict the realm of what the human mind and spirit can experience.

Kant perhaps best articulated the Enlightenment conception of rational, scientific knowing in his *Critique of Pure Reason*.

> This domain [human understanding] is an island, enclosed by nature itself within unalterable limits. It is the land of truth—enchanting name!—surrounded by a wide and stormy ocean, the native home of illusion, where many a fog bank and many a swiftly melting iceberg give the deceptive appearance of farther shores, deluding the adventurous seafarer ever anew with empty hopes, and engaging him in enterprises which he can never abandon and yet is unable to carry to completion. Before we venture on this sea, to explore it in all directions and to obtain assurance whether there be any ground for such hopes, it will be well to begin by casting a glance upon the map of the land which we are about to leave, and to enquire, first, whether we cannot in any case be satisfied with what it contains—are not, indeed, under compulsion to be satisfied, inasmuch as there may be no other territory upon which we can settle.[16]

As for Kant, so for secular, rational thinking today: academic inquiry must remain on the island of the finite world and of secular, rational discourse. Venturing out is not a legitimate activity and is to be excluded from the academy. Kant's island can serve as a metaphor for modern academic disciplines. The human mind is limited to studying the phenomenal world, beyond which there is nothing knowable. Only what is available to the human reason can be considered true knowledge; religious knowledge is outside the scope of human reason and therefore not accessible.

Remarkably, some Catholic college leaders in the late twentieth century adopted a similar view: that the border between island and ocean ought to remain impermeable within academic inquiry itself, and spiritual life must be restricted to the margins of campus life—to the chapel, to campus ministry, or perhaps to centers or institutes separated from the ordinary academic life of the university. Michael J. Buckley, S. J., recounts how the late Timothy Healy, S. J., former president of Georgetown University, suggested that the life of the church and the life of the academy are extrinsic to one another. Healy wrote, "Education [is] principally a secular business, and the university a secular entity with a secular job to do," while conceding that "the Church can deeply influence how that secular job is done."[17] In other words, the church, representing the religious dimension, works on the university from the outside. Healy's extrinsicist position is no anomaly in the modern Catholic university;[18] indeed, some say it has become the norm, and no one seems quite sure whether or how the religious dimension ought to be integrated into the core of academic life itself.

In spite of such reticence and uncertainty, integrated learning remains the ideal, if not the reality, in many Catholic institutions, as it was for John Henry Newman. In an 1856 sermon preached at the Catholic University of Ireland, Newman said that the various human faculties (intellectual, moral, spiritual, and emotional) were, in the beginning, "blended together" by God and made to "conspire into one whole, and act in common toward one end." Human sinfulness sunders their integrity. The consequent separation of faculties within each individual has its counterpart in the external world, where each faculty is served by a separate institution. The university is the institution that serves the intellectual faculty. Newman would have his hearers recognize how detrimental this situation is for the health of our souls. Moreover, "what makes [this situation] worse is, that these various faculties and powers of mind have so long been separated from each other ... that it comes to be taken for granted that they cannot be united."[19] The reason the church creates Catholic universities, says Newman, is "to reunite things which were in the beginning joined together by God [i.e., the intellectual, spiritual, and moral], and have been put asunder by man."[20] He then gives us his ideal.

> I wish the intellect to range with the utmost freedom, and religion to enjoy an equal freedom; but what I am stipulating for is, that they should be found in one and the same place, and exemplified in the same persons. I want to destroy that diversity of centers, which puts everything into confusion by creating a contrariety of influences. I wish the same spots and the same individuals to be at once oracles of philosophy and shrines of devotion. It will not satisfy me, what satisfies so many, to have two independent systems, intellectual and religious, going at once side by side, by a sort of division of labour, and only accidentally brought together. It will not satisfy me, if religion is here, and science there, and young men converse with science all day, and lodge with religion in the evening. It is not touching the evil, to which these remarks have been directed, if young men eat and drink and sleep in one place, and think in another: I want the same roof to contain both the intellectual and moral discipline.[21]

Newman was not responding specifically to Kant but to the general philosophical currents of his day. Over a century later, the German theologian Karl Rahner, using Kant's island metaphor—and in explicit disagreement with Kant—maintained that everyone is called to explore beyond the island.

> In the ultimate depths of his being man knows nothing more surely than that his knowledge, that is, what is called knowledge in everyday parlance, is only a small island in a vast sea that has not been traveled. It is a floating

island, and it might be more familiar to us than the sea, but ultimately it is borne by the sea... Hence the existentiell question for the knower is this: Which does he love more, the small island of his so-called knowledge or the sea of infinite mystery? Is the little light with which he illuminates this island—we call it science and scholarship—to be an eternal light which will shine forever for him? That would surely be hell.[22]

Christopher Schiavone summarizes the difference between Kant and Rahner: "For Rahner, to be rational is to acknowledge that the limits of all those finite particulars found on the island, as well as of the island itself, are only known in relation to the unlimited depth and breadth of the sea."[23] Paul Tillich maintained that Kant confined modern thought to a "prison of finitude,"[24] to what Rahner might have called a "hellish island" where truth, goodness, and beauty are caged in a phenomenal world devoid of transcendence. The island metaphor is illuminating for our topic, and I will employ it regularly in this book when discussing disciplinary specialization and the intellectual secularization of the academic mind and curriculum in both Catholic and non-Catholic colleges. The metaphor has limitations, though, suggesting a boundary where the spiritual world of God begins and the "natural" world ends. This too, is inadequate. The light of God is not outside the island. It is the light that illuminates its very life; it is the light of the mind, as Augustine proclaimed,[25] that generates a desire to know the island in its full relation to what is ultimate. Switching metaphors, the divine is the ocean that surrounds and undergirds the island; it is also the source of the rain that falls on the island, of the springs that well up in it, and of the streams that flow from it. Ultimately, they all come from one source.

The current understanding of academic freedom (and its practice) is inadequate for the Catholic university. True academic freedom must be founded on the theological principle of the human being as made in the image of God, as oriented to God. The human mind possesses a dynamic desire for the divine that cannot rest until it knows and understands the subject of its study in relation to God. This dynamic orientation to and desire for God is a form of spirituality—a spirituality of the inquiring and wondering mind.[26] Hence, spirituality must be a foundational component of academic inquiry, not only in theology, but in all inquiry. Integrating spirituality into academic inquiry and basing academic freedom in the desire of the mind for God does not undermine the secular principle of academic freedom commonly understood in American society; rather, it builds on, completes, and *transforms* it.

As noted earlier, the attempt to couple intellectual and spiritual effort in the academy evokes anxiety in those who fear heteronomy. I propose an alternative to the fruitless dialectic between an absolute autonomy on the part of scholars, on the one hand, and a heteronomous control of academic inquiry by religious authorities, on the other. This alternative is a *theonomous* approach to academic inquiry. Theonomy, a term coined by Paul Tillich,[27] refers to a spiritual dynamism operating from within intellectual effort, grounding reason in its own spiritual depth.Theonomous reasoning does not undermine the autonomy of reason; rather, it refers to a process in which the Spirit immanent in everyone steadies, guides, and orients reason, not as an extrinsic power working through external authorities but as *the immanent, divine ground of reason* within each scholar. It is in this general sense that I use the term "spirituality" in this book.

Tillich, of course, views theonomy from a Protestant perspective: there is a direct, unmediated relationship between the individual and God. Catholics would view it as not only including direct relation to and awareness of God but also grounded in and mediated through tradition. Theonomous thinking within the Catholic tradition means more than the isolated individual in direct and personal relationship with God through his or her subjective awareness. It involves that awareness as a *prius* but then finds itself inextricably immersed within the framework of an ongoing tradition that informs one's subjective spiritual consciousness. Direct spiritual experience is inevitably mediated and formed by language, culture, and tradition. The presence of God—the Word as image at the center of our being—is, as it were, implicit and inchoate. Inculturation into a theological tradition forms an explicit awareness of that inner Word, and this affects the way Catholics view the world and approach their inquiry into it.

Some will say that the influence of a tradition obviates any possibility of independence of mind. But such a claim is belied by the many profound and independent minds throughout Christian history who developed tradition in new and fruitful ways, yet encountered opposition from ecclesiastical authorities.[28] Moreover, if postmodernism has taught us anything, it is that there is no consciousness that is not influenced by some tradition. Everyone is raised in a tradition—whether religious or secular— that helps form one's experience and serves as a background understanding of life, so much so that most people assume their background view is objective reality. If Catholic perspectives do not influence students in the Catholic university, some other philosophical perspective will.

Theonomy implies an integration of both theology and other academic disciplines with spirituality as a basic element of academic inquiry. Here I am referring to spirituality, not as external practices and rituals unconnected to intellectual life (as important as those are) but as a quest for truth guided by a spiritual dynamism, an *eros* toward God that illuminates the mind and prevents scholarship from resting on merely finite ends, even while including such finite ends as stations along the way.[29] It requires grounding academic freedom in a theological anthropology that understands humans as having a desire for knowledge of God because they are made in the image and likeness of God. This is the foundation for understanding the dynamism of inquiring into and knowing the nature and cause of all things in relation to God. This desire may be either implicit or explicit, but it is always present. There is an unthematic awareness of God present in the mind that propels the desire for ever fuller knowledge. God illuminates the mind right from the start, is the engine driving inquiry, and is the direction toward which inquiry ultimately moves. In the felicitous phrase of Michael Buckley, God is "the direction toward which wonder progresses."[30] And who will argue that academic inquiry does not have its origins in wonder?[31]

This idea of the mind's dynamic drive is not new; in fact, it is almost as ancient as the church itself. Catholic thinkers have always attempted to appropriate what was true and good in the thought of non-Christian sources and to adopt truth arrived at by natural reason. According to Justin Martyr (ca. 114–165 AD), truth can come from non-Christian sources because all humans participate in the Logos, or reason, of God. Seeds of this Logos (*logos spermatikos*) are spread throughout the universe and implanted in the minds of all human beings. As a result, everyone has access to this divine reason, or Word—even non-Christians.[32] For Origen (ca. 185–254 AD), each intellect was created in the image of God—as a participation in the Logos—and can therefore recover the "original state of contemplative likeness to God."[33] All education and culture (*paideia*) should be oriented to leading us on this ascent to and reunion with God. A dynamism in the movement from one academic discipline to another orients and guides us toward an ultimate horizon. The basis of this dynamism is love or, in Origen's term, *eros*.[34] Eros designates the longing and desire that impel us dynamically toward the object of our desire; we are not satisfied until we have achieved union with it.

Gregory of Nyssa (ca. 332–395 AD), like his predecessor Origen, emphasized the role of desire in the search for God. All rational creatures desire goodness, beauty, and wisdom, which can never be attained fully; hence, we never grow weary of searching for them. Whoever "pursues true virtue participates in nothing other than God, because He is Himself absolute virtue. Since, then, those who know what is good by nature desire participation in it, and since this good has no limit, the participant's desire itself necessarily has no stopping place but stretches out with the limitless."[35] This concept of limitless desire of the intellect and soul pervaded the writings of many of the church fathers and extended well into the thought of the high Middle Ages (see chapter 2).

The concept of the desire of the mind for God, once a commonplace for patristic and medieval thinkers, became suspect and all but rejected by scholastic thinkers in the early modern and modern periods. When acknowledged at all, it was presented as a mere velleity or "non-repugnance" for God rather than as an active, spiritual, and intellectual dynamism operating within the human mind. The concept was retrieved by authors in the twentieth century, and I will draw on it as the basis for formulating a Catholic foundation for academic freedom and autonomy.

When speaking of theonomous thinking, I am not referring to the science of theology as it is normally conceived and practiced today: as a separate science reflecting on Christian revelation. In the thought of Thomas Aquinas, theology, whose source is supernatural revelation, is a science set off from philosophy, whose source is natural reason. Theology as a science based on supernatural revelation is a form of knowing superadded to the kind of knowing that occurs through natural reason. In contrast, by "theonomous thinking," I mean an awareness of the divine as both the source and end of all knowledge.[36] It refers to the desire of the mind for God as it moves through all reality. In this sense, it is closely related to spirituality.

Thomas Aquinas had distinguished the natural from the supernatural and reason from revelation, but he also recognized the natural orientation of the mind to the divine. In numerous writings, he points out that the mind has a natural desire to know God, that we must pursue this desire until it is satisfied.[37] Moreover, God's light is present in all knowing. "All knowers," he writes, "know God implicitly in all that they know."[38] This is an insight founded in the theology of Augustine. God is the light of the mind that enables us to know the truth of any particular thing, says Augustine.[39] This guiding and illuminating presence of the divine in all intellectual activity is what I mean by *theonomous*. Theonomous thinking should be active in all inquiry. By this I do not mean that all scholars must integrate spirituality and theology into their studies; only that some, in every department, should (more on this in chapters 7 and 8).[40]

God's light is always present as a criterion and orientation to the mind. Joseph Pieper reminds us that the close link between intellectual attainment and spiritual wonder has always characterized the best thinking in the Catholic tradition.[41]Gerald McCool points out that "the activity of the human mind, ordered to truth by its very nature, [is] a participation in the light of truth communicated by the Word of God himself," and that Word is, as Clement said, the "Universal Pedagogue."[42] Such thinking is the ideal to which the Catholic university should aspire.

Most scholars stop short of incorporating theonomous thinking into scholarship within their disciplines. That is a loss to the academy. Can we regain such a theonomous approach when the norms of contemporary, mainstream academic inquiry systematically exclude it? I believe we can, but it will be no easy task. To do so, I propose to reappropriate the Christian concepts of divine illumination (from Augustine) and of the desire of the mind for God (from the church fathers and Thomas Aquinas) as foundations for articulating the intimate relation between spirituality, theology, and finite academic disciplines.[43] These concepts can also help us move toward an understanding of academic freedom that is more productive and comprehensive than assumptions currently prevalent in academe.

After the Second Vatican Council (1961–1965), Catholic universities made tremendous academic progress. Their academic quality improved dramatically—they cast off heteronomous control by the church and became places of robust academic inquiry. These are positive developments to be praised by all. Hesburgh's goal of integrating disciplines in a theological vision remains a key goal of Catholic universities. This goal, however, is yet unrealized and I will argue that there is a reason why this is so. As Edwards, Schindler, and the Jacobsens point out, the very structure of the modern American university prohibits that integration from taking place. Even in Catholic colleges and universities, we see the discipline of theology sitting alongside, and largely unconnected to, other academic disciplines that have become largely secularized. I contend, therefore, that academic freedom in the modern Catholic university requires a more sound theological foundation.

At present, serious discussions about the nature of the Catholic university and about the relation of spiritual life to academic inquiry are at an impasse, trapped in a fruitless dialectic between claims of autonomy and fears of heteronomy. How have we arrived at this impasse, and what can be done to move the discussions forward and foster both true academic freedom and a linkage among spirituality, theology, and other areas of academic inquiry? How are we to integrate academic disciplines into a broader philosophical and theological vision in an academic world dominated by presuppositions that would exclude such views as illusory, nonintellectual, and intrusive? How might we do so without repeating the mistakes of the past? I will attempt to show a way.

Chapter Summaries

I will challenge three major assumptions often taken for granted in Catholic higher education today. First, I challenge the assumption that we should base the modern Catholic university on the secular university in its current form. Second, I challenge the assumption that the term "modern" university implies an essentially secular research university to which religious knowledge may be added. Finally, I question the adequacy of the prevailing concepts of autonomy and academic freedom as developed in America during the twentieth century. In the Catholic milieu, we cannot rely solely on contemporary theories and educational realities when trying to assess the telos of the Catholic university. We must also draw on wisdom from the Catholic tradition—not as a trump card—but as a partner in conversation with contemporary thought and realities.

In chapter 2, "The Medieval Liberal Arts and the Journey of the Mind to God," I examine the ways in which three medieval thinkers—Augustine, Bonaventure, and Thomas Aquinas—conceptualized the relation between the spiritual life, theology, and academic studies. My goal is to analyze their theories of the liberal arts to see if we can gain insights into the purpose of higher learning that can be appropriated today. I will also examine their attitudes on how the scholar ought to approach studies. Even though they lived in different historical and cultural circumstances than our own, we find principles in their work that can help us think more fruitfully about the proper telos of the modern Catholic university. Appropriating the wisdom of the tradition does not mean reverting to curricular forms that existed in earlier periods; rather, it means appropriating timeless principles to use in contemporary settings. For example, Thomas Aquinas held that our intellectual drive cannot be satisfied by knowledge of things finite and must always go beyond the finite to knowledge of God. Nonetheless, he gave the disciplines plenty of "elbow room" to work. Augustine and Bonaventure believed the mind is made in the image of God, with a desire to know all things in relation to an ultimate horizon, or God. These remain valid principles today.

Having reappropriated principles from the tradition, we must acknowledge the validity of Hesburgh's insistence that we take the modern university as a norm in its own right. We must, however, carefully scrutinize what is meant by the "modern" university or the university "in the modern sense." In chapter 3, "Berlin: The Prototype of the Modern University," I explore the question of whether we should accept the modern, American, secular university as the norm and standard for Catholic universities and then try to graft a Catholic dimension onto it. My answer is no. I argue that we can find alternative principles in the creation of the University of Berlin, the first modern research university, founded in 1810. I focus particularly on the German idealist philosophers J. G. Fichte, Friedrich Schelling, Friedrich Schleiermacher, and G. W. F. Hegel. The German idealists were concerned about the fragmentation of knowledge, the severance of reason and faith, and the detachment of the finite from the infinite and attempted to reunite them within the university curriculum. Their goal was to create a comprehensive philosophical system that would encompass and orient all particular sciences within the totality of knowledge. The scholar was to grasp how the finite world was related to the infinite, or Absolute, integrating all the fragmented disciplines of the university into a unity. Scholars required the freedom to pursue the whole of knowledge, not merely some finite corner of it, and this was an essential aspect of academic freedom.

The German idealists were not without their flaws, and I critique those flaws. Their overarching philosophical systems tended to predetermine how the various other sciences should be approached and even what constituted valid findings in the sciences. Their commitment to academic freedom was not always firm. In spite of their flaws, however, there is much we can learn from them. They advocated the unity of knowledge. They believed that the Absolute, or God, is what is disclosed in all of nature, in human history, and the workings of the human mind. Specialization, they held, is necessary and fruitful as long as a unity of vision holds together the ever-diversifying array of particular knowledge. Philosophy, they believed, and for some theology as well, must be not just one discipline alongside others, but must play an architectonic role in the circle of sciences.

In chapter 4, "Academic Freedom and Religion in America," I trace how the concept of academic freedom developed in America. The German ideal of the unity of knowledge, and the ideal of placing specialized studies within a broader philosophical and theological context, did not long survive in America. The ideal of academic freedom took on uniquely American historical characteristics. The ideal was transformed and, I contend, seriously restricted, confining freedom of inquiry primarily to scholarly work within academic disciplines. This had several causes. First, conflicts between science and religion increased during the nineteenth century. To avoid conflict, scientists began limiting their research to natural phenomena. At first this did not imply a rejection of religious teachings, but merely a prescinding from consideration of religious and philosophical questions in favor of focusing on finite phenomena. This was perfectly legitimate. Methodological agnosticism and methodological atheism could be compatible with either theism or atheism. It was not long, however, before naturalistic methodologies, valid in themselves, became naturalistic philosophies, and many scientists began openly to deny the existence of the divine.

Second, there was increasing disciplinary specialization. Throughout most of the nineteenth century, scholars had the freedom to adopt scholarly methods from any field and to conduct research across disciplines as they wished. This freedom to roam began to change gradually in the late nineteenth century. Scholarly competence required restricting oneself to one's discipline, as Jon Roberts and James Turner have shown.[44] The unity of knowledge began to be divided into separate territories. Freedom to inquire on disciplinary islands without interference gradually came to imply prohibition against inquiry beyond them.

Third, Catholic scholastic thought contributed in its own way to the severance of scientific inquiry from theology. Some forms of scholasticism contained a dualism of orders: the order of nature and the order of the supernatural. In the cognitive realm, there was a correlative epistemological dualism: knowledge that has its source in the natural reason, on the one hand, and knowledge that has its source in supernatural revelation, on the other. The order of nature has its own laws, its own finality, and natural beings seek merely natural ends. The natural reason, in turn, has its own ends and scope that do not extend to the divine unless illuminated by supernatural grace. Catholics, therefore, no longer searched for the divine presence in the world; instead they searched for it outside the world in a separate realm or in a highly subjective and affective interior realm. This, too, contributed to secularism, to the concept of a natural world devoid of the divine.

Finally, Catholic thought in the late nineteenth and early twentieth centuries was largely antithetical to modern thought. Catholic intellectuals who engaged modern thought were sometimes censored, and modern culture was often condemned. Non-Catholic academics in America could not help but observe the attitudes and repressions in the Catholic intellectual world, so they instinctively rejected as heteronomous the religious dimension of academic life. As a consequence, they developed their methods of inquiry and principles of academic freedom largely without regard to, and sometimes in hostility to, religious ways of knowing.

In chapter 5, "The Pursuit of Intellectual and Spiritual Wholeness, 1920–1960," I examine developments in American Catholic higher education during the period when Catholic educators attempted to integrate knowledge into a coherent Christian worldview. Closely connected to this was a renewed emphasis on the spiritual dimension of all learning and an attempt to integrate spiritual and intellectual life. They often did so awkwardly, though, attempting to force all knowledge from the various disciplines into a procrustean bed of neoscholastic philosophy. What didn't fit that neoscholastic framework was to be excluded. The problem with these approaches was not the desire to integrate the religious with the academic, but the fact that they did not give the academic disciplines "elbow room," to use Newman's term. Some Catholic educators blurred the distinctions between their own disciplines and scholastic philosophy to such an extent that they confused them. They also blurred the distinction between education and catechism in their zeal to integrate all knowledge within a theological vision. They claimed to be basing their views on the thought of Thomas Aquinas, but Thomas allowed wide leeway to academic disciplines to explore reality according to their subject matter and particular methods. Unfortunately, many American Catholic educators were not well grounded in Thomas's own thought. Because of these shortcomings, and the poor academic quality of Catholic colleges and universities in general, many Catholic educators rebelled against the Catholic educational system following the Second Vatican Council.

In chapter 6, "The Consequence of Caesar's Gold," I focus on some of the dramatic changes—both positive and negative—in Catholic colleges and universities following the Second Vatican Council. On the positive side, the Council called on Catholics to engage modern thought and culture, and to collaborate with their non-Catholic peers for the betterment of society. Catholic colleges liberated themselves from heteronomous church control, improved their academic quality, and adopted principles of academic freedom.

There was also a negative side. Because Catholic educators did not have their own theological framework for understanding academic freedom— or better, didn't employ the principles they did have in the tradition—they adopted the dominant secular principles, often uncritically. A major spur to this ready adoption of secular principles was a series of court cases in which Catholic universities were challenged in their right to receive public funds. To be eligible for these funds, Catholic college leaders across the country severed their ties with their founding religious orders, downplayed their emphasis on the spiritual dimension of academic life, and adopted secular principles of academic freedom. The results of these court cases were profound and far reaching, moving Catholic universities in the direction of secularization.

However, an opposite trend was occurring simultaneously. During the same time that these court cases were taking place, leaders of Catholic universities worldwide began meeting to discuss the implications of Vatican II for Catholic higher education. In a series of documents beginning with the "Land O'Lakes Statement" in 1967, Catholic educators reaffirmed the spiritual dimension of academic life and insisted that theology must assist in the development of the individual disciplines, to help them move beyond their finite concerns to theological concerns. Ironically, while these college leaders were affirming the spiritual and theological dimension of academic life in these documents, many of them were simultaneously removing such language from their mission statements and catalogues in order to qualify for federal and state funds.

That is where Catholic universities find themselves today, on the one hand, wanting to integrate the religious with the academic and, on the other, dependent on federal funds, on rankings, and on the desire for prestige from their secular counterparts, and therefore often downplaying the religious. Morey and Piderit's recent study of Catholic higher education shows that most administrators and faculty in Catholic universities are poorly trained in connecting knowledge in the various disciplines with the Catholic intellectual tradition.[45] Most Catholic universities have strong departments of theology, but these sit alongside, though mostly unconnected to, other academic disciplines. The other departments remain, for the most part, confined to Kant's island. In the final two chapters, I offer an alternative vision.

In chapter 7, "The Direction toward Which Wonder Progresses," I argue that academic freedom in the Catholic university must refer to a specific instance of religious freedom: the freedom to pursue the spiritual dynamism of the mind wherever it will go, as well as the freedom not to go there. Grounding academic freedom in theological principles will enable Catholic universities to foster a robust Catholic intellectual and spiritual life that permeates scholarly inquiry without undermining freedom of inquiry and expression. In this concluding chapter, I draw on the work of Henri de Lubac, Karl Rahner, and Michael Buckley to develop a theology of academic freedom and to formulate a theonomous alternative to the fruitless dialogue between autonomy and heteronomy, moving us beyond the current impasse.

This theonomous alternative can be stated as follows: there is at the heart of all inquiry, whether the inquirer is explicitly aware of it or not, a dynamism whose source and goal is the divine. To claim that scientists and other scholars must remain within their specialized domains, in the realm of the finite, is to make a philosophical and epistemological claim about the human mind. I challenge that claim from a Christian perspective. An inner teleology drives us toward ever-greater understanding, toward completeness of understanding within an ultimate horizon. And although scholars cannot discover divine reality in its fullness through their disciplinary methods of inquiry, their inquiries, if not truncated, lead up to the limits of scientific knowledge and to the larger questions about God. They lead to the edge of disciplinary islands, where the infinite sea of the divine beckons. This movement of the mind toward an ultimate horizon is the true telos of the Catholic university. Not all scholars *must* pursue this trajectory toward an ultimate horizon, but all must be free to do so. That is the essence of a theologically grounded understanding of academic freedom.

I will argue for a structure, a framework, in which teaching and inquiry in a Catholic university ought to occur. The Catholic intellectual, artistic, and theological tradition must be in regular dialogue with all academic disciplines. No one thinker or school of thought within the Catholic tradition should dominate or exclude all others, as did neoscholastic thought in the late nineteenth and early twentieth centuries. Instead, authors from the entire tradition (e.g., Justin, Origen, Augustine, Thomas Aquinas, Bonaventure, Nicholas of Cusa, Newman, et al.) should be studied in any Catholic university, for both their content and their method of approaching different subject matters. None of them should be the sole lens through which we must view the world. Rather, their views are among the various lenses through which all students in a Catholic university explore the world.

For the past 40 years, and especially since the publication of *Ex Corde Ecclesiae* in 1990, Catholic colleges and universities have struggled to enhance their Catholic character, to integrate faith and reason, and to maintain scholarly excellence and academic freedom. Morey and Piderit's 2006 work demonstrates that they are struggling without much success, notwithstanding their public relations statements to the contrary. They are, for the most part, stuck at an impasse. In chapter 8, "Implications for Faculty Development and the Curriculum," I attempt to move the discussions forward and offer some general, but practical, suggestions for improving Catholic institutions.

A few clarifications about terms used in this book are in order. First, by "university" I mean Catholic higher education generally, both Catholic research universities and Catholic liberal arts colleges. I believe the principles I advocate are applicable to all, though colleges and universities may certainly adopt and incorporate them differently. My proposals are aimed primarily at undergraduate rather than graduate education, though I believe the principles may also be applied, in appropriate disciplines, at the graduate level. Among these Catholic colleges and universities, I have some in mind more than others. Catholic higher education is not monolithic: there are research universities and liberal arts colleges; there are traditional, conservative colleges and more liberal, pluralistic institutions. Some have the liberal arts at their core, while others focus more on professional training. Morey and Piderit have developed a typology of the various kinds of Catholic institutions of higher education: (1) Catholic immersion universities, (2) Catholic persuasion universities, (3) Catholic cohort universities, and (4) Catholic diaspora universities.

Catholic immersion universities seek to be pervasively Catholic; to recruit committed Catholic students, faculty, and administrators; and to thoroughly integrate spiritual, moral, and academic life. Residential dorm life is expected to follow church teachings, and students are strongly encouraged to attend Mass regularly. These universities, though now few in number, seek to create a strong Catholic culture amid a secularized—and,

I might add, increasingly pagan—society.[46] Examples of immersion universities are Franciscan University of Stuebenville (Ohio), Ave Maria University (Florida), Thomas Aquinas College (California), and Thomas More College of Liberal Arts (New Hampshire).

Catholic persuasion universities attempt to appeal to both Catholic and non-Catholic students and faculty and to present the teachings of the Catholic faith gently but persuasively while respecting and fostering the pluralism of modern intellectual, cultural, and religious life.[47] They are concerned with conforming to mainstream academic standards and trends within American higher education generally, but they seek to add a significant Catholic component to that education and to maintain a majority of Catholics on the faculty and in the student body. Most mainstream Catholic colleges and universities belong in this category: most Jesuit colleges and universities, the University of Notre Dame, St. Bonaventure University, the Catholic University of America, and the majority of Catholic liberal arts colleges that do not fit into the immersion type.

The Catholic diaspora and cohort universities are characterized by increasing dilution of Catholic teachings and identity. Demographically, only a minority of students and faculty are Catholic, but these institutions seek to give students at least some background knowledge of Catholic teachings. They also seek to instill in their students moral values that are consonant with church teachings in the hope that students will carry these values into life after graduation.

It is the Catholic persuasion universities that I have primarily in mind in this book. They have moved, to varying degrees, down the path toward secularization and are struggling today to define and strengthen their Catholic character. Many of the changes these institutions have made during the past four decades—openness to and engagement with modern thought, respect for and fostering of pluralism, ecumenism, and a dramatic increase in academic quality—have unquestionably been beneficial. Nonetheless, by most accounts—and by their own admission—these institutions are in an uphill battle to maintain their Catholic character.[48] I believe my proposals will be equally useful for the more traditional, immersion universities, though their challenges are different. In their case, it is not secularization and loss of Catholic identity that they must struggle against but heteronomous tendencies and resistance to a serious engagement with modern life, thought, and culture.

Second, a disclaimer is in order. In parts of this book, I critique the current state of Catholic higher education, leaving me open to the suspicion that I might be working from a conservative, pre-Vatican II perspective. I am not. I do not long for some "golden age" of Catholic higher education that, in fact, did not exist. I do not think a return to neoscholastic dominance is the answer to what ails Catholic higher education. On the contrary, I believe neoscholasticism had many defects, and it is no surprise that many Catholic educators rebelled against it after the Second Vatican Council. So while I criticize some aspects of the contemporary Catholic university scene, I praise others. I also criticize many aspects of Catholic higher education prior to the Second Vatican Council, while I commend others. My goal is to draw on the best of the Catholic tradition (and other traditions) in hopes we might move beyond the conventional conservative-liberal dichotomy that characterizes much discussion of Catholic universities today.

I draw on Catholic thinkers throughout the tradition, even from traditions within Christian history that many consider rival or incompatible traditions (e.g., Augustinian and Thomistic, *Nouvelle Theologie* and Transcendental Thomism). In spite of differences in their approaches, they have far more in common than in what separates them, and I draw on the commonalities to frame the argument of this book. Rival schools of thought in the Catholic tradition argue over how knowledge of God becomes known to us. Do we have direct access to divine illumination, or does illumination come only through institutionalized mediation and special revelation? Is knowledge of God immediate or remote? Is it somehow connatural to us, even if only unthematically and implicitly—as the presupposition of all search for truth—or must it come in mediated form, through the church's avenues of grace? Does this illumination arise at the beginning of our search for truth or at the end? Or both?

Countless volumes have been written on these questions, and I have no intention of rehearsing the controversies or taking sides. Both perspective contain valid elements. Catholic thinkers from the Patristic period have held that God is present to the mind, unthematically and amorphously, right from the start, as the source of wonder, the engine driving inquiry, the criteria by which we judge truth from falsehood, and the direction toward which inquiry ultimately moves. This view is more characteristic of the Augustinian-Bonaventuran tradition. At the same time, what is unthematic and dimly intuited, seeks to become explicit and thematic. Therefore, a fuller understanding of God emerges only at the end of our inquiry and searching, and even then, only through Revelation vouchsafed through the church. This view is more characteristic of the Thomistic school of thought. These positions, though they have different emphases, are not mutually exclusive. Elements of both traditions can be found in the writings of Thomas, and are present in both the *Nouvelle Theologie* and Transcendental Thomism of the twentieth century. Both dynamics are present in the process of knowing and understanding, as they are in most of the great theologians—Augustine, Bonaventure, Thomas, Henri de Lubac, Karl Rahner, and Michael Buckley, on whom I draw equally to frame this book.

Finally, a note about what this book does and does not cover. The intent of the book is to formulate an understanding of academic freedom that ensures scholars in nontheological disciplines the freedom to pursue knowledge beyond the limited domain of their academic disciplines (beyond Kant's "island of finitude") and move toward the theological and spiritual. All scholars must be free to follow their innate sense of wonder beyond their academic disciplines toward an ultimate horizon, or God. The book does not address controversies over the relation between theologians in Catholic universities and the church's Magisterium. The extent to which Catholic theologians may dissent from the church's official teachings is a highly contested issue that has been debated exhaustively over the past four decades, without definite resolution. It will, and must, continue to be discussed. This issue, however, is not the focal point of this book. This topic is complex and highly controversial, deserving of a thorough separate treatment; indeed, it would require an entire volume to treat it fairly and thoroughly. The more limited scope of this book should generate sufficient discussion and controversy for one short volume.

Chapter 2

The Medieval Liberal Arts and the Journey of the Mind to God

This chapter examines the ways in which three medieval thinkers—Augustine, Bonaventure, and Thomas Aquinas—conceptualized the relationship between the spiritual life, theology, and academic studies. Many scholars today would question whether it is legitimate to examine ancient and medieval texts to help illuminate our current academic situation. Even Theodore Hesburgh claims that the medieval university was an altogether different reality from the modern university. In order to build great Catholic universities, he says, we must begin by building great universities in "the modern sense."[1] After all, our mental and cultural horizons today are totally different from what they were in the patristic and medieval periods. The horizons of the past may be of historical and antiquarian interest, but do they have relevance for fashioning a Catholic university today? Must we not instead bring contemporary realities and thought structures to bear on contemporary issues? For certain, we must attend to contemporary experience and realities in the work of Catholic universities. Yet in the Catholic intellectual milieu the teachings of the tradition must also have a place in any discussion, not as a trump card or a model to which we must blindly adhere but as a partner in conversation. How then shall we draw on the tradition for enlightenment and guidance?

Michael Buckley's writings on Catholic universities can serve as a point of departure. In *The Catholic University as Promise and Project*, Buckley highlights three ways of attempting to understand the distinctive nature of a Catholic university.[2] First, one may simply describe Catholic universities as they exist today and conclude that their common characteristics are what make for a Catholic university. The weakness of this descriptive approach, says Buckley, is that it fails to take into account degradations from long-standing Catholic ideals that may have taken hold in universities due to excessive accommodation to the *zeitgeist*. A second option is to adopt a prescriptive definition or model, based on idealized characteristics, which all particular institutions should seek to realize. The weakness of such ideal models is that they seldom take into account cultural, economic, and intellectual realities existing at any given time in history. They aim to fashion institutions in conformity to some "eternal" or theoretical model, which may never come about in reality.[3]

In distinction to these two options, Buckley argues for a third way, a "dialogic" approach, which combines the de facto situation of Catholic universities as they presently exist with normative statements of origins and finality from the tradition. Drawing on Hans Georg Gadamer, he claims we must create a "conversation" or "dialogue" in which "classic statements of purpose, often from the past, are presented to the questions that emerge from the present; and at the same time the present situation is itself questioned and opened by the issues that these great and classic articulations of purpose pose."[4]

I will follow such a dialogic approach in this chapter, reviewing classic texts of Augustine, Bonaventure, and Thomas Aquinas to see what we can learn from them. Can we find, in spite of the vast differences in historical and cultural reality that separates our way of thinking from theirs, something in common among them that might serve as a conceptual framework for Catholic higher education, something that will serve us better than the norms and standards of the modern, secular university?[5] I argue that we can and that this norm is a theonomous approach to inquiry. There is a dynamism in the movement from one academic discipline to another that orients and guides us toward an ultimate horizon. Desire impels us dynamically toward complete knowledge and truth, and it is not satisfied until we attain it, even though only asymptotically. This concept of limitless desire of the intellect and human spirit pervaded the writings of the church fathers and extended well into the thought of the high Middle Ages.

Augustine: The Restless Desire of the Mind

For Augustine, God is the light by which all things are known. All acts of knowing, including the sciences, are possible because of the Truth that resides already within our minds. Because we are made in the image and likeness of God, the eternal Logos dwells in the depths of our spirit, making us able to discern the truth not only of what lies within us but of the world around us. God's wisdom is everywhere and comes to us from everywhere because the Word became flesh and dwells in the world. God "externalizes" his wisdom in the created world, just as we externalize our thoughts in the form of speech and writing or in creative works.[6]

The natural world points to God, yet before the human mind can even know and understand things in the natural world fully, one must turn inward, to the inner self. One can only hear and understand the "spoken word," or Logos, of the natural world if one tests created realities against the truths within oneself. In other words, there is a Logos structure to reality that the human mind can discover and recognize because that structure is also in our minds, enabling us to recognize the truth of things when encountering them in the external world. Without the image of Truth that resides within each of us, we could not discern the truth of the natural world. We would have no criteria to judge the adequacy of our concepts of reality.[7] Were it not for the Truth within us, we could never pronounce judgment regarding the truth or falsity of any theorem or conclusion. The eternal Logos, in Augustine's thought, is that Truth. The Logos, or Word is "the *principium* or the beginning point of knowledge"; it is "the precondition of all *scientia*," for all knowing.[8]

Inquiry must take us beyond knowledge of the natural world in itself. Whatever subject matter the scholar attends to and loves, he must move beyond it to the wisdom of God, which is the true culmination of his progress in knowing. Augustine here implies a dynamism in the human mind that leads ever toward God, regardless of the subject matter one studies. This does not mean that we neglect to focus our minds on the material creation; we must do so to get on in life. But we must do it in such a way that the mind's attention is not limited to investigating and understanding the natural, social, and cultural realms as ends in themselves. The goal is to "do whatever we do in the reasonable use of temporal things with an eye to the acquisition of eternal things, passing by the former on the way, setting our hearts on the latter to the end."[9] There are traces of God infused everywhere in the universe, and anyone with an attentive mind can discover them. Even the ancient Egyptians, with their "abominable practices" and beliefs, were nonetheless able to mine nuggets of truth from "the ores of the divine providence" that they discovered in the natural world.[10]

Theology and philosophy (which in ancient times included the natural sciences) are a unity in Augustine's thought.[11] Intellectual work is always joined and subsidiary to spiritual effort. Augustine distinguishes between the mind's knowing of finite reality and the knowing of the divine, and he gives separate names to the different ways of knowing: *ratio inferior* (science, or *scientia*) and *ratio superior* (wisdom, or *sapientia*). *Scientia* is a rational cognition of the finite, temporal world; *sapientia* is cognizance of the full or eternal Truth. The former uses the method of investigation, the latter, intuition. They have different ends: *scientia* has practical ends of improving agriculture, curing the sick, and building better societies, while the end of *sapientia* is the contemplation of God.[12] But while Augustine was willing to separate these functions of the mind analytically, he insisted that they are not "two parallel or concurrent mental procedures, nor ... two distinct and autonomous spheres of intellectual activity." Rather, they are "two consecutive steps in the only valid field of intellectual activity there is, which is the quest for saving, divine truth."[13] They work "in a helpful partnership."[14] We must not separate rational activity about finite things from contemplation of the divine. We must look at the mind *in its wholeness* not its logically separate functions.

Augustine had high regard for natural reason, but reason was never "to be taken in isolation from the illuminating activity of God. Even reason wholly occupied with creatures and directed away from the Creator by the power of the will is yet empowered by divine illumination to apprehend the creatures which enthrall its interest."[15] Augustine's general conception of knowledge is that God, as the uncreated light within us, is that which illuminates all that we know; is the Truth by which we judge the truthfulness or falsity of all things in the sciences, aesthetics, and ethics. As the sun is to our perception of sensible things, so God, the uncreated light, is the cause of all certain knowledge in the sciences. All intellectual knowing presupposes "the *informing* of our minds by the Truth apprehended *a priori*."[16] Reason is never unaided in its quest for Truth. "The divine informing by the eternal Word is the precondition of all *scientia*."[17] This is true even though we are fallen. The image of God in human minds can never be completely erased. There is always some awareness of God in our consciousness, even if at a subconscious level. There always remains a trace of love for the Truth, a desire for God.

The error that scholars commit is to use the divine light within them to learn about the natural world through *scientia,* but then forget to give thanks to the divine Light itself, and fail to pursue their scholarship beyond the natural world to its ultimate end.[18] For Augustine, reason is flawed because our will and actions are corrupted, and until we can submit our pride and will to Christ, our knowledge will always remain defective, imprisoned, and enthralled in things finite.[19]

Full knowledge, according to Augustine, cannot be had through rational thinking alone. Desire, or love, must precede knowing. This desire (eros) leads to wonder, exploration, and understanding. Rational thought is driven by desire and the affections, even though we may be unaware that they are the engine behind our intellectual pursuits. The practical and theoretical functions of the mind are integrated, not separate, aspects of the mind.[20]

Augustine discusses how the liberal arts themselves may be a pathway to divine Wisdom, and his epistemological principles in *De Trinitate* and the *Confessions* provided the foundation for his successors to do so. Bonaventure and St. Thomas built on that foundation in theorizing about the curriculum in the schools and universities of the thirteenth century.

Bonaventure: The Mind's Journey to God through the Liberal Arts

Bonaventure considered the spiritual life the foundation of all academic inquiry, as he makes clear in *The Journey of the Mind into God*. I emphasize this point because there is a common misconception today that the *Journey* is directed primarily to those engaged in a spiritual journey rather than to scholars in the academy. This misconception is based on the assumption that intellectual and spiritual journeys are necessarily separate, even opposed to one another. Today's theologians often place the *Journey* in the category of "spiritual theology," appropriate for those on a spiritual quest but not for academics in the university.

Ewert Cousins's translation of the *Journey* helps maintain this misconception by translating the title of Bonaventure's work to *The Soul's Journey into God*, even though the original Latin is *Itinerarium mentis in Deum*. He defends his translation of the Latin word *mens* (mind) as "soul" by arguing that our current word "mind" has connotations of purely cognitive and abstract thinking, whereas the medieval word *mens* "encompassed the soul in its three faculties of memory, intelligence and will, which constitute the soul as image of God."[21] Cousins has a valid point, and we must bear it in mind when we use the word "mind" in the medieval context. However, translating the Latin word *mens* as "soul" is equally misleading because the word "soul" today has a spiritual and affective as opposed to intellectual connotation. For Bonaventure, the word *mens* integrates the intellectual and spiritual. In the *Journey,* he was indeed describing a spiritual journey, par excellence, but even more, he was describing an integrated spiritual and intellectual journey for scholars in the academy.

This is apparent in the way he holds intellectual and spiritual effort in balance in the prologue, in which he urges the reader to not believe "that reading is sufficient without fervor, speculation without devotion, investigation without wonder, observation without exultation, intelligent work without piety, knowledge without love, understanding without humility, and study without divine grace."[22] These pairings, or poles, when analyzed closely, reveal how Bonaventure sees their relation:

Reading	is not sufficient without	Fervor
Speculation	is not sufficient without	Devotion
Investigation	is not sufficient without	Wonder
Observation	is not sufficient without	Exultation
Intelligent Work	is not sufficient without	Piety
Knowledge	is not sufficient without	Love
Understanding	is not sufficient without	Humility
Study	is not sufficient without	Divine Grace

If we glance down the list of activities in the left-hand column, we see at once that they are activities undertaken by scholars. Bonaventure is not telling his readers to abandon those academic activities in favor of the spiritual virtues in the right-hand column. Rather, he urges students to integrate the poles. The *Journey* itself, with its elements of scholastic theological concepts and its motifs and images of spiritual journey and desire, is an excellent integration of the two.

For Bonaventure, the liberal arts are more than a tool for helping us better understand and teach Scripture (as Augustine taught). When approached rightly, they are themselves a pathway to God. In *De reductione artium ad theologiam,* Bonaventure says that God is the source of all illumination of knowledge in the world: "The *manifold Wisdom of God,* which is clearly revealed in Sacred Scripture, lies hidden in all knowledge and all nature...It is likewise evident how wide is the illuminative way and how in everything which is perceived or known God Himself lies hidden within."[23] By sharing in God's light, we are able to investigate and know the various aspects of reality on which the liberal arts focus. For Bonaventure, divine illumination allows the investigator to better understand reality in the context of the divine economy. This is the meaning of the *reductio*: tracing all knowledge in the liberal arts to its source in the divine light. It is the eternal light of the Godhead that informs the various sciences, and so even the liberal arts, often conceived as secular sciences, must be placed in a broader spiritual framework.[24]

The presence of God suffuses creation and readily offers itself to those who study it attentively. Created things, says Bonaventure, lead us to God; they "signify the invisible things of God...because God is the origin, exemplar and end of every creature, and every effect is the sign of its cause, the exemplification of its exemplar and the path to the end."[25] Therefore, students in a Catholic university, even those in nontheological sciences, should be taught how to be attentive to those hints.

Bonaventure considered God to be present in our mental processes as we explore the liberal arts. If fact, human creativity and intellection are a *participation in* the very life of the Trinity in its own creativity and are, at their core, deeply spiritual endeavors. Therefore, Bonaventure's ordering of the various branches of knowledge does not present a curriculum composed of "secular" sciences followed by a study of theology. Rather, he demands that we integrate a theological dimension—what I have called a theonomous approach—to the study of all aspects of reality and the various sciences, both theoretical and practical. In this regard we can see that Bonaventure's journey into God through the liberal arts is an intellectual journey and a spiritual journey simultaneously.

Bonaventure's thought on higher studies is an excellent example of a theonomous approach to the intellectual life: one's entire being is suffused with the divine light. That light both orients the mind's journey and is the journey's end. His close-knit integration of intellectual and spiritual effort combines both Platonic and Aristotelian Christian traditions, which were sometimes perceived as antagonistic during the twelfth and thirteenth centuries. Bonaventure's contemporary, Thomas Aquinas, also attempted to integrate these two strands.

Thomas Aquinas and the Natural Desire of the Mind

A common theme in Thomas Aquinas's writings is that the human mind naturally desires to know God. This desire cannot come to rest in any knowledge of finite things in themselves. The mind must continually move forward to ever-greater knowledge of both the finite world and the divine reality that generates, founds, and completes the finite.[26] The intellect does not reach its goal until its natural desire comes to rest in God.[27] The mind has proximate ends toward which it is temporarily oriented. Proximate ends in cognitive understanding possess real value. The various sciences differentiate themselves according to their subject matter, which is abstracted from the whole of reality and must be studied in accordance with methods appropriate to that subject matter. Nonetheless, knowledge of any subject matter, *in itself,* cannot satisfy the mind because that knowledge is incomplete apart from its relation to God.[28] The ultimate end—knowledge of God—subordinates all proximate ends, and nothing moves toward a proximate end except insofar as it is a step on the way toward the final end.[29]

Jean-Pierre Torrell claims that, for Thomas, the natural human desire to know the divine essence "*is one with the very being of man*, such that his intellect cannot stop before being filled with the knowledge in itself of the Being who is at the source of his [own] being and every being."[30] The result, writes Torrell, is "an irresistible attraction inscribed in man's very nature to become like God in the way that an image resembles the model on which it is made."[31] It is God's free gift that awakens this desire and prompts the mind's journey toward its fulfillment.

On these principles, Thomas bases his view of the architectonic role of philosophy (understood as metaphysics, or divine science) among the sciences. The practical arts and sciences, he says, are valuable goals and objects worthy of our attention because they are means to something greater. Philosophy "is wholly ordered to the knowing of God as its ultimate end; that is why it is also called *divine science.*" So divine knowledge is "the ultimate end of every act of human knowledge."[32]

The sciences, of course, have their own distinct subject matter and methods. The fact that the ultimate goal of the sciences is always knowledge of God does not mean that every act of knowing and each inquiry into a given subject matter must explicitly refer to God, to the first and final cause. Most of the time, students and scholars will focus on proximate ends and secondary causes. In the overall scheme, though, the ultimate end must be kept in view. For Thomas this is done sequentially, beginning with the natural sciences and progressing to more abstract disciplines as the student matures. Learning, then, is a continuum through which we seek knowledge of different aspects of the one reality, the entire natural-divine continuum, if you will. We begin with natural sciences because they focus on physical objects in the world and are readily understandable to the student. To study physical objects, we abstract them from their surroundings, from all the other things to which they are related, so as to better focus on the essence and function of the object at hand. Mathematics abstracts lines, numbers, and shapes from physical objects and focuses only on those abstractions. Philosophy abstracts the essences—the regularities, the constants, the universal elements—from particular things to understand their essence rather than their changing and accidental manifestations. So one progresses through natural science to mathematics, philosophy, and finally to theology. Each of these fields of study has its own subject matter and methods. That does not mean, however, that we should disassociate the sciences from philosophy and theology. Philosophy and the sciences may be distinct from theology, but God is never far from the human mind. In all knowing, said Thomas, God creates a natural light within us and directs it to the truth.[33] In *De veritate*, Thomas writes that "all knowers know God implicitly in all they know."[34] This idea has similarities to Augustine's theory of illumination, in which God's light is the medium through which all learning occurs and the criterion by which all approaches to truth are judged.[35] God is always at work in the mind.[36] So much is this the case that all perception of truth on the part of the human mind should be ascribed primarily to God.[37]

Truth, said Thomas, is the conformity of mind to reality. All things are related, ultimately to God, so cannot be separated in reality. The analytical reason—what Thomas called the *ratio*—can abstract things temporarily from their broader context and from the things they are related to. It can prescind from considering their relation to other things and study what things are in themselves, in their finite manifestations. That is what natural scientists do. The synthetic reason, on the other hand—what Thomas called the *intellectus*—functions differently. It may distinguish the various characteristics of things but must always relate things to essential being. For "when that which constitutes the intelligibility... of a nature and through which the nature itself is understood, has a relation to and a dependence on something else, clearly we cannot know the nature without the other thing."[38] Synthetic reason, or *intellectus*, places all knowledge gained from the particular sciences into a broader philosophical understanding.

In Thomas's thought, it is primarily philosophy that inquires into the questions of meaning and the divine. But not only philosophy. "Really to possess a science," says Ralph McInerny, commenting on Thomas, "consists not only of mastery of a subject matter but also in seeing its relation to the ultimate end of human life, such knowledge as we can attain of the divine."[39] The basic and comprehensive principles that underlie an understanding of all things, said Thomas, must be studied not only in one particular science, that is, in philosophy or theology, but rather must "be investigated in *every* particular science" even though they properly belong to philosophy.[40] The question, from a Thomistic perspective, is not whether the continuum of learning should be followed to its full extent, to its end in philosophy and theology. The question is how much the philosophical and theological aspects should be integrated into nonphilosophical and nontheological parts of the curriculum in order to set the stage for further studies in philosophy and theology.

The Science of Theology

Though the focus of this book is not on the science of theology per se, Thomas's description of how theology relates to other disciplines illustrates how he conceived the overall trajectory and goal of the curriculum.

Theology as a discipline incorporates the other sciences into itself without becoming subsumed by them or intermingled in such a way that it loses its character. Some of Thomas's contemporaries feared that by using and engaging philosophical and scientific currents of thought, theology would be diluted or made to conform to philosophical principles. Thomas disagreed, and he used the metaphor of water and wine to make his point (wine being understood as theology and water as the philosophical sciences). Theology does not mix water with wine but transforms it into wine.[41] By incorporating philosophy—understood in the medieval period as encompassing all the sciences—into a broader theological framework, theology transforms philosophy.

Thomas accomplishes this incorporation of all sciences into theology within both the *Summa Theologia* and the *Summa Contra Gentiles*, in which all subjects are subsumed under and viewed from a theological perspective. Both summas follow a threefold, Trinitarian framework. First, they treat of God in himself; second, they treat of the coming forth of the universe—of creatures, including human beings—from God; and finally, of the "ordering of all things to God as to their end," that is, the return of all things to God through Christ.[42] There is no subject matter that does not fit into this order of things. Theology studies God in himself and his relations to the world. The natural sciences—natural philosophy during Thomas's time—cover the physical universe, its forces, the motion of planets and stars, the way elements combine to form larger wholes, and biological life. The social sciences—to apply the principle to today's academic disciplines—study humans in their intrapsychic development, their social organization, and their political structures and then attempt to discern which structures will best facilitate human flourishing.[43] The humanities study the human spirit and its various expressions in literature, the arts, and philosophical reasoning.[44]

In each academic discipline, scholars must study their subject matter in accordance with the methods best suited to understanding one portion of the continuum of reality abstracted from the whole. They must often prescind from relating their subject matter to other areas of reality and to the divine life. But if inquiry is not to be frustrated, they must ultimately move beyond disciplinary knowledge to an all-encompassing theological framework. Once they do that, the academic disciplines are transformed into good wine.The entire curriculum of the Catholic university, therefore, should be directed to theological ends, with all academic disciplines incorporated into a broader theological framework in which theology serves as the culmination of, and framework for,university studies. Integral to Thomas's thought was a vigorous engagement of theology with non-Catholic forms of thought—with the philosophical and scientific currents of his time. Thomas took these currents seriously, engaged them, and attempted to respond to the challenges they posed to Christian theology. He did not merely exclude, ignore, or condemn them. He incorporated them dialogically into his broader Christian thought.

The Autonomy of the Sciences and the Mind's Desire

How are we to square the medieval concept of the mind's journey to God through the arts and sciences with the modern notion of the autonomy of the sciences? Is it not a settled principle that each academic discipline is autonomous, with its own defined subject matter and methods? Are scholars not free to pursue knowledge within their disciplines without taking theological concerns into account? Is not the modern university founded on this principle? The answer is yes, but a brief examination of the principle underlying the autonomy of the sciences is warranted here. This principle is not problematic in the abstract sense, but in the concrete, we must bear in mind that it is not the "science" or "academic discipline" itself that possesses autonomy.[45]

The sciences are abstractions conceived by scientists, who, in agreement with one other, have decided to focus on, and limit their inquiries to, a restricted dimension of reality. The study of that specific dimension of reality and the methods used to study it constitute a science or an academic discipline. We cannot, however, claim that the sciences are agents in possession of autonomy: they possess no free will, desires, or goals; they make no decisions on which they act. It is the individual scholars in those academic disciplines who possess autonomy and who have a right to freedom of inquiry. This means they must be able to freely investigate the particular area of reality that falls within the scope of their discipline in accordance with the methods agreed upon by scholars in the field. This is what is normally meant by "academic freedom." Yet we must not lose sight of a deeper truth: these individual scholars are oriented to God. In their minds is implanted a natural desire to know reality beyond their limited academic disciplines. The offer of God's self extends to them in their total human existence not just to some self-enclosed "spiritual" corner of it. The dimension of reality they investigate is not independent of other dimensions of reality. The subject matter they study is part of a continuum, connected to the whole of material and divine reality. These scholars therefore must be equally free to explore the relationship of the restricted dimension of reality that is the object of their academic discipline to ever-wider and deeper dimensions of reality, and to pursue their inquiries to their ultimate end. That means asking and exploring the larger questions about the relation of a particular realm of reality to the whole, and to its divine ground. This does not mean that *every* scholar must pursue inquiry to its ultimate end, but that everyone must be free to do so, without impediments of narrow disciplinary strictures.

I believe it is more fruitful to speak of the autonomy of the individual scholar to pursue his or her inquiries to their ultimate end than to speak of the autonomy of the sciences. For Thomas, each science grasps its object using a mental abstraction by which it focuses only on some features of an object or realm of reality, while excluding from consideration other features that also belong to that object or realm of reality. That does not mean, however, that scholars should remain imprisoned in the realm of a particular science, or even of several sciences studied in an interdisciplinary fashion. Indeed, if Thomas is right that we have an insatiable desire to know more, then every scholar is called to move beyond all disciplines to the whole of knowledge.

Eros and Telos

The three Catholic thinkers explored in this chapter lived in very different cultural and historical circumstances from ours. They wrote largely for those dedicating their lives to a religious vocation rather than for laypersons, who today make up most of the faculty in Catholic universities. Moreover, they do not agree with one another on all things. Nonetheless, some timeless principles emerge from their writings that can be applied to Catholic higher education today.

First, Christian thinkers must be open to non-Christian thought and must display a willingness to discern what is good and true in it, even while rejecting what is false. As a tradition develops, it must be able to incorporate the thought, cultures, and practices it encounters into a unity, transforming them, purifying them, and enlarging itself in the process. This power of assimilation forbids any peremptory dismissal of ideas contrary, or even foreign, to one's tradition. There is no justification in the Christian tradition for closing our minds to the streams of thought in the surrounding culture, no matter how unsettling those streams may be.[46] We must study and know those streams of thought, feel their sway over us, and finally discern their flaws and know where they contradict Christian principles. Then we must appropriate what accords with the tradition and reject what is corrupt and pernicious.

Second, desire, or eros, guides intellectual inquiry. There is no such thing as disinterested scholarship unmoved by some dynamism.

Third, and following logically on the second principle, there is a telos to intellectual inquiry that takes one beyond the finite, a goal toward which eros moves. That goal is a comprehensive, ever-widening realm of knowledge that terminates only when we gain a knowledge of God, or wisdom.

Fourth, any inquiry that stops short of that ultimate goal must be considered an aborted instance of the intellectual drive desiring to come to full term.

Finally, one cannot reach that goal without integrating spiritual and intellectual effort. In none of these authors do we find the idea of a university (or school of higher learning) with purely secular learning unconnected to spiritual effort and limited to the finite, temporal realm. There is a telos to academic inquiry that incorporates proximate ends of a specific academic discipline, but also leads to an ultimate end—God.

By insisting that we begin with the autonomy of the academic disciplines, as understood in the modern, Kantian sense, Catholic universities are at a disadvantage, for in that modern university, theology and spirituality are already proscribed, and the individual sciences are considered totally autonomous and unrelated to theology.[47] By overdetermining the foundational role of autonomy, the engagement of theology with other academic disciplines that many Catholic educators advocate rarely occurs. The ideal of an education completed by philosophy and theology sits side by side with different and often contradictory principles: increasing specialization and the fragmentation of knowledge; independence of the empirical sciences from any philosophical or theological framework; research as the dominant goal of the scholar to the neglect of teaching and integrative knowledge; and the use of strictly disciplinary criteria rather than broader philosophical criteria in judging scholarly competence, teaching, and research.

Appropriating the wisdom of the tradition does not mean reverting to a curricular form that existed in earlier periods. We must, as Hesburgh insists, take the modern university seriously. At the same time, we must keep the realities of the modern university in creative dialogue with wisdom from the past. This dialogue with tradition is the Catholic way.

Chapter 3

Berlin: The Prototype of the Modern University

In the previous chapter I examined the thought of three medieval thinkers in order to discover if there are principles from the Catholic tradition that can help inform Catholic higher education today. In doing so, I made clear that ideals from the past must not be used to hinder or suppress knowledge and inquiry in the present. Nor can we merely replicate curricular forms from the past, such as the *trivium* and *quadrivium* or the *Ratio studiorum* as models for today. We must draw on principles from the tradition, but we must also build on universities as they exist in the modern world, and that means taking core principles of the modern university seriously. But which core principles?

The University of Berlin is universally considered the first modern research university, and its founding in 1810 provides us with a logical starting point for discussing the nature of the modern university and the modern ideal of academic freedom during their formative stages. All subsequent research universities were, to some extent, modeled on Berlin. In this chapter I will explore the philosophical principles underlying the founding of Berlin, focusing particularly on the unity of knowledge (i.e., the relation of specialized knowledge to the whole of knowledge), academic freedom, and the role of theonomous thinking in specialized academic disciplines. My purpose is not to propose the University of Berlin or German Idealism as the paradigm for the modern Catholic university; rather, it is to demonstrate that the "modern university" has a deeper, and even more spiritual, foundation than that which has developed in American higher education.

In the late eighteenth and early nineteenth centuries, German intellectuals recognized the need for serious reform of existing universities for a number of pressing reasons. New developments in science and philosophy, and a growing interest in fostering research began to replace existing views of science and philosophy, which were based on an amalgam of Aristotelianism, classical studies, scholasticism, and orthodox Protestantism. Traditional teaching methods and curricula were no longer suitable for the spirit of the new scientific age. The new educational theories of Rousseau and Pestalozzi had arisen, causing scholars to rethink and transform teaching methods. Many Enlightenment thinkers wanted universities to become purely research academies, with theology excluded entirely, since it dealt with realms of knowledge inaccessible to critical reason. Scholars and intellectuals therefore called for major reforms of education.

Carrying out substantial reforms of existing institutions with entrenched ways of thinking and acting was no easy task. The French Revolution, however, had undermined traditional power structures and institutions, and educational reformers in Prussia found an opportunity to create an entirely new institution based on modern principles. The creation of the University of Berlin gave the philosophers Johann Gottlieb Fichte, Friedrich Schelling, and Friedrich Schleiermacher an opportunity to propose blueprints for an ideal university. In the first decade of the nineteenth century, all three wrote brief treatises setting forth the philosophical principles on which the new university should be founded.[1] I will examine these principles, the order of the curriculum arising from them, and their concept of academic freedom. I will also examine the thought of G. W. F. Hegel, who, though not one of the contributors to the founding of Berlin, taught at Berlin beginning in 1818, attempted to influence its course, and wrote extensively about the ideals of a university education.[2]

Berlin was founded on several principles that affected its organization: (1) the unity of research and teaching; (2) academic freedom, encompassing both the freedom to learn (*Lernfreiheit*)and freedom to teach (*Lehrfreiheit*), which grew directly out of the Enlightenment principle of the autonomy of reason; and (3) the centrality of the arts and sciences,[3] with philosophy as the architectonic discipline.[4] Equally important, the German idealists were concerned about the fragmentation of human knowledge, the severance of reason and faith, and the detachment of the finite from the infinite, of subjective from objective, and of thought from reality—separations within the consciousness of Western thought that had been developing for some time as religious thought became severed from philosophical and scientific thought. How did they attempt to reconnect these poles in the university? Which subjects should be included and which left out? How should knowledge be organized, and how should the various branches of science relate to one another? What is the relation of philosophy to other sciences, and what is the place of theology in the circle of sciences? I will explore their answers to these specific questions in this chapter, with a primary focus on their concepts of the unity of knowledge, academic freedom, and how theonomous thinking should affect inquiry in nontheological disciplines.

The Goal of Education and the Circle of the Sciences

The German idealists share a number of philosophical presuppositions. Among the most important of these is the concept of *Bildung*. Like the ancient Greek word *paideia, Bildung* refers to the education or formation of "the whole person" in his or her intellectual, moral, and social unity. It is variously translated as "education," "formation," or "character formation," none of which adequately translates its full range of meaning.[5] Fostering autonomous, self-developing individuals is central to forming character, and so *Bildung* takes on the character of self-development as opposed to the inculcation of a *paideia* imparted by others, no matter how wise. Indeed, it is the spirit within one that motivates and directs this self-development. Central to the academic side of this formation is a broad education in all the arts and sciences and an understanding of the unity of all knowledge. Students in a university need an *encyclopedic* knowledge of all academic disciplines in their interrelations and unity. The root meaning of encyclopedia comes from the Greek words *encyclos* (circle) and *paideia* (or learning and formation in the liberal arts and sciences as a whole). Hence, "encyclopedia" refers to the circle of the sciences, or education and culture encircled within a whole.

For Fichte, Schelling, and Hegel the encyclopedia is a comprehensive philosophical system that encompasses and orients all particular sciences within the totality of knowledge. Philosophy is the organizing or architectonic discipline that orders all others. In the philosophy of Fichte, the goal of human life is to come freely to consciousness of the divine transcendence within the world and in human consciousness.[6] The university is the ideal place for this knowing to occur.[7] Moreover, one must show the organic interrelation of the sciences and their mutual relations. This means understanding how scientific and philosophical concepts must be organized, the order in which they should appear, and their place in the whole. To do this effectively, a philosophical encyclopedia must be created to order the curriculum and orient teachers and students. Particular subjects must be treated in accordance with the principles of the encyclopedia, and all faculty must comprehend the nature of the overall curriculum.

Encyclopedias have the function of both unifying and ordering scientific disciplines in themselves, and also of ordering the various disciplines to one another and to the whole. Philosophy is the discipline that structures the encyclopedia because it grasps the broader context of knowledge into which the particular branches fall.[8] The scholar in any particular science must possess a broad philosophical vision and must be trained in philosophy right from the beginning. He or she in turn will be able to transmit knowledge, in its philosophical context, to students.[9] Fichte contends that the motivation behind scholars' reluctance to adopt an encyclopedic vision is due to their inability to give an account of the whole; they are able to focus only on the details of their particular science.[10] Only scholars who are able to place knowledge from their particular science in a broader philosophical framework belong in the university.

Closely connected to the intertwined concepts of encyclopedia and circle of the sciences was a new vision of learning, one based not solely on the study of classical authors—though that is important for all the German idealists—but on the new scientific spirit of the age. *Wissenschaft* is the term they use to describe this scientific spirit. *Wissenschaft* is normally translated as "science," but this is inadequate because it means more than our limited idea of science as an investigative procedure into natural phenomena using the scientific method. According to Walter Metzger, "the very notion of *Wissenschaft* had overtones of meaning utterly missing in its English counterpart, *science*. The German term signified a dedicated, sanctified pursuit. It signified not merely the goal of rational understanding...not merely the study of the 'exact sciences,'...but the study of things for themselves and for their ultimate meanings."[11] Scholarly inquiry is to be allowed "to push against any of the frontiers of knowledge," and not just for pragmatic purposes.[12] Philosophy is the chief discipline that gives form and meaning to all others. In contrast, philosophy in American thought "was only one of a heterogenous group of divisions," sitting alongside others.[13] The German idealist philosophers connected with Berlin felt free to range broadly from philosophy per se. In fact, they would have rejected the very notion of philosophy as a discipline alongside others.

Like our concept of science, *Wissenschaft* refers to critical inquiry conducted in an ordered and disciplined way. It also means to investigate and understand something not only in its particularity but also in its relations to other phenomena, to grasp how it is situated in the circle of natural and historical relations that make up a larger whole. The scholar is to be free to pursue these connections to the whole. Indeed, the very inner being and drive of the mind requires this pursuit, and hence, it is an essential component of academic freedom. A great university implies catholicity.

To understand the educational theories of the German idealists, we must grasp this broader meaning of "science" or "the sciences."

The Infinite within the Finite, the Whole within the Part

In chapter 1 we saw how Kant attempted to explore the "land of pure understanding," which he likened to an "island" enclosed within the unalterable boundaries of nature. The understanding can know only the world of phenomena—that which is accessible to human reason. There may be a "land" beyond the island of the phenomenal world, but it is outside the realm of human knowability. After Kant, belief in a "supernatural" realm outside nature and a realm of "revealed" knowledge outside reason became problematic. The German idealists accepted Kant's critique of the *externality* of the divine, noumenal world, but they rejected the notion of a self-enclosed island. Friedrich Schelling (1775–1854) held that the spiritual world of the Infinite is neither some separate realm accessible only through supernatural revelation nor a "land of illusion." The Infinite is manifested in the finite. "Revelation" does not come through intermediaries but is directly available to everyone. The Absolute is immanent in the human mind. The Absolute is the presupposition of all knowledge, and it precedes all concrete knowing, which it makes possible—a reality that Augustine had recognized but which Kant had not.[14] The awareness of limits to knowledge presupposes an implicit acknowledgment of something unconditional.[15] Individual insights and individual sciences constitute an organic part of the totality of knowledge. If scholars are to engage competently in a given discipline, they must possess the freedom and ability to relate particular, disciplinary insights to a greater whole.[16]

Schelling attempted to create a system of knowledge, or meta-philosophy, that could integrate all the fragmented disciplines into a unity of consciousness. Take the natural sciences, for instance. In Schelling's philosophy, nature embodies spirit; it is the objective aspect of spirit.[17] Knowledge of the finite in itself is impossible without also knowing the infinite soul that permeates nature. The empirical approach in natural science focuses solely on the finite world as something existing in itself, separating objective reality from its grounding in the divine, making nature something merely finite while utterly negating its infinite, spiritual dimension, leaving us with a dualism.[18] Here Schelling is criticizing Descartes's diremption, or division, of reality into two separate spheres—*res cogitans* and *res extensa*—without any intrinsic relation between them. This

Cartesian view fundamentally changed humans' attitude toward nature, leaving us with a purely mechanistic rather than an organic view of nature. The mechanistic approach begins with observed effects and infers causes from these effects. It is an approach that goes hand in hand with materialism and naturalism. As such, it can explain only a limited realm of reality, ignoring or denying the spiritual dimension.

Contrasted with a purely empirical approach, a more holistic philosophical approach views nature as the embodiment of a divine ideal. The science of nature, says Schelling, must go beyond particular phenomena and "investigate their common source, the Absolute, in which they are one."[19] The purpose of philosophy is to show that all things originate in God and that "nature is inherently one...Nothing in nature is purely material"; everything is infused with spirit. The science of nature is one, and the parts into which it is divided by the understanding are *branches of one absolute knowledge*."[20] So the natural sciences (chemistry, physics, biology, astronomy) study primarily the material aspects of the Spirit's self-manifestation in the form of nature. Nonetheless, the scholar who is truly a philosopher is not so timid as to remain on the island of the finite. Desiring truth in its fullness, he or she sets out on the infinite sea to explore it.

The Absolute manifests itself not only in the form of nature but also in the form of history.[21] History is sacred because it is "a great mirror of the world spirit, an eternal poem of the divine mind."[22] It is a more advanced stage of the process that is called nature. Both the course of nature and the course of history are the work of divine Providence.[23] History, when viewed as a whole, is itself a revelation that gradually discloses the Absolute or, better, is the Absolute's self-disclosure. True history is a synthesis of the empirically given and the ideal. Through the empirical approach historians uncover events of the past, organize data, and analyze it. But human reason is not fully satisfied until the empirical causes are placed in the context of a broader understanding. History, says Schelling, is like a great drama that "only an infinite mind could have composed."[24] The goal of historical processes is the actualization of "an objective order of freedom, that is, the state."[25] The science of the state is jurisprudence, which is not merely a knowledge of particular laws and an understanding of the objective organization of society but also the embodiment of a political philosophy. The goal of history and law as academic disciplines is to uncover the workings of the Absolute within human history and social organizations, and to lead the state toward a perfect unity of social and historical reality with the will of the Absolute.[26]

Friedrich Schleiermacher's 1808 *Occasional Thoughts on Universities in the German Sense*[27] assumes a foundation in the circle of the sciences and advocates the architectonic and central role of philosophy in it.

A community of scholars is necessary because nothing can be properly known but in relation to and in combination with all else. "All scientific endeavors pull together, tending toward oneness," because of the inner unity of all science.[28] There can be no such thing as a solitary scholar, and scholars are united by their awareness of the necessary unity of all knowing.[29]

> At the point when they have just ascertained only what is most necessary about an object, they draw it into the domain of science, searching for the inner unity out of which all the manifold of experience admits of conceptualization, striving to see the whole in each particular and every particular only in the whole. So do they direct every person whom they would similarly cultivate…likewise to this highpoint of scientific unity and form, accustom that person to see in this fashion, and only after one has gained a firm grasp on this permit one to go deeper into particulars. They do this because for them the task for each thing is really to know it in the stricter sense. Otherwise all accumulation of particular information would simply be an unsteady groping about.[30]

Schleiermacher presents an idealized vision of the cooperative spirit that must exist among all scholars, regardless of discipline, and assumes their desire to participate mutually in this communal project of pursuing and integrating knowledge rather than jealously staking out turf that they defend from outside influences. "They feel at one through their lively sense and enthusiasm for knowing as such, and through their insight into the interconnectedness of all parts of the process of knowing."[31] This may seem an overly idealized hope today, something more appropriate for university catalogues or public relations material than a realistic expectation, but that was the ideal of the time, even among many natural scientists. Schleiermacher's vision is to overcome the strife among the faculties that Kant had written about in his *Conflict Among the Faculties*.[32]

The splitting of scholars into subdisciplines is beneficial, allowing each branch to gain more knowledge of a special area. The whole is more complete the more this division into branches occurs. The unity of the whole is not jeopardized but strengthened by this increasing division into specialties, for scholars' love for their own specialized discipline and their participation in the progress of knowledge as a whole are mutually stimulating activities.[33] Only students who combine both the talent for specialization and a sense for the whole in which his or her special field belongs should go forward to specialized research academies after completing university studies. The curriculum cultivates each academic discipline while also ensuring that they are related "to knowing as a whole," within a coherent, unitary vision.[34] Philosophy is the proper discipline for attaining this unity of knowledge and all students must study it alone during their first year at the university, for it is preferable for them to pursue general studies first, "to get a firm hold on principles and to acquire an overview of all the genuinely scientific disciplines."[35] Only once they have attained a coherent philosophy should they go on to specialized studies. Schleiermacher is responding to the realities of his time, when many educational reformers wanted to do away with universities as such and transform them into specialized research institutes or academies, as happened in France. He wants to protect the university from this trend and preserve a place where the integration of knowledge could still take place.

Schleiermacher believes faculty in all disciplines should also be members of the philosophical faculty in some way because "wandering from one field into the others" now and then is a sign of intellectual vitality as long as scholars do so competently. The "mutual jealousy of the faculties over their respective fields" is outmoded and injurious, for "new life comes to any branch of the sciences when it is once more treated by others afresh," especially those who are expert in other academic fields.[36] Schleiermacher expects scholars to learn outside their disciplines and even to teach an occasional course in another field so as to maintain a sense of the whole of university studies and of how their own disciplines fit in with the entire circle of the sciences. Academic freedom implies that ability, and even obligation, to roam, not aimlessly, but purposefully and holistically. Academic freedom is violated if scholars are prohibited or discouraged from going beyond the bounds of their specialized disciplines.

G. W. F. Hegel (1770–1831) attempts to overcome the radical divisions and fragmentation of thought and life, of subjective and objective worlds, and of religion and science that prevailed in his day. Building on Schelling he held that the infinite is not separate from the finite, natural world but is manifested in it. His *Encyclopedia of the Philosophical Sciences* (1817) attempts to encompass all the individual academic disciplines within a more comprehensive circle of the sciences.[37] Philosophy is the soul of this circle and its relation to other sciences is analogous to the interpenetration of the spirit of a whole living organism and its parts. They mutually permeate one another.The scholar requires freedom to reach beyond particular branches of knowledge and expand outward toward the broader circle of sciences. Academic strictures that attempt to contain thought within a closed sphere impinge on academic freedom.

The whole that comprises philosophy is divided into three parts: (1) the science of logic; (2) the philosophy of nature; and (3) the philosophy of spirit.[38] Hegel's core vision is one of the unity of God and world, of spirit and nature, of the infinite and finite. Like Schelling, he views the universe as the theater in and through which Absolute Spirit (*Geist*) goes forth from itself, becomes other than itself (objectifies itself) in the form of nature, and then becomes reconciled with itself through the works of human spirit, such as law, art, religion, and philosophy. One will immediately notice the triadic structure of these three major divisions of his system and its connection to Trinitarian thought. Each division is, in turn, divided into triads: the science of logic into being, essence, and concept; the philosophy of nature into mathematics, inorganic nature (physics), and organic nature (physiology); and the philosophy of spirit into subjective spirit, objective spirit, and absolute spirit.

The science of logic includes everything that once fell under the rubric of *metaphysics*, or the study of Being itself, of God (intra se), and logical thought.[39] Hegel begins with logic as the science of thought, which studies being-in-itself, or thought's essence. It is, in a sense, the study of the mind of God in its inner dynamics prior (logically, not temporally) to its movement toward self-objectification in the external world. In the beginning, there is an original unity within God, with no division between subject and object, thought and reality, finite and infinite. God's internal being is like a seed, an acorn still enveloped in its shell, with its full potential for outward expression contained within, but initially only in and for itself. In Christian terms, this is akin to what is referred to as the immanent Trinity in itself prior to creation.

In the *Philosophy of Nature*, Hegel notes that a necessary diremption occurs because the Spirit of God cannot fully become explicit and fully know itself unless it expresses itself *outside* itself in the form of nature. The Absolute is like a seed with its potential contained within itself, ready to be realized. The seed splits open, grows out of itself, and spreads into the world. Spirit objectifies itself by becoming its own "external world," that is, nature.[40] Nature emerges when God's internal idea presents itself as otherness, as its own external objectification. This is the essence of nature.[41] All the natural sciences—mathematics, physics (astronomy, chemistry), and organics (physiology, biology, geology)—therefore, fit within the philosophy of nature. One must study these sciences in the context of their place in the whole, as expressions of God's self-externalization.

Finally, there must be a reconciliation, or reunification, of what has been severed into a new, more complex, and comprehensive unity at a higher level.[42] The tree growing from the seed has become in reality what it was implicitly while still encased in itself.[43] Hegel describes the process by which Spirit develops in and transforms the natural world to create the works of civilization: social organizations and government (law). So all the human sciences—psychology, anthropology, history, ethics, government, law, art, religion, and philosophy—fit within the *philosophy of spirit* because they are all manifestations of the Spirit's work of reconciliation with its own original concept. This work of the Spirit occurs through humans as they refashion nature in varying ways, aiming always at the self-actualization of Spirit in the world through human flourishing.

The Trinitarian foundation that structures Hegel's philosophy has Christianity as its metanarrative, if you will. It is worthwhile to note the isomorphism between Hegel's thought and that of certain trends in Catholic theology, for example, the *exitus* from and *reditus* to God found in medieval Catholic thought, especially the philosophy of Nicholas of Cusa in *De Docta Ignorantia* (*On Learned Ignorance*),[44] and the plan of Thomas Aquinas's *Summa Theologiae*.[45]

Understanding and Reason

Hegel draws on Kant's distinction between the understanding and reason. The "understanding" is the mode of the natural sciences and mathematics; it analyzes, draws distinctions, measures. It is technical, analytical reasoning. This form of thinking Hegel identifies with "secular science," a knowledge of finite objects. It searches for "causes and grounds" of finite phenomena, but these causes and grounds are reduced to mere efficient causes.[46] Analysis and understanding of the finite are necessary and essential aspects of thought, but they reach completion only when drawn into a broader, more comprehensive form of thinking. The understanding, when used as the supreme principle and sole form of thought, is separate from the form of divine reason in us (the Logos) and tends to elevate knowledge of the finite world as the goal of thinking. When this occurs, the scholar or researcher finds himself confined on Kant's island.[47] The understanding (analytical or scientific reasoning) alone, therefore, is not able to function architectonically.

Reason, on the other hand, is more synthetic and philosophical. It has a drive for completeness, for integrating what has been understood through separation, abstraction, and analysis, and it moves dialectically toward synthetic integration.[48] A corollary of this is that all findings of analytical science must be placed in a broader system of philosophy for them to be complete. The finite, Hegel says, is that which is "not true in itself." [49] Any genuine search for truth in a university must place the finite within its infinite context. Anything short of that will be inadequate, a mere approximation to truth. And while the finite world has its own form of independence,[50] that independence is not complete. When we view finitude "as something contradictory to God [or wholly separate and independent from God], then we take the finite as something fixed, independent—not as something transitional, but rather as something essentially independent, a limitation that remains utterly such."[51] God is everywhere present, says Hegel: "the presence of God is just the element of truth that is in everything." The "true is the whole."[52] Therefore, "what is universal or abstract must precede everything else in scientific knowledge; scientifically, one must start with it," not with the determinate reality of the finite world.[53] The university as a whole, in its orientation and overall requirements for the curriculum and hiring of faculty, must begin with a comprehensive, universal framework, knowing that scholars and students in different disciplines may either begin from it or move toward it, variously, depending on their special nature and methods. From whichever starting point they begin, they must have the freedom to pursue the whole of knowledge.

Theology within the Circle of the Sciences

The German idealists are not unanimous as to the role theology should have in the modern university. Fichte believes it should be excluded entirely. The purpose of religious thought is to instruct us in how to live in accordance with God's will. God's will, however, can be known to us without any special revelation. In this he is following the thought of Kant in *Religion Within the Bounds of Reason Alone.* There is not a realm from which supernatural revelation comes externally and heteronomously. For Fichte, as with all the German idealists, the divine is immanent in the human mind. If theology is to be considered at all for inclusion in the circle of the sciences, it must relinquish its claims to "incomprehensible mysteries" and unique revelations known only through "special ambassadors,"[54] that is, clergymen. Rather, theology must be interpreted through the lens of proper philosophical understanding and be subordinated to philosophy. In fact, the teacher of religion must be trained by the philosopher and must form his system of religion in the school of philosophy. Fichte tends to downgrade theological tradition to the extent of rejecting it entirely. Tradition, which seeks to obstruct innovation in science and thought, is akin to darkness, he says.[55]

Schleiermacher's assessment is more ambivalent. The circle of the sciences is composed solely of the *philosophical* faculty. The three faculties of theology, medicine, and law are specialized schools that do not belong in the circle even though they are based within the broader university. They are pragmatic, not pure, and do not "possess their unity in knowledge specifically" but rather gather what they need from various other disciplines.[56] If theology *is* to be included in the university, it must take a place subordinate to philosophy, which must remain the superior faculty in which all others are rooted. Schleiermacher says that the grounding of theology in philosophy requires theologians to give lectures now and then within one of the other academic fields. Without such a linkage of the theological to the philosophical faculty, theology's existence as part of a university would have no justification. An individual theologian who lacks the desire and motivation to gain expertise in some science other than theology does not deserve to be on a university faculty.[57] He prefers, however, that philosophy not even be mingled with theology, medicine, and law for fear it would lose its unity and become subordinate to them.[58]

To a large extent, the separation of theology is a logical consequence of the fragmentation and specialization of branches of knowledge. Theology is narrowed to a limited area of the real, to the exposition of Christianity or to the study of Christian revelation as a separate sphere of knowledge, rather than as a grounding, pervasive feature of all knowing and all inquiry. In part, Schleiermacher adopts this solution in order to justify the inclusion of theology in the university at all. Many of the cultured despisers of religion during the Enlightenment believed it absurd to include theology, with its reliance on special revelation inaccessible to reason, in a university (this was Kant's and Fichte's position). Even so, he makes a sharp distinction between theology and other branches of knowledge.

> [Religion's essence is] found over against morals and metaphysics...In order to take possession of its own domain, religion renounces herewith all claims to whatever belongs to those others...It does not wish to determine and explain the universe according to its nature as does metaphysics; it does not desire to continue the universe's development and perfect it by the power of freedom...as does morals. Religion's essence is neither thinking nor acting, but intuition and feeling.[59]

Metaphysics, he says, "proceeds from finite human nature and wants to define consciously, from its simplest concept, the extent of its powers, and its receptivity, what the universe can be for us and how we necessarily must view it."[60] Here he is referring to Kant's "reduction of metaphysics to the realm of finite human experience" in the *Critique of Pure Reason*.[61] As a consequence, religion remains in its own domain, withdrawing from speculative sciences. It sits side by side with metaphysics and morality, in a complementary way, but sharply opposed to them at the same time.[62] The intellect, through metaphysics, considers what is on Kant's island. Feeling and intuition—associated with religion—deal with what is beyond it.

Schleiermacher, like Kant, came from a pietistic background in which religion was largely equated with private and personal feeling. Intellectual, cognitive work is different in kind from the feeling of absolute dependence on the divine that characterizes religion. As such, one can see how Schleiermacher would relegate theology to a separate professional school rather than consider it an integral component of the circle of the sciences. Theology, following Schleiermacher, was no longer integral to the circle of the sciences, at least in Protestant universities; it was moved to the margins of academic life and studied only in separate divinity schools. This remains the heritage of divinity schools in America that reside in Protestant or once-Protestant universities, such as Harvard, Yale, Princeton, and the University of Chicago: they are separated from the core liberal arts curriculum, unintegrated into the broader circle of arts and sciences. This is what Protestant universities have inherited from Schleiermacher.

Schleiermacher's thought is inconsistent, though. For example, shortly after writing that religion is sharply opposed to metaphysics, he writes,

> The universe exists in uninterrupted activity and reveals itself to us every moment. Every form that it brings forth, every being to which it gives separate existence according to the fullness of life, every occurrence that spills forth from its rich, ever-fruitful womb, is an action of the same upon us. Thus to accept everything individual as a part of the whole and everything limited as a representation of the infinite is religion.[63]

If one accepts this statement, then theological studies surely would be an integral part of understanding and exploring that rich, fruitful womb of the universe. Not for Schleiermacher, though, who goes on to say that "whatever would go beyond that and penetrate deeper into the nature and substance of the whole is no longer religion."[64] By "religion" he means piety, the feeling of unconditional dependence on the Absolute, which is not a cognitive or speculative act. Yet the science of theology is cognitive and speculative, and since it reflects on God's relation to the universe through Christ, why would it not be a part of the circle of the sciences? His own later statements suggest it should be.

> Everything is ornately connected and intertwined. That is the spirit of the world that reveals itself in the smallest things just as perfectly and visibly as in the greatest; that is an intuition of the universe that develops out of everything and seizes the mind. But only the person who in fact sees it everywhere, who, not only in all alterations but in all existence, finds nothing else but a production of this spirit and a representation and execution of these laws, only to him is everything visible really a world, formed and permeated by divinity.[65]

He also claims that the intuitions of the universe come from "the interior of the mind." Moreover, there is a Logos structure to the universe and to the human mind that observes and ponders the universe, and everything external to us "is merely an other within." Everything is the reflection of the human spirit, and the spirit is the reproduction of everything external.[66] Since university students, as we saw above, are to seek the interrelations of all things within the whole, it is curious that Schleiermacher separates theology from the other sciences. For him it is philosophy that does this investigation of the whole. Here was one symptom of the split in modern thought and the diremption of intellectual and spiritual life, based on a pietistic separation of feeling and thought (Hegel strongly criticized this separation and sought to overcome it).

Schelling, unlike Fichte and Schleiermacher, considered theology a part of the circle of the sciences. His view of the university curriculum and how subjects ought to be organized constitute the framework for a metahistory of the cosmos, a study of the processes that make up God's selfobjectification and return to unity with self through the many elements of the universe, including human history. The different sciences merely focus on different aspects of this process, with philosophy providing the overarching framework."Theology," he says, "is the highest synthesis of philosophical and historical knowledge."[67] In Christianity, the entire universe is viewed as history. The history of the universe has a theological dimension; in fact, Christian history is the comprehensive metahistory of the universe.[68] God becoming human is a process that has been going on from eternity. When God took on human form through the Incarnation, God then became truly objective.[69] Christianity sees "*through* nature conceived of as the infinite body of God, and penetrates to its innermost core, to God's very spirit,"[70] and this is the ultimate goal of university education. This is quite different from a scholastic conception of theology as a distinct science based on a separate, supernatural revelation. Although Schelling places great importance on theology, he considers philosophy rather than theology the architectonic science. Theology is a penultimate rather than ultimate discourse.

Hegel, like Schelling, is much more accepting of the role of theology. Philosophy is often considered antithetical to theology, but Hegel sees them as much the same process, as did the church fathers and some of the scholastics of the Middle Ages for whom philosophy was largely identified with theology.[71] In fact, the "science of religion is one science with philosophy."[72] Thinking and conceptual knowing were not regarded as injurious, but as necessary, to theology. Hegel, then, is seeking to overcome the divide between philosophy and theology, to reconcile them and once again to think theonomously in the manner of the church fathers.[73] Hence, not only is theology a part of the circle of the sciences in Hegel's thought, it is, because it is synonymous with philosophy, its very soul.

Hegel's was a theonomous system: the human mind is that in and through which *Geist* does its thinking. Study of the natural and human worlds are *Geist's* coming-to-consciousness of its own objectification in the form of nature, and then its attempt to come to full self-consciousness through the works of civilization (law, art, religion, philosophy). Our duty is to lay the structural framework in the human world (good laws, social order, and cultural and educational institutions that foster human flourishing) that best enables this emerging to self-consciousness to be achieved. Indeed, the concept of *Bildung* itself goes through a reconceptualization in Hegel, moving away from the individual in his or her development to "the universal Spirit's stages of *Bildung*" as this occurs through human development.[74] This means that academic freedom requires the freedom of the human mind so that *Geist* can come to consciousness within any scholar called to pursue truth in its fullness. Any restrictions on a scholar's freedom to do that would be to place a restraint on *Geist*, on the Spirit of God.

Weaknesses in the German Idealist Conception of Academic Freedom

Berlin provides an alternate model for the modern university from which Catholic educators can draw. They must, of course, draw carefully and with discernment. That means critiquing the German idealists' model in addition to borrowing on its strengths. I now offer that critique.

The encyclopedia, as conceived by the German idealists Fichte, Schelling, and Hegel, is an all-encompassing worldview into which all particular knowledge was to find its place or to be fitted. Coherence of vision and integration of knowledge are desirable, in Catholic higher education no less than German idealism. The greatest weakness of the encyclopedic vision, however, is that the overarching philosophical system can become a dominating frame that predetermines how one approaches and interprets reality. Perception and observation are formed, to a significant degree, by assumptions and concepts that predispose one to see things in a certain way. This cannot be avoided entirely. This does not mean that a scholar with prior beliefs and commitments cannot approach a subject fairly and with a degree of detachment. It does mean though, that scholars should be aware of their preconceptions and how they may influence one's observations and interpretations, so as to reduce the way prior philosophical frameworks—whether implicit or explicit—determine the outcome and interpretation of data.

Some of the German idealists tend to be uncritical regarding their own philosophical preconceptions. All knowledge in particular academic disciplines has to fit into the philosophical system governed by the encyclopedia. For Fichte, there is to be but one such philosophical system in the University of Berlin, and it is *his* system. The tributary encyclopedias, which are to be produced by scientists in the various disciplines, have to fit into the philosophical framework of the general encyclopedia, which, presumably, Fichte would write. The authors of the tributary encyclopedias would receive their philosophical training and principles from a master philosopher (again, Fichte), who would teach the proper philosophical principles by which to orient all subject matter and guide all inquiry. The tributary authors are obligated to accept the authority of these philosophical principles and agree with them. If they do not accept this authority, they should not be appointed.[75] The goal, in Ficthe's view, is for them to arrive at the same philosophical position presented in the general encyclopedia.[76]

As for a healthy pluralism in thought, Fichte is against it. As we saw, he recognizes the diversity of philosophical positions and potential for conflict, but his goal is not to take in the diverse perspectives and then foster debate and conversation among them, seeking a higher synthesis. On the contrary, his goal is to suppress them in favor of one dominant perspective. "Controversy," he writes, "quite destroys the nature of a philosophical academy and must therefore be denied all entrance thereto."[77] Fichte insisted there must be only one philosophy to frame and govern all other disciplines in order to avoid the multiplicity of competing philosophies. We can only juxtapose this assertion to Newman's belief that controversy and the meeting of mind with mind in disputation are essential aspects of university education.[78] In Fichte's desire for coherence and wholeness, he prohibits legitimate diversity of opinion and method. While seeking integration and coherence is a good thing, *forcing* knowledge into a unified theory ends up creating a procrustean bed into which data is forced to fit.

Schelling has similar tendencies. Like Fichte, he contends that the various sciences take their guidance from philosophy. Facts discovered by scientists are relevant, but not as important as the overarching philosophy. This is equally true of history. History, in Schelling's view, is a revelation that discloses the workings of the Absolute. The object of history (as a process, not the academic discipline of history) is the actualization of "an objective order of Freedom, that is, the state," and it is clear that the results of historical inquiry, rightly interpreted, must show this.[79] The correct ordering and interrelating of events is important, but these events must always be placed in an interpretive framework that sees history as a drama disclosing the workings of the divine mind. This can too easily lead to selecting historical facts that fit the "script" of the preconceived drama. Schelling displays little awareness of this potential shortcoming.

For Hegel, the attempt to force knowledge into a preordained system manifests itself especially in relation to the natural sciences. He is well aware of the distinction between philosophy and the empirical sciences, and knows that the empirical sciences approach their subject matter from a limited, finite perspective that prescinds from broader philosophical questions. He also rejects any reliance on supernatural causes to explain the workings and design of nature. He insists that the philosophy of nature must "presuppose" and be "conditioned by empirical physics."[80] The philosophy of nature cannot present a view of nature contrary to what the empirical sciences have discovered. Nonetheless, he insists that nature cannot be reduced to a mechanical system, as the Newtonians of his time held. Instead, it must be understood as a coherent whole that includes mechanical and chemical systems and also *spirit*. Though claiming not to offer alternatives to scientific explanations of natural phenomena, he frequently violates the boundaries between philosophical reflection and scientific explanations of phenomena.[81] His dialectic is at the base of this problem.

The dialectical movement is central to Hegel's entire philosophy. The indwelling tendency of all things is outward, toward self-externalization, which becomes the "negation" of their essential "idea" or concept and thereby becomes the concrete "other" of that idea. For instance, nature is the self-objectification and self-externalization of *Geist*'s own self-concept. "Nature has presented itself as the idea in the form of otherness. Since in nature the idea is as the negative of itself, or is external to itself, nature is not merely external in relation to this idea, but the externality constitutes the determination in which nature as nature exists."[82] In Hegel's philosophy of nature, each natural phenomenon must replicate this dialectic. All things must "produce" their own negation, and the joining of the thing and its negation is what constitutes a fuller whole.

This dialectic so overdetermines his interpretations that he sometimes provides explanations of natural phenomena that are quite at odds with scientific explanations of the same phenomena. For instance, he rejects the Newtonian conception of light as bundles of lightrays and particles, a concept he calls "barbarous,"[83] because it is at odds with his own system. Light, he maintains, cannot be conceived as rays or particles generated by some source, which then bounce off material objects, but is simply the way in which matter manifests itself to an "other" as its own self-externalization. Light is the "abstract self of matter," according to Hegel.[84] "Light, as universal physical identity, relates itself to the matter qualified by the other moments of the Notion. It does this in the first instance as something different from this matter, and therefore as something which is distinct from and external to it. The matter is therefore determined as the negation of light, or as a darkness, and in so far as it also subsists for itself, and is different from light."[85] Matter, Hegel says, is weighted, while light, as its negation, is weightless. These come together to form "specific gravity," sound, and heat as further determinations of matter.[86] Thus, the correct interpretation of scientific data has to fit his dialectical theory. When the scientific explanation conflicts with his own, he rejects it. He even claims that physicists were wrong to claim that the sun produces heat by consuming hydrogen, and he claims that "finite physics" cannot explain phenomenon such as lightning, heat, or rain because it does not take into account the whole of nature and reality.[87] To the scientists of his day, Hegel's explanations seemed absurd, and his philosophy of nature had almost no influence on natural scientists.

Schleiermacher avoids this kind of philosophical imperialism and is more willing to allow the various disciplines their differentiation. He does insist that all academic disciplines must be related to one another, with philosophy serving as the architectonic science, but not to the extent that the findings of science must conform to a prior conceptual framework determined by philosophers. His main flaw is that he severs theology from the circle of the sciences, thereby omitting what Newman referred to as a crucial branch of knowledge, with a subject matter related to all else.[88] Schleiermacher does not omit theology because he believes it an unworthy or unscientific discipline (like Fichte). Quite the contrary, he has high regard for it. His position is to keep it in a separate professional school, because its purpose is primarily to train professional ministers for the church. Theology is still a *Wissenschaft* that must be related to and draw insights from other sciences, but this relatedness and influence go in one direction only: *from* the various sciences in the school of philosophy *to* theology. He does not insist with equal force that scholars in the sciences should be also well accomplished in the theological dimension of reality.

Schleiermacher is also too sanguine about the harmonious, noncompetitive nature of academic disciplines. The differences in outlook, the conflict between scholars and worldviews, are great, and we cannot naïvely assume scholars in various academic disciplines will work together harmoniously. We must recognize the differences between disciplines and allow them their free exercise, even while seeking dialogue among them.

Hegel's commitment to academic freedom had its limits. Like other educators and philosophers of his time, he upheld the principles of *Lehrfreiheit* and *Lernfreiheit*, but he was not unwilling to see it abridged for scholars with whom he disagreed. This became clear over the dismissal of one of his colleagues, Wilhelm de Wette, from the University of Berlin in 1819. The

German government had become wary of academics suspected of fomenting revolutionary ideas among students and the population. Europe had
experienced turmoil during waves of revolutionary ferment since the French
Revolution, and German leaders were concerned about subversive actions
within their own realm. De Wette, a theologian sympathetic to political
reform, was considered just such a subversive and was dismissed from his
university position. Many professors at Berlin, including Schleiermacher,
protested his dismissal. Hegel, however, maintained that the state had the
right to act as it did. The state, not the individual, was the concrete realization in history of the Absolute Spirit, so its interests superceded those of
any individual. In fairness to Hegel, he did insist that the university had
an obligation to continue paying De Wette's salary, yet he did not object
to his dismissal.[89]

One final critique of German idealism. Because the theonomous philosophy of the German idealists was rooted in Protestantism and, hence, in
a personal, subjective relationship of the individual with the divine within
the interior of the mind, there is no recourse to a Great Tradition—a deep
spiritual-theological tradition—to help orient and anchor one amidst the
welter of ever multiplying and competing philosophies. This was less the
case for Hegel, and of course they all referred their thought to the history
of Western philosophy, but the foundation of their thought was highly
subjective; sometimes (as in Schelling) wildly eccentric, and sometimes (as
in Fichte) imperial.

Implications of the Berlin Model for Modern Catholic Higher Education

Given these flaws, and the different cultural and educational world of
early-nineteenth-century Germany, we must be cautious about adopting
German idealist principles in Catholic higher education. Nonetheless,
I believe many of the philosophical principles on which the University of
Berlin was founded can shed light on the attempt to integrate religion and
scholarship in Catholic universities today. Thinkers such as Schelling and
Hegel rejected the notion of "secular science" as a foundational principle,
although that option was available to them. There could not be a "great
university" based on excellence in the purely secular sciences, that is, in
the exploration of the finite world alone. Such exploration is necessary
and should be done at an advanced level, but not in isolation from the
whole, that is, from the Absolute that permeates the cosmos. The exploration of the whole was the *prius* of all scholarship for the German idealists.

They did not merely advocate secular study followed, or supplemented, by a separate study of theology, as did the Jesuit *Ratio Studiorum* of previous centuries and as do most Catholic universities today.[90] Philosophy and/or theology were to be integrated, to some extent, with all the sciences, in a more theonomous approach to study.

The standards and canons of research and academic freedom in America today turn out not to be something foundational on which all modern university research and education must be based; instead they are a contingent feature of academic life that developed in the American research university from the mid-nineteenth century until now, as we will see in the next chapter. They can by no means be said to constitute the foundational principles of the modern university. The German idealists explicitly repudiated the idea of a secular approach to the sciences as the basis of the university. At least in the origins of modern university education, the notion of a great university as a *secular* research university, and the idea that the secular university is what defines a university qua university, was far from the mark. That notion had its advocates during the eighteenth and early nineteenth centuries, but I believe Schelling, Schleiermacher, and Hegel would have considered the idea of a "secular university" a contradiction in terms.

There are several constants in the views of these four authors: the circle of the sciences forms a whole of which all individual sciences are a part. They share the belief that the Absolute, or God, is disclosed in all of nature, in human history, and in the workings of the human mind. Specialization is necessary and fruitful as long as a unity of vision holds together the ever-diversifying array of particular knowledge. Some of the key principles guiding the foundation of Berlin—the unity and integration of all knowledge, for example—remain to some degree part of the announced mission of many Catholic universities today.[91] But these principles sit side by side with different and often contradictory principles, such as increasing specialization and the fragmentation of knowledge; independence of the empirical sciences from any philosophical or theological framework; research as the dominant goal of the scholar to the neglect of teaching and integrative knowledge; and the use of strictly disciplinary criteria rather than broader philosophical criteria in judging scholarly competence. In chapters 7 and 8, I will offer a way of overcoming these contradictions.

Chapter 4

Academic Freedom and Religion in America

During the nineteenth century, scholars and administrators in America's elite colleges and universities looked to the University of Berlin as a model for their own institutions. Many of them studied in Germany for a year or more to imbibe its atmosphere of openness, freedom, and research. They inevitably brought back aspects of the highly vaunted German academic ideals to America. This German influence had a profound and transformative effect on American universities. Previously, higher education in America was characterized by small, denominational, liberal arts colleges founded on classical humanism, where Greek and Latin classics stood at the center of the curriculum. Grammar, rhetoric, logic, mathematics, natural philosophy, and moral philosophy rounded out the curriculum. This was the case for both Protestant and Catholic colleges, both of which had inherited the educational ideals of Renaissance humanism. In Catholic colleges, theology was studied only by those advancing beyond the basic collegiate level, most of them students entering the priesthood. The primary goals of American colleges were the formation of character and the training of the intellect.

This curricular foundation began to change after the Civil War. The explosion of scientific knowledge and technological advances meant rapid progress in the sciences and the formation of new scientific disciplines. Following the Berlin model, American colleges began transforming themselves into universities, focusing heavily on research and the advancement of knowledge for the benefit of society. Johns Hopkins University, established in 1876, was the first university created primarily as a graduate research institution. Other colleges soon transformed themselves into research universities: Michigan, Chicago, Harvard, and Yale, to name a few.[1] In the Catholic fold, the Catholic University of America in Washington, DC, was established in 1889 as the first Catholic research university.[2] American colleges and universities began to grow and change rapidly in the late-nineteenth century. James Turner has referred to the late nineteenth and early twentieth centuries as the "age of universities" in America, because of their rapid growth and expansion.[3]

A key element in the development of universities was the evolving understanding of academic freedom. We have seen how academic freedom in Germany was conceived as both a freedom *from* governmental and ecclesiastical intervention in academic affairs and a freedom *to* fully pursue the truth of the finite in relation to the Absolute. Unfortunately, the latter ideal of placing specialized studies within a broader philosophical context—a necessity assumed by the German idealists—did not long survive in America. In fact, nineteenth-century educators—and the historians who have studied their thought—rarely, if ever, mention the concept of academic freedom as pursuing the truth of specialized knowledge in relation to the whole of knowledge. The development of the ideal of academic freedom took on uniquely American historical and social characteristics. The ideal was transformed and, I contend, seriously restricted, confining freedom of inquiry primarily to scholarly work *within* academic disciplines.

Academic Freedom and Kant's Island

Most American universities of note were Protestant in origin and orientation until the late nineteenth and early twentieth centuries. During much of the nineteenth century, liberal theological concerns were closely allied with scientific progress. Scripture was an integral part of higher education, as was natural theology. Natural theology arises from the belief that God is manifested through his works in creation (based on Romans 1:20). The created world is wondrously intricate and intelligible, clearly the work of an intelligent designer. Moreover, if one traces the causes of all effects in the world, and the origin of all movement back to their ultimate origin, one is led to posit a First Cause and a First Mover. These arguments have their roots in both Aristotle's *Physics* and Romans 1:20, and became a standard principle in Christian thought through Thomas Aquinas's proofs for the existence of God.[4] Natural theology was distinct from revealed theology: through the former, the unaided reason could know of the existence of God; through the latter, we know of God through his revelation, especially

Scripture. Throughout Christian history, Christian thinkers have regularly linked knowledge of God gained through Scripture to knowledge of God through study of the natural world. Since the medieval period, Christian scholars have referred to "the two books of God": the book of Scripture and the book of Nature, both of which reveal and point to God.[5]

William Paley's *Natural Theology, or, Evidences of the Existence and Attributes of the Deity: Collected from the Appearances of Nature* (1802)[6] was a common text used in American colleges during the nineteenth century. Paley wanted to prove the existence of God from the evidence of design and beauty in nature. Comparing the world to an intricately designed watch, he argues that its design provides clear evidence of a divine "Watchmaker." He then provides examples of order and design from the sciences of biology, anatomy, and astronomy in order to demonstrate the intricate design of the natural world—a design that could come only from a wise and intelligent God.

This perspective was widely adopted by American educators during the nineteenth century. Science and religion were closely aligned. Roberts and Turner point out how scientists generally believed that "a study of natural phenomena would be spiritually edifying: it would attest to the glory, wisdom, power, and goodness of the Creator."[7] The scholar who studies nature also studies the mind of God, which is revealed in his works, said Charles Eliot, the future president of Harvard.[8] Another writer of the period referred to the "doxological" view of science, "the view that the investigation of nature constituted a means of praising God."[9] This melding of religion and science was common among liberal Protestant educators during the period. Religion and science were merely two differentiated but complementary functions within a broader Christian cultural worldview. Each function allowed one to learn and understand aspects of the truth. The differentiated function of the research university was to promote truth through science. Daniel Coit Gilman, the first president of Johns Hopkins University, said that religion focuses on and interprets the word of God, while science focuses on and interprets the natural laws established by God.[10]

In the course of time, however, conflicts between the two "books" arose. Science was discovering laws about the natural world that showed a universe hitherto unimaginable. The age of the earth was far older than the biblical account of creation suggested. The theory of evolution showed a mechanism for the origin and development of life forms quite different from that contained in the book of Genesis. Inevitably, literal biblical accounts of creation would collide with scientific discoveries of the origins and development of the natural world. Rather than a harmoniously designed world adapted for the happiness of man, Darwin showed nature as a brutal struggle of the fittest for survival, obeying laws of natural selection governed by chance. Scientific understandings of cause and effect would contradict biblical and religious understandings of miracles. Gradually, educators increasingly held that the Bible was not intended to be a scientific account of the world. This gave freer reign or "elbow room" for scientists to conduct their research and arrive at conclusions that came into conflict with biblical-literalist accounts of the origin and workings of the natural world. Eventually, even natural theology gave way and was undermined by science.

By the late-nineteenth century, scientists in American colleges and universities began limiting the range of their discussions and explanations to natural phenomena, effectively severing their scientific pursuits from the natural theology prevalent at the time, just as they had previously severed their inquiries from biblical perspectives.[11] All phenomena were to be brought under the domain of natural laws and secondary causes.[12] Kant's philosophy played a role in this severance. If the island of human understanding is confined within "unalterable boundaries" and limited to knowledge of phenomena, then the inference of God from the observation of natural phenomena cannot be made. Natural theology is not a possibility. We are confined to a "prison of finitude," a phrase that Paul Tillich used to describe Kant's confinement of human thought.[13] Supernatural explanations for all phenomena had to be excluded from scientific research, which focused purely on the natural realm through empirical investigations. Natural phenomena were governed by principles of cause and effect, detectable through our natural senses and the tools we build to enhance our perceptions.[14] There was no room left for miracles or revelation. Reason could study and understand these natural processes and explain them scientifically.

At first, empirical investigations did not imply a rejection of religious teachings. Rather, scientists merely prescinded from considering religious and philosophical questions in favor of focusing on finite phenomena, the better to understand them within a limited sphere. This was, of course, perfectly legitimate. Methodological agnosticism and methodological atheism became compatible with either theism or atheism; it seemed to many to be theologically neutral.[15] It was not long, however, before such naturalistic methodologies, valid in themselves, became naturalistic philosophies and entered the realm of metaphysics. It was then that some scientists openly denied the existence or influence of the divine. This, of course, led to even more conflict with religion.

Once this process of intellectual secularization had progressed far enough, there was no cogent intellectual link between ordinary causal operations and the divine. Nor was it necessary to find such links, because these operations could be understood and explained through naturalistic explanations. Only sustained observation and testing were needed to achieve true knowledge of things. For something to pass as true knowledge, it had to be verifiable and reproducible through testing by other researchers.

The goal became to narrow one's investigations to narrower and narrower slices of reality that are susceptible to testing and verification, thereby building up a well-established body of knowledge over time and through the effort of many scientists. The benefits of this method have been enormous: the scientific understanding of the mechanisms of life, technological advances that made for a better quality of life, improvements in medicine and health, and an understanding of social processes. There has also been a negative side: the excision of disciplinary knowledge from the whole of knowledge, leading to intellectual and curricular fragmentation.

Another area that created hostility between religion and science was religious opposition to Darwin's theory of evolution. Historian Walter Metzger asserts that this opposition was a factor in the movement toward an increasingly narrow concept of academic freedom as the freedom to inquire and publish within one's narrow field of competence without regard to the opinions or pressures of those outside who lacked expertise in that field. Attempts to silence or censor Darwinian scientists inevitably led to conflicts. One means of dealing with these heteronomous threats was to withdraw into an autonomous scientific realm unconnected to larger philosophical currents. Metzger claims that evaluation of academic performance became the "private" domain of scholars in a specific discipline, rather than of administrators or a broad range of knowledgeable scholars, in order to ensure that external groups, especially religious obscurantists and governmental agents beholden to political powers, could not exert pressure or control.[16]

Disciplinary Specialization and Intellectual Secularization

Most private universities in America were founded as denominational colleges for the education and training of Christian ministers. As science progressed, and as science and theology separated, these colleges began to sever their ties with their founding religious bodies. This was one element in the secularization of universities. Secularization, however, involved more than severing ties with founding religious bodies. Roberts and Turner maintain that it was disciplinary specialization, more than anything else, that led to secularization of the curriculum and the academy. Prior to the American Civil War, research was conducted and fostered but not in the form of exclusive specialization within a given field. Only in the late nineteenth and early twentieth centuries did disciplinary specialization become prominent to the extent that a scholar was discouraged from roaming from one academic field to another, gaining a coherent sense of the interrelatedness of knowledge from many fields. Reality is one and scholars in academic disciplines focus on carefully delineated aspects of the whole. Yet the different aspects are interconnected. Roberts and Turner note that, throughout most of the nineteenth century, scholars in most academic disciplines had the freedom to adopt scholarly methods from any field and conduct research across disciplines and into areas as they wished.[17] We have already seen that this freedom to pursue knowledge in all its interconnections and wherever it may lead characterized German university ideals. Even Darwin "roamed from zoology and botany (where he was expert) into philology (where he was an amateur) without perceiving any methodological barricade."[18] This freedom to roam became progressively restricted in American universities during the late nineteenth century.

Free-roaming scholars were eventually replaced by a younger generation of scholars in the latter half of the nineteenth century who were themselves disciplinary specialists, and they began to raise barriers between disciplines. Previously, specialization "neither limited authority over [a] subject to a distinctive cadre of methodologically acculturated experts nor restricted a scholar from pursuing very different subjects."[19] In the hands of the new specialists, though, "scholarly competence required restricting oneself to one's 'discipline.'" Thus, according to Roberts and Turner,

> Disciplinary specialists...began to snip apart the previously undivided map of knowledge into separate territories. Between these "disciplines" they started to erect methodological fences hard for nonspecialists to scale. They declared...two revolutionary dogmata: that knowledge does *not* form a whole but, on the contrary, properly divides itself into distinct compartments, and that unique methodological principles and scholarly traditions govern life within each of these boxes.[20]

Specialization has many positive benefits, but it has the negative effect of narrowing the realm in which a scholar could speak authoritatively—and dared to speak at all in many cases. One was to be judged only by those competent in the same specialized realm, not by others outside it. Certainly not by ecclesiastical authorities or officials of the state. Not even scholars who possessed a broad philosophical understanding of the sciences but lacked specialized knowledge in the discipline of the scholar in question were deemed competent. Academic freedom in America, then, came more and more to mean freedom to inquire and publish within a specialized realm only, a development noted with concern even by John Dewey.[21] Freedom to inquire on disciplinary islands without interference gradually came to imply prohibition against inquiry beyond it, of relating knowledge gained in it to other areas. The dark underside of academic freedom willy-nilly became academic constraint.

The only proper way a scholar could venture outward was to gain additional formal training, that is, an advanced degree in another academic discipline. The creation of these separate disciplinary islands became dominant in the twentieth century, so much so that by the late-twentieth century terms like "multiversity"—indicating that the oneness of knowledge implied in the word "university" was no longer valid—came to be applied to large universities. Indeed, one may think of the modern American research university as an archipelago of disciplinary islands that are in close proximity but unconnected by bridges. In the increasingly constrained situation in which the scholar resides, the freedom to focus on specialized matters within a narrow disciplinary framework and the freedom to prescind from pursuing questions to their ultimate end became a prohibition *against* pursuing them beyond the island. On the one hand, this displayed a desirable sense of intellectual modesty and humility, a recognition of the limits of one's knowledge. On the other, it became a means of suppressing a scholar's natural desire to move beyond his or her area of competence, especially if the movement was toward the religious. Indeed, growing hostility to religion characterized science. Moreover, the legitimate methodological decision to prescind from considering finite phenomena in relation to the divine soon became a philosophical assertion that there is no connection between knowledge on the disciplinary island and religious knowledge. Given these developments, TheodoreHesburgh's model for Catholic higher education—first building a great university in the modern sense (as in modern research university), then adding a religious dimension—is constrained from the very start.

By the late-nineteenth century, open hostility by scientists to traditional religious views gained cachet. John William Draper's *History of the Conflict Between Religion and Science* (1874) and Andrew Dickson White's *A History of the Warfare Between Science and Theology* (1896) proclaimed the need for unfettered freedom of scientific investigation untrammeled by the constraints of Christian theology.[22] This metaphor of warfare between science and religion has been a dominant metaphor in academia ever since. In fairness, it must be acknowledged that Christians, Catholics included, played a role in engendering this hostility.

Catholic Thought and the Realm of Nature

Catholic scholastic thought, ironically, also contributed to the severance of scientific inquiry from theology. Some forms of scholasticism contain an inherent dualism of orders: the order of nature and the order of the supernatural. In the cognitive realm, the corollary of these two orders is an epistemological dualism: knowledge that has its source in the natural reason, on the one hand, and knowledge that has its source in supernatural revelation, on the other. This division is rooted in the theology of Thomas Aquinas.[23] Thomas, however, while distinguishing between these forms of knowing, did not make the kind of fateful, ontological separation between orders that later scholastics, such as Cajetan and Suarez, did. In Thomas there remained a natural desire of the mind for God, and a natural orientation of all things to the divine. In the university, all subjects were to be ordered in such a way as to lead to a knowledge of God. Later scholastics undermined this idea of the natural desire of the mind for God. The order of nature, they claimed, had its own laws, its own finality, and natural beings sought merely natural ends. Natural reason had its own ends and scope that did not extend to the realm of the supernatural unless illuminated and moved by supernatural grace. Cajetan wrote that "reasonable nature is a closed whole within which the active capacities and tendencies are in strict correspondence." The natural desire of the mind does not extend beyond the natural faculty of human reason ("*Naturale desiderium non se extendit ultra naturae facultatem*").[24]

Eventually the concept of "pure nature," entirely separated from the divine, began to emerge. Both nature and humans, previously understood as having an orientation toward God, were now considered independent realms, all but devoid of divine presence. They had purely natural ends. Only through supernatural intervention, working as an efficient cause external to the world, did the divine influence the natural and human world. The divine was placed in a distant, supernatural realm, inaccessible to most people except through the mediation of the church. Or it was to be found in a highly subjective and affective interior realm of the subjective self, as one finds in many mystics of the sixteenth and seventeenth centuries. The divine presence became known to the subjective, interior self through inner experience, but the inner experience was not connected to intellectual developments.[25]

Catholics, therefore, no longer searched for divine presence in the world; rather, they searched for it outside the phenomenal world in a separated realm. These developments led, over the centuries, to secularism, to a natural and human world where God is irrelevant. It was Kant who argued that this supernatural realm, severed from the natural and connected only heteronomously, was a sea of illusion, and he declared the natural realm accessible to human reason to be an island "enclosed by nature within unalterable limits."[26] Human reason is sufficient; we do not need to look beyond it to revelation. The Catholic concept of "pure nature," then, led inexorably to Kant's island, where the realm of the supernatural is a deceptive sea of illusion on which the wise person does not set sail. For Catholics, of course, there remained a superadded layer that can intervene in the affairs of the island, heteronomously. In such a view, the realm of the sacred can influence the natural only from without, as an intrusion. The realm of thought is influenced by religion only through the intervention of external religious authorities. As the severance of theology from other forms of intellectual thought advanced, the church claimed to rule over all realms and "to control them from the outside," leading to the fight between "autonomous secularism and religious heteronomy," in the words of Paul Tillich.[27] Theology began focusing on a highly abstract supernatural world largely unrelated to the discourse of scholars in other academic disciplines. Kant had rejected the added-on layer and proclaimed the island of human understanding alone sufficient. Non-Christian rationalists merely ignored the added-on layer and excluded it from their considerations and from academic thought.[28]

Henri de Lubac, as much as any other historian in the twentieth century, uncovered the detailed history of these developments. Once the supernatural is severed from a "pure nature," he asked, "what misgivings could the supernatural cause to naturalism? For the latter no longer found it at any point in its path, and could shut itself up in a corresponding isolation, with the added advantage that it claimed to be complete." Catholic philosophers and theologians of the sixteenth and seventeenth centuries, in their attempt to protect the transcendence of the supernatural realm, ended up "banishing" it from the world, thus ceding the world to secularism. "The most confirmed secularists found in [this separated realm of the supernatural]...an ally."[29] It was but a short step from the dualism of Catholic scholasticism to the agnosticism of Kant, and another short step from Kant to philosophical atheism.

A curriculum based on such a dualistic order would, of necessity, make the natural sciences and other nontheological disciplines separate and autonomous from theology, disconnected from theonomous thinking. The sciences readily asserted their autonomy and independence. They grew independently of theology, sometimes indifferent to it (what impact could a separated theology have on science?), and often in hostility to it. Nonetheless, Catholicism still attempted to censor and control modern scientific development and thought, naturally provoking hostility, as we will see in more detail below.

Catholicism, Modern Thought, and Academic Freedom

Anti-Catholic hostility was a pervasive feature of American life in the late nineteenth and early twentieth centuries.This created a defensive posture on the part of American Catholic academics, who often reacted in kind, with condemnation of progressive American life and modernity generally. We may rightly criticize secular academics for their narrow understanding of academic freedom and their hostility to religion, but we must also acknowledge that religious leaders and educators—both Catholic and Protestant—played a major role in engendering hostility to religion and inducing academics to close off ranks to religious considerations. Religious leaders were often as hostile to modern trends in scholarship as scientists were hostile to theology. Moreover, sectarian disputes, by fomenting bitter strife over the teaching of religion in public colleges and schools, played into the hands of secularists. Roman Catholics' objection to the teaching of religion in the public schools, which they (rightly) considered Protestant, led many public institutions to banish Bible study and theology from the curriculum altogether, as too divisive and sectarian. Charles Eliot, the president of Harvard from 1869 to 1909, even noted how "the supreme subject of theology has been banished from the state universities" and from many private universities because of sectarian religious conflicts over how religion should be taught.[30]

Academic disputes over religion between Protestants and Catholics were common in the nineteenth and twentieth centuries. Protestants even found common cause with secularists in trying to keep the state from funding Catholic colleges and schools, by promoting the theory of a "wall of separation" between church and state. Protestants believed that such a separation would not hurt their own version of Christianity because the general cultural ethos of society at large, and the schools in particular, were Protestant. Hence, prohibiting religious schools and programs from receiving public funds, they reasoned, would not affect Protestant Christianity because the schools were broadly Christian (Protestant) in ethos. In the end, even the Protestant versions of theology and religion were banned from public schools, leaving the secularist agenda triumphant.[31]

There were other sources of conflict between Catholicism and modern American culture. In the early-twentieth century, optimism about enlightened modernism had been shattered. The killing fields of Europe during World War I undermined optimism about progressive advances. Trends in cultural and intellectual life trended toward nihilism. Music and art expressed increasing angst, while education became progressively fragmented and society alarmingly secularized. Given these realities, Catholics reacted negatively and strove to fashion a Catholic educational system that would counter the insidious influences of modernity.

The Vatican also saw developments in society, education, and philosophy during the nineteenth and early twentieth centuries in a negative light. A number of papal encyclicals were issued in the period from 1879 to 1950 calling attention to the destructive nature of modern philosophical developments and recommending Catholic philosophy as the alternative. Pope Leo XIII's *Aeterni Patris* (1879; hereafter AP) constituted a vigorous renewal and assertion of Catholic philosophy and its enduring value for intellectual culture.[32] A key component is an insistence on the value of natural theology—of the ability of the mind to know God through the visible universe. The universe reveals a maker, and the pope was concerned that the integrity of the faith was being corrupted by modern philosophies that deny this.

Leo insists that the church does not oppose the advancement and development of natural science, but promotes it, since study of the natural world leads to awareness of things divine. Indeed, he says there is no conflict between the natural sciences and scholastic philosophy worthy of the name (AP 30). He writes that "all studies should accord with the Catholic faith, especially philosophy, on which a right interpretation of the other sciences in great part depends" (AP 1). This meant adopting one overarching philosophy that would overcome the multiplication of philosophical novelties (AP 24). That overarching philosophy is the thought of St. Thomas Aquinas. The pope contrasts the unity and coherence of Thomas's philosophy with what he perceives as a chaotic multiplication of "novelties" and conflicting philosophies (AP 24). The effect is a narrowing of Catholic intellectual life because of the almost exclusive focus on scholasticism and the philosophy of Thomas Aquinas.[33] A strong heteronomous impulse is also present: scholars must subject their reason to divine authority. This means primarily to the teachings of the church, given by religious authorities.

The condemnation of modernism in 1907 by Pope Pius X in *Pascendi Domenici Gregis* (*Against the Modernists*; hereafter PDG) had a chilling effect on scholars in Catholic colleges and universities.[34] In *Pascendi* many strands of modern thought are condemned. First among them is agnosticism, which denies that we can know the divine through natural means and argues that we must rely on human reason alone for what we can know and understand. Agnosticism maintains that human reason must be confined "entirely within the field of phenomena" to things that are perceptible to the senses. Human reason, in the view of modernists, has no right and no power to "transgress these limits" (PDG 6). In the intellectual and academic realm God must be excluded from inquiry because God is not something in the phenomenal world, a position in conformity with Kant's *Critique of Pure Reason*. Pius X points out that such an approach undermines both natural theology, through which the mind is led to God through contemplation of the visible universe, and external revelation, which comes through mediation of the church. The pope was within his rights (and duty) to criticize this philosophy and point out its shortcomings. He did more than this, though: he condemned it outright and forbade the consideration and discussion of modern philosophies in Catholic seminaries and institutions of higher education. He also reiterated Leo XIII's recommendation of Thomas Aquinas. In fact, *Pascendi* required the teaching of Thomas's thought in all Catholic colleges and seminaries. This tendency to condemn rather than engage modern thought, unfortunately, conflicted with Thomas's own approach to non-Christian philosophy. Thomas had actively engaged the thought of his time, assimilated what was compatible with Christianity, and debated what was not.

Agnosticism was not the only idea that met Pius X's censure. Equally condemned was the idea that the church must come into line with modern thought and institutions, and rid itself of encrusted forms of thought and life that were not essential to the faith. Furthermore, he condemned the argument that some doctrines of the church were not based on the teachings of Scripture or the early church; rather, they were later additions and therefore not integral to Catholic life and faith.

Pascendi condemned modernism as the "synthesis of all heresies" (PDG 39) in language that oozed sarcasm on almost every page. The encyclical was criticized by many as authoritarian and repressive of freedom of thought. Philip Gleason and others believe the condemnation had long-term, damaging effects on Catholic intellectual life, creating what some have called an "intellectual reign of terror."[35] Any faculty member suspected of harboring modernist thought was to be fired from his or her teaching position (PDG 48).Catholic college libraries either were purged of modernist books or had them locked up, available only to those who had special permission to use them. Books were to be censored by bishops before publication if they did not meet standards of orthodoxy (PDG 52). If they were already published, they were to be suppressed and kept away from Catholic students (PDG 51).[36] Catholic priests were forbidden to be editors of journals or periodicals without the prior written permission of their bishop (PDG 53); and they were not allowed to attend academic conferences at which any hint of a modernist topic might be discussed (PDG 54). Diocesan "watch committees" were set up to monitor publications and teachings of Catholics.

The overall thrust of *Pascendi* was repressive and dictatorial. Catholic educators—taking their cue from the Vatican—suppressed certain kinds of knowledge that challenged Christian doctrine. This occurred by proscribing certain authors, placing their works on the Index of Prohibited Books, and excluding certain ideas and authors from college syllabi. One would be hard pressed to find a clearer example of heteronomy, in the sense of authoritarian leaders proscribing what those under their charge can do, think, and explore. A declaration of autonomy from such heteronomous control is a proper response. But autonomy without reference or relation to God degenerates into a mere humanism wherein humans are enclosed within themselves. Kant's version of autonomy, as we saw, leads to a "prison of finitude."[37] The church is right to criticize this aspect of modernity. On the other hand, forbidding autonomy—in the sense of using one's own reason without someone else telling one what to think (Kant's definition of enlightenment)—is a violation of the dignity of those who are made free in the image of God.

Pius X's stance may be summarized as follows. Humans are necessarily dependent on the divine; they are not autonomous creatures independent of God.[38] An exaggerated autonomy leads to agnosticism and atheism, devoid of God. Dependence on God implies obedience to church authorities, who are representatives of Christ on earth. The corollary to this is that Catholics must rely on church authorities for the proper way to think about the world. This outline is perhaps too simplistic, but it summarizes a consistent thread woven through papal documents during the late nineteenth and early twentieth centuries.

In the encyclical *Humani Generis* (1950; hereafter HG), Pope Pius XII wanted to refute ideas that threatened to undermine Catholic doctrine.[39] Among these were the theories of evolution, existentialism, and historicism. Each of these, writes Pius XII, in some way considers only existing things in the world. Evolution considers living beings only in their material and biological development, but not their spiritual dimension. Existentialism considers humans in their subjective consciousness alone. Historicism limits its purview to the verifiable historical events in human life without consideration of divine providence or of history as a response (good or bad) to God's will. These theories base knowledge on these finite realms while neglecting their "unchangeable essences" (HG 5–7). Such philosophies, the Vatican feared, inevitably undermine theology itself because of its dependence on the reality of divine revelation. Hence the constant concern over what many saw as purely secular disciplines: those disciplines frequently affected the theological doctrines held by the church and, inevitably, a movement arose to change those doctrines to conform with whatever the current philosophies were. Again, the ideas of Thomas Aquinas were promoted as the antidote to these false philosophies (HG 31). Pius XII did ameliorate his criticism of evolution by saying that those who are experts in the field of biological evolution had the right to conduct research and discuss the findings regarding the development of the human body from preexistent material, but not the development of the soul. They were warned to be sure to give reasonable positions on all sides of the debate and ultimately to be prepared to submit their work to the judgment of the church (HG 36).

It is clear that all these papal documents are arguing against some version of Kant's restriction of cognition to the island of human understanding alone. Human knowing, limited to the finite realm and to "natural" knowledge alone, is not adequate. On the one hand, there is nothing problematic, from a Catholic perspective, of this critique of the relegation to knowledge to the finite. On the other hand, these Vatican documents went well beyond a critique of certain philosophical positions. They condemned modernity so strongly and thoroughly that they created an atmosphere in which Catholics hesitated and even feared to engage in conversation with modern currents of thought. The overall tone and thrust of these encyclicals was to confront and correct modern thought, not to engage it; not to leaven and steer it from within, but to correct it from without.

It would be a gross exaggeration to claim that hostility toward modern thought and academic freedom characterized all Catholic scholars during this period. It did not. It did, however, find frequent echo in the writings of a number of American Catholic educators during the first half of the twentieth century. For example, Hunter Guthrie, S. J., inaugurated president of Georgetown University in 1949, derides modern concepts of academic freedom, calling them a false liberty leading to license. The liberty to teach profane subjects, he says, is accompanied by a prohibition against informing students about the divine dimension of reality. Such license allows scholars to mistake "the part for the whole." Secular notions of academic freedom, he writes, afford the atheistic view the same standing as the Catholic, and the secular viewpoint receives an equal hearing with the religious. The autonomous mind, severed from objective truth assured by authority, cannot know truth "without the controlling assistance of Revelation."[40] The authority of the church's Magisterium, of course, determined what constituted revelation. Academic freedom had become "a sacred fetish," and "the sooner it is armor-plated by some sensible limitation," the sooner will America be secure against flawed systems of thought.[41] On the one hand, Guthrie means by this that modern scholars fail to look beyond the particular knowledge of their disciplines to the larger whole. In this regard he is justified in criticizing the modern university. The German idealists would have done no less. Intertwined with Guthrie's criticism, however, is a rejection of much of modern thought in favor of an emphasis on classical learning. Classical learning in ancient times, according to Guthrie, is what prepared "the intellect of the world for the advent of Christ," and a curriculum based on classical learning is what will lead students to Christ today. With the exception of science, modern thought has little to offer.[42] This amounts to a refusal to allow students to learn modern trends in thought, understand those trends, and assess their strengths and weaknesses in light of Catholic thought.

For Guthrie, revelation is restricted to an objective body of doctrine but does not include the spiritual awareness in the mind of the scholar. This has not always been the case in Catholic thought. Yves Congar has shown that, in earlier centuries, revelation referred not only to Scripture and doctrine, but also to "the idea of a divine illumination, active in all knowledge, even in what we should regard now as coming under the heading of purely natural knowledge."[43] This idea of illumination was assumed by many of the church fathers, including Augustine. Scholastic thought progressively narrowed the idea of revelation to "supernatural" revelation, that is, that which comes through an objective body of texts and authoritative pronouncements.[44]

The idea of including thought adverse to Catholic teachings in the curriculum did not sit well with many Catholic educators. Edward Rooney, S. J., wrote in 1941 that "the Catholic educational institution may not tolerate in its classrooms or in its publications advocacy of doctrines or practices that are in contradiction to its own fundamental tenets."[45] By "advocacy" he clearly means to include even "consideration" and "discussion" of problematic ideas. This position held sway in many Catholic institutions. Fairfield University, a Jesuit university, stated on the opening page of its 1959 catalogue, "Fairfield University refuses to subscribe to the doctrine that 'academic freedom' may be used as a pretext to teach systems which destroy all freedom. It proudly boasts that as a Catholic institution it has taught and will always teach the principles on which rest all law, order, and right government."[46] That meant excluding many aspects of modern thought that questioned the traditional order.[47]

The University of Notre Dame faced charges of antiintellectualism during the 1920s under the prefecture of Father John O'Hara. O'Hara believed that "error whether doctrinal or moral simply had no rights, and the godlessness of the secular campus and the libertinage that was fostered by modern American literature could be banished from Notre Dame without any great loss."[48] He considered the culture outside campus adversarial to morality, and he wanted to protect students from it. They were to avoid the movie theater and the dance hall. In his effort to strengthen the spiritual life on campus, he suggested to the Notre Dame president that students be forbidden to live offcampus. "My judgment is that the off-campus residence of a large body of our students is detrimental not only to the off-campus students themselves, but to the student body as a whole. The infiltration of the spirit of the world in our students is one of the things our cloister is intended to combat."[49] The *Bulletin* of the University of Notre Dame in 1920 states that students are "expected to take their recreation on the large, park-like campus" rather than "in loitering about the city" of South Bend.[50] This kind of suspicion and hostility toward modern thought and culture was common among American Catholic educators—common, but not universal.

Others were more open to modern thought. John Courtney Murray, S. J., for example, was aware of the deficiencies of modern secular thought, yet he held that the Catholic intellectual's task was to analyze and understand it rather than merely denounce it. The goal was "to seek and love and liberate the truth that is at the heart of every error."[51] Many Catholic educators wanted to shut out the modern world and keep Catholic students enclosed in the protective embrace of the Catholic college, as if it were a fortress against danger. Murray protested this tendency.

> Is the Catholic scholar a self-inclosed spiritual monad in a secularist world? And is the Catholic institution of learning simply a citadel, a fortress of defense, or an asylum of escape? Does it exist on the periphery or at the center of the present cultural crisis? Has it an orientation rather sectarian than Catholic in the adequate sense? Is it the focus of purely centripetal movements, all its currents incoming, none out-going?[52]

Unfortunately, the answers to those questions at many Catholic colleges during the early-twentieth century were affirmative. Against this centripetal tendency, Murray held that the Catholic college "ought to be the point of departure for a missionary effort out into the thickening secularist milieu…It is not enough to stand firm against the [secularist] drift; for after one has stood firm, the drift itself still continues to sweep other minds and souls off into the shallows and on to the rocks."[53] Rather than defensiveness, the Catholic college needed to develop an "intellectual apostolate" that would nurture both mind and soul, producing spiritually mature, committed young scholars who would be a leaven to the world they entered upon graduation.

Jacques Maritain, one of the leading Thomist philosophers of this period, insisted that the liberal arts curriculum must be recast and enlarged to integrate modern advances in the natural and social sciences; indeed, he considered physics as among "the chief branches of the liberal arts." Instead of censoring or excluding the natural sciences because of difficulties they pose to Christian doctrines, he wanted them included because they "provide man with a vision of the universe and a sense of the sacred, exacting, unbending objectivity of the humblest truth." The social sciences must also be taught, though from a sound philosophical perspective rather than from the biased positivistic perspectives with which they are normally approached.[54]

Unfortunately, views like those of Murray and Maritain did not predominate in Catholic higher education during the period. Instead, heteronomy, hostility to modern thought, antipathy toward academic freedom, and academic weakness prevailed. Overall, we see a failure of openness to the thought and development of surrounding cultures on the part of Catholic college educators. This was not always the way with Catholic thinkers. In the nineteenth century, John Henry Newman articulated a case for academic freedom in the Catholic university: "[The university] is a place . . . in which the intellect may safely range and speculate, sure to find its equal in some antagonist activity, and its judge in the tribunal of truth. It is a place where inquiry is pushed forward, and discoveries verified and perfected, and rashness rendered innocuous, and error exposed, by the collision of mind with mind, and knowledge with knowledge."[55]

Newman was himself caught personally between forces advocating the autonomy of the scientific endeavor, on the one hand, and a heteronomous control of the academic enterprise by church leaders through authoritarian means, on the other. He equally rejected both poles. This was a profoundly personal issue for Newman. In his own life, he had to answer charges that, on becoming a Catholic, he forfeited his right to think independently and freely. His response to that charge was to claim that the church has always allowed for the free airing of ideas. Scholars, he insisted, must have due freedom to pursue their subject matter wherever it leads. The church "fears no knowledge, but she purifies all; she represses no element of our nature, but cultivates the whole." Her principle is "not to prohibit truth of any kind, but to see that no doctrines pass under the name of Truth but those which claim it rightfully."[56] Scholars need "elbow room" and freedom to explore the specific line of inquiry to which they have devoted their intellectual talents.[57] He claimed that the church has always been willing to allow this elbow room and has hesitated to pronounce on matters until an idea has been thoroughly discussed and critiqued, and then only when the matter impinges on matters of faith and morals.[58]

Newman's idea was not, unfortunately, the dominant one in Catholic higher education circles. During the first half of the twentieth century one frequently finds positive references to Newman's *Idea of a University*, especially to the idea of developing in students a wide-ranging philosophical habit of mind. But one seldom finds references to his statements on the freedom of the scholar to pursue his studies freely and to test his ideas out through publications and scholarly debate. On the contrary, Catholic scholars were often punished for doing so. For example, efforts by Catholic scholars to come to terms with the theory of evolution were suspect and authors silenced. John A. Zahm, C. S. C. and Pierre Teilhard de Chardin, S. J. were two of the more well-known figures. Zahm attempted to reconcile the theory of evolution with ancient Christian thought. Teilhard attempted to synthesize Christianity and evolution by showing Christ as the source, driving force, and end of evolution. John Courtney Murray was silenced for his attempt to reconcile religious freedom in a pluralistic democracy with Catholic thought. Henri de Lubac was silenced and exiled from his university position in France for his attempt to recover the rich but forgotten (and suppressed) traditions of Catholic thought. Their thought could have had a significant leavening effect on Catholic intellectual life had it been published and made widely available in a more timely way. Given the tradition within Catholicism of openness to and engagement with the intellectual currents of the time, and the fact that freedom and institutional autonomy found a home in the medieval universities,[59] it is a tragedy that Catholic colleges in the early-twentieth century were hostile to it.

Non-Catholic academics in America could not help but observe these attitudes and repressions in the Catholic intellectual world, so they instinctively rejected as heteronomous the religious dimension of academic inquiry. As a consequence, they developed their methods of inquiry and principles of academic freedom largely without regard to, and sometimes in hostility to, religious ways of knowing. An examination of the definitions of academic freedom in America during the twentieth century will illustrate this.

Defining the Meaning of Academic Freedom in America

Historical tensions between religion and science have played a major role in shaping our current understanding of academic freedom, which is defined largely in terms of protecting scholars from undue encroachments from nonacademic interests, both church and state, and even other academics outside one's specialization. It is seldom defined as the right to follow one's intellectual proclivities to other realms, especially if that broader realm touches on the religious.

The American Association of University Professors (AAUP), founded in 1915, played a leading role in advocating establishment of the principle of academic freedom in America. The AAUP issued its first report on academic freedom in 1915, declaring that academic freedom comprises three elements: "freedom of inquiry and research; freedom of teaching within the university or college; and freedom of extra-mural utterance and action."[60] The AAUP wanted to ensure that scholars have the freedom to inquire and publish "without fear or favor." The scholar must be "absolutely free not only to pursue his investigations but to declare the results of his researches, no matter where they may lead him or to what extent they may come into conflict with accepted opinion."[61] The report encourages competent and patient inquiry, temperateness in expression, fairness and balance when dealing with controversial topics, and considerateness of both the students' level of maturity and their inherited beliefs.[62] The report recognizes the need for research in dealing with the natural world (through natural science), the human world (through social science), and "ultimate realities and values" (through philosophy and religion).

> In the spiritual life, and in the interpretation of the general meaning and ends of human existence and its relation to the universe, we are still far from a comprehension of the final truths, and from a universal agreement among all sincere and earnest men. In all of these domains of knowledge, the first condition of progress is complete and unlimited freedom to pursue inquiry and publish its results. Such freedom is the breath in the nostrils of all scientific activity.[63]

The committee then describes the important service scholars can render the commonweal. It details the vital function social and natural scientists carry out, but it does not follow up on its statement, just cited, about the freedom to pursue religious truth. Nor does it suggest a trajectory from the natural and social sciences to the religious and philosophical. In fact, the only other reference to religion is to encourage religious colleges and universities to state clearly in writing their limitations on scholars' academic freedom.

In subsequent developments in the concept of academic freedom, freedom becomes narrowed to scholars working within their disciplines. For example, in 1930, Arthur O. Lovejoy provided the following definition of academic freedom:

> The freedom of the teacher or research worker in higher institutions of learning to investigate and discuss the problems of his science and to express his conclusions, whether through publication or in the instruction of students, without interference from political or ecclesiastical authority, or from the administrative officials of the institution in which he is employed, unless his methods are found by qualified bodies of his own profession to be clearly incompetent or contrary to professional ethics.[64]

Lovejoy was one of the founding organizers of the American Association of University Professors in 1915, and his definition has carried considerable weight since its promulgation. This statement rightly rejects heteronomy ("without interference from political or ecclesiastical authority"). A scholar with a proclivity for broader studies, however, would be struck by the narrowness of the definition: academic freedom is confined to investigating and discussing the problems of one's *particular* science. It is a freedom from interference and pressure from anyone lacking competence in one's specialized field or subfield, not a freedom to explore beyond it and connect it with other aspects of the whole of reality. It was the latter freedom, we will recall, that characterized the ideal of academic freedom in the German model. In the American setting this freedom would be especially prohibited if one attempted to venture into the theological realm and make connections between God and his creation. Roberts and Turner point out that specialization served to exclude religious knowledge "as an *intellectual* tool within the university."[65] The justification for this exclusion is the assumption that religious belief limits intellectual freedom because it is based on acceptance of an authority other than one's own reason.

The American Association of University Professors' 1940 "Statement of Principle on Academic Freedom and Tenure" is silent on the freedom to pursue truth beyond one's disciplinary boundaries. The statement claims that "the common good depends upon the free search for truth and its free exposition," and that "teachers are entitled to full freedom in research and in the publication of the results."[66] There is no indication in the statement of a freedom to inquire into the relations of one's specialized field to a broader philosophical or theological framework. Such limiting vision consistently characterized thinking on academic freedom in America throughout the twentieth century.

During the 1950s American academics became alarmed by increasing threats to academic freedom from many quarters of society. Senator Joseph McCarthy's investigations of Communist infiltration into institutions of American society was one major threat. A number of scholars were either Communists or Communist sympathizers, and the threat of Communist infiltration into the academy worried many Americans. Many powerful leaders in society wanted them dismissed from their academic positions. There were also threats from economic interests that disliked scholarly criticism of corporate policies and criticism that shed light on the negative impact of laissez-faire capitalism. Finally, there was the threat from religious authorities who wished to censor viewpoints that did not conform to specific religious orthodoxies.

A spate of publications appeared during the 1950s addressing the issue of academic freedom.[67] The thrust of these books and articles was to define academic freedom and to defend it against threats both external and internal to the university. Among them was that of Sidney Hook.

> [Academic freedom] is the freedom of professionally qualified persons to inquire, discover, publish and teach the truth as they see it *in their field of competence*, without any control or authority except the control or authority of the rational methods by which truth is established. Insofar as it acknowledges intellectual discipline or restraint from a community, it is only from the community of qualified scholars which accepts the authority of rational inquiry.[68]

One's freedom is limited to one's "field of competence" and does not extend to include the freedom to pursue truth beyond that field, to the full truth in connection to other areas and to the divine.

Robert MacIver makes the same limitation on the pursuit of truth. Academic freedom for MacIver means that the scholar and the student are free to learn for their own sake, to seek truth. A statement is true when it is "in accord with the facts," with the way things can be shown to be, using methods of scientific and rational inquiry. The scholar observes the phenomena, gathers data, and applies the "logic of evidence" using his or her own ingenuity and reason. Truth derived from revelation or faith does not constitute this kind of knowledge, in MacIver's view, and therefore is to be discounted in the academy. Truth "is relevant only to knowledge that depends on investigation, that can always be questioned and retested, and that is never accepted on the ground that it is the deliverance of any authority, human or divine." Faith then becomes an "invasion" of this realm of scientific investigation.[69] Faith is always understood as something accepted blindly without critical thinking, without assessment of facts and experience. This perspective defines faith as belief based on acceptance of an extrinsic authority, not an intrinsic divine illumination of the mind.

"Academic freedom is…a right claimed by the accredited educator, as teacher and as investigator, to interpret his findings and to communicate his conclusions without being subjected to any interference, molestation, or penalization because these conclusions are unacceptable to some constituted authority within or beyond the institution."[70] This definition rightly seeks to exclude heteronomous interference by ecclesiastical, governmental, or economic interests. The alternative it presents, however, is that only truth derived through one's own ingenuity and autonomous reason counts. There is no consideration of an alternative to both autonomy and heteronomy.

As examples of an optimistic modernism, these definitions do not entertain the possibility that the very philosophical framework that believes truth is only what comes through scientific investigation is itself the offspring of a philosophical position that limits the human mind to a small island. Freedom for the student became "freedom of the student within his field of study"[71] rather than the freedom to pursue truth beyond one's field to a more encompassing reality. Outside authority is rightly barred from interfering in academic pursuits; scholars, both professors and students, are rightly afforded the freedom to pursue their specialized realm of reality in accordance with the accepted methods of their disciplines and to publish the results of their findings without censorship. What is missing is any recognition of the right of these scholars to move off of Kant's island to the sea of mystery, not because an outside authority demands this of them but because there is an orientation of the mind to know the full truth of things, a desire of the mind for God[72] that demands of some scholars that they freely seek to know the full reality of the realm they study.

That freedom is precisely what is missing from our modern understandings of academic freedom. That freedom is seldom, if ever, discussed in the modern university. Robert MacIver even claims that the academy must exclude any conclusions that "lie apart from or beyond the test of investigation" because it is "at odds with the scientific spirit."[73] Only empirical investigation into phenomena is valid. In fact, MacIver states that no area of reality must be fenced off from scientific investigation. He argues that religion usually contains a cosmology and teaches that there are social consequences to the violation of moral codes, or that there is a divine force at work in the world with efficacious action on natural processes and human history. These teachings are ascertainable or falsifiable through investigation, MacIver asserts, so they are proper subjects of academic study.

The divine is here treated and understood as something objective in the phenomenal world, not as a spiritual reality and awareness brought to bear on all studies, as the spiritual depth dimension of inquiry. Indeed, MacIver rejects the idea that religious consciousness may legitimately be brought to bear on science. Science may study and criticize religion as a phenomenon, but not the reverse. Religion as a spiritual knowing may not be brought to bear on or criticize "secular" inquiry. MacIver did assert that "the search for knowledge cannot, without injury and distortion, be confined, divided, or regulated by any boundaries of faith, race, party, or nationality."[74] His purpose in this statement is to criticize those universities that hire only those who think like themselves. In this he is right, but he fails to see how he has himself already placed boundaries around Kant's island to negate the influence of the religious and to prohibit inquiry from going off the island. Freedom of mind must never be suppressed or truncated in the academy—not in the name of religion, nor in the name of irreligion. Boundary fences built to ensure that outside intruders stay out also serve to keep explorers confined to the inside, unable to venture out.

Walls meant to prohibit external powers from binding the reason can also be used to constrain reason's drive toward ultimacy.

Let us contrast this limiting perspective on academic freedom in the literature of American higher education with a statement articulated during the same period by an international conference convened by UNESCO in 1950. At this conference, leaders of universities worldwide developed three interrelated principles that every university should uphold.

- The right to pursue knowledge for its own sake and to follow *wherever the search for truth may lead*.
- The tolerance of divergent opinion and freedom from political interference.
- The obligation as social institutions to promote, through teaching and research, the principles of freedom and justice, of human dignity and solidarity, and to develop mutually material and moral aid on an international level.[75]

It is the first of these principles—the right to pursue knowledge wherever the search for truth may lead—that is of interest.[76] This statement leaves open the possibility of pursuing knowledge beyond one's disciplinary island. This reflects an influence perhaps more European than American. Interestingly, the First Global Colloquium of University Presidents in 2005 based its own declaration of academic freedom on the UNESCO statement. They made a slight alteration to the UNESCO principle, however, defining academic freedom as "the freedom to conduct research, teach, speak, and publish, *subject to the norms and standards of scholarly inquiry*, without interference or penalty, wherever the search for truth and understanding may lead."[77] While the addition of the qualifying phrase "subject to the norms and standards of scholarly inquiry," may seem innocuous, we must understand that these norms and standards are often quite constraining in practice. In fact, the Colloquium goes on to state that scholarly competence "must be subject solely to the professional judgment of scholarly colleagues."[78] One may ask, however, what if those colleagues are so narrowly specialized that they have no appreciation for the whole within which their specialized knowledge fits? What if their viewpoint is founded on a narrow ideological position from which they view all differing perspectives as offensive and worthy of exclusion? No serious scholar will dispute that many academics are dismissive of religious perspectives. The pursuit of knowledge too often turns out to mean "wherever the search for truth may lead, *as long as the search remains on Kant's island*."

It was this narrow and truncated ideal of academic freedom as a freedom from pursuing truth in its wholeness to which many Catholic educators objected. Unfortunately, in rejecting its narrow manifestations, they often rejected its legitimate aspects as well.

According to Philip Gleason, the established norms of academic freedom had been evolving for a century or more and were doing so quite apart from religious considerations. Not only that, but they were developing "in actively hostility to" religious influences. Consequently, academic freedom became bound with a worldview that labels religious thought as outmoded and inimical to the progress of science and scholarship. Indeed, many of the principal advocates of academic freedom in America have been social and natural scientists with a "predominantly secular and positivistic bent of mind." Gleason even refers to this worldview as a "quasi-religion."[79] This attitude is deplorable, but we must acknowledge the role religious thinkers of the past few centuries—animated by their own hostility to scientific findings and their own attempts at censorship—contributed to it.

Chapter 5

The Pursuit of Intellectual and Spiritual Wholeness, 1920–1960

Catholic thought during the period prior to the Second Vatican Council is often depicted as backwards and obscurantist by both liberal Catholics and secularists. Andrew Greeley referred to Catholic higher education in this period as a "backwater."[1] The terms "ghetto Catholicism" and "fortress mentality" are often used to characterize Catholic attitudes toward modernity during the period. These criticisms are based on a strong foundation in reality. It is necessary, however, to distinguish the negative from the more promising developments. One of the promising developments was a strong emphasis on the integration of knowledge into a coherent Christian worldview as a counter to the increasing fragmentation of knowledge found in secular universities. Closely connected to this principle of integration was a renewed emphasis on the spiritual dimension of all learning. Many Catholic educators during this period believed that Christian spirituality must permeate all aspects of the Catholic university: the curriculum, student life, and the administration. In this chapter, I will examine those developments; specifically, I will investigate how Catholic college and university educators viewed the relation between spiritual and intellectual life and how they saw the relation of religious thought to other academic fields. Finally, I will examine their attitudes toward research.

The Imperative for Integration of Thought, Life, and Spirituality

A major impulse for integration was Pope Pius XI's 1929 encyclical *Divini Illius Magistri* (*On the Christian Education of Youth*; hereafter DI).[2] One of the main thrusts of the encyclical was that religious instruction should be taught not merely at fixed times but must permeate the entire curriculum (DI 80). A sacred spirit must pervade the entire academic community. The goal was to form morally upright citizens who could then help infuse the spirit of Christianity into society once they graduated. The proper end of Christian education was to cooperate with divine grace in forming the true and perfect Christian, formed in the image of Christ. Christian education was to take in the entirety of human life—physical and spiritual; intellectual and moral; individual, domestic, and social—and to elevate and perfect all these dimensions. The graduate of Christian schools was to be "the supernatural man who thinks, judges and acts constantly and consistently in accordance with right reason illumined by the spirit and teaching of Christ" (DI 96).Another thrust of *Divini Illius Magistri* was its insistence that the ultimate goal of education was the formation of the "whole man," complete in body, mind, and soul (DI 58). Any education that excludes the religious dimension is seriously defective (DI 60).

Great deference was shown to magisterial teachings on education and the ideals expressed in *Divini Illius* were readily adopted by most American Catholic colleges. Echoes of the language from the encyclical could be found in the writings of Catholic educators and in the mission statements of many Catholic college catalogues during the period. Educators proclaimed a "Catholic Renaissance" of philosophy, literature, and art. Slogans such as "education of the whole man" and "permeation of the curriculum" with religious truth were commonly found in Catholic college literature. In the decades prior to the Second Vatican Council, writes Philip Gleason, the Catholic Church boldly promoted "an organically unified Catholic culture in which religious faith constituted the integrating principle that brought all the dimensions of life and thought together in a comprehensive and tightly articulated synthesis."[3] Catholics took a newfound pride in their own tradition, and Catholic artists and writers flourished, especially in Europe. The sense of renewal in Catholic culture also came to America and was a major spur to attempts at reformulating educational principles.

The principle of integration became central to Catholic higher education during this period. All knowledge and all reality were seen to be interrelated. Everything fits together into a coherent scheme framed by a Catholic worldview, informed by Catholic philosophy. The theme of integration harkens back to the third discourse of John Henry Newman's *Idea of a University*, where he writes,

> All knowledge forms one whole, for its subject-matter is one; for the universe in its length and breadth is so intimately knit together, that we cannot separate off portion from portion, and operation from operation, except by a mental abstraction; and then again, as to its Creator, though He of course in His own Being is infinitely separate from it, yet He has so implicated Himself with it, and taken it into His bosom, by His presence in it, His providence over it, His impressions upon it, and His influences through it, that we cannot truly or fully contemplate it without in some main aspects contemplating Him.[4]

Integration implied several things. First, there must be coherence in the curriculum because all subjects are interrelated, and students must be led to grasp this truth. Second, spiritual life must not be severed from the intellectual. The intellectual and religious should be a unity within "the whole man," that is, students should be unified in body, mind, and spirit. Religion should permeate all aspects of college life, including the academic. Finally, it implied a telos to academic study: that all subject matter, when pursued far enough, leads to philosophical and theological questions that can be answered only by Christian truth.

These ideas pervaded the educational literature of the time. Catholicism, says Fordham professor George Bull, S.J., should be viewed as a culture, not merely a creed; as "an attitude, a whole complexus of things taken for granted, in every activity of life and not in the sphere of the strictly religious alone."[5] The function of the Catholic college, he writes, is to graduate students "who are so steeped in the Catholic mood, that it colors their every activity." Catholic principles must permeate their thought to such a degree that they are able to help transform the world for Christ.[6] Every sphere of human life is "related essentially to every other," and no activities can be understood in isolation from others and from the totality of life, the universe, and God.[7] In Bull's view, this understanding of the interrelatedness of knowledge and its relations to God is what sets Catholics "at odds with the whole modern outlook on life."[8] Bull's vision of Catholicism as a comprehensive culture that must permeate every aspect of the curriculum and of life as a whole was adopted almost verbatim in the statement of objectives at Mount St. Mary's College in Emmitsburg, Maryland.

> Mount St. Mary's remains what its founders had envisioned—a Catholic Liberal Arts College, concerned primarily with producing a man who can see each aspect of life in its relation to life as a whole. Such an objective embraces several points. As a Catholic College, Mount St. Mary's is

concerned with training its students in the principles of their religion so that they may go forth intelligently equipped with the Catholic formula in religion, in philosophy, in science and the arts. To a much greater degree, however, the College aims at imparting to the student the Catholic attitude toward life as a whole. In this way the college authorities hope to graduate students who are so steeped in the Catholic way of life that it colors their every activity, not their religious activity alone, and who are stamped with certain traits which come into play and govern their approach to life in every sphere. Such an attitude gives true definition to the term liberal education since it emphasizes that there must be unity and totality by emphasizing that every sphere of life is essentially related to every other, and that in the conscious activity of man there is no action that can be evaluated as an isolated entity.[9]

Such sentiments were widespread at the time. The 1940–41 catalogue of the Catholic University of America stated that the university aims to "bring the Catholic student to learn...that the only education is self-education and that the only life worth living is one lived personally with God...that the Catholic philosophy of life is not locked up within the confines of certain courses labeled religion and philosophy but that it properly pervades every intellectual and moral action."[10] The College of St. Thomas, in St. Paul, Minnesota, proclaimed in 1939 that religion "permeates every portion, function, and purpose of the Catholic college as a philosophy of life."[11] Not only in religion courses but also "in other courses and activities of the campus the imitation of Christ is proposed as the supreme principle of the truly Catholic life."[12] Similar language can be found in the catalogues of most Catholic colleges and universities in the four decades before the Second Vatican Council.

The language of "permeation" was also commonly found in the writings of Catholic educators. Virgil Michel, O.S.B. (1890–1938), a major figure in liturgical reform in the United States, believed that the "exposition of Catholic ideals and ideas should not be the special object only of a separate class but should be the all-pervading atmosphere of the entire educational work," and that "all teaching of whatever subjects must reflect Catholic truth." If a subject does not contribute to that truth, it should be dropped from the curriculum. Moreover, the college must present a unified and "all-pervading" Catholic atmosphere that would be "absorbed consciously at times, but always breathed in unconsciously."[13] The "ideal of Catholic life must shine forth in the teacher," who should have "a universal sympathy for all things human...and breathe forth in his every action the full conviction of the Catholic ideals of life." This ideal extends to the entire staff of the Catholic college, who must be "not a well-drilled army of technicians, but a well-unified, cooperative family spontaneously breathing out a common atmosphere."[14] The Catholic college is to be an educational institution and a sort of missionary training ground at the same time, engaged in spiritual and moral formation of young adults, who, after graduation, would help transform a troubled world.

Fulton J. Sheen (1895–1979), a scholastic philosopher by training, also advocates a complete rearrangement of all college courses through which "some one 'vital principle' gives unity to the distinct courses in the same way the soul gives unity to the body." For Sheen, that vital, unifying principle is religion.[15] Sheen, who taught philosophy at Catholic University of America from 1926 to 1950, attempted to strengthen the religious vigor of students by integrating the "vital principle" of religion into the college curriculum. This "principle of vitalization" means "the presentation of Christian truth, not as a mechanical unity... but as an organic whole, and the practical adaptation of that truth to the student's own experiences in such a way as to make it the very soul and vivifying spirit of those experiences."[16] Religion is central to every aspect of the Catholic college.

The thought of John Courtney Murray, S.J. (1904–1967), perhaps best articulates the theoretical foundation of this Catholic intellectual and spiritual renewal, combining as it does the integration of spiritual and intellectual knowledge into a coherent whole. He also advocates the engagement of Catholic thought with modern developments in science and philosophy. Murray is best known for his controversial writings on religious freedom and church-state relations in a pluralistic democracy, but he also wrote occasional essays on the topic of Catholic higher education. Some scholars have been tempted to apply Murray's thought on church and state—wherein all creeds and ideas in a pluralistic democracy have equal opportunity to make their case in a neutral and civil forum provided by the state—to the Catholic university.[17] Murray does apply this concept to the *public* university, but his writings on Catholic higher education reveal the opposite: the Catholic university, while open to all ideas, must be grounded in traditional principles of Catholic thought and spiritual life. These principles include the following: theology is the architectonic science that provides the basic principles on which education is founded, giving the various subject matters their direction and goals and bringing a coherent unity to the course of studies in college;[18] the telos of Catholic education is to bring students to intellectual and spiritual wholeness; Catholic higher education is to be based on the doctrine of the Incarnation; and a purely temporal end for education is a profanation of the spiritual dignity of each student.[19]

Murray says that the Incarnation sanctified human nature in its entirety by elevating it toward the divine. This means any purely temporal end of education is a profanation of the spiritual dignity of each student. The Incarnation means that human nature is not enclosed in itself, defined by its purely natural and human possibilities. It is also directly related to the divine because Christ, both human and divine, has assumed humanity into his nature. Christian educators therefore must cooperate with the Spirit to fashion an integral person who is intellectually, morally, and spiritually whole. This is the telos of Christian education.[20]

Christ is the Truth in which all truths are ultimately one. The Logos, the Word of God, came as the light of the world and is the same light that illuminates the philosophical and scientific intelligence. The Catholic university therefore must encompass universal knowledge, founded on a broad range of sciences and learning and integrated into a philosophic view that, in turn, is related to a coherent body of Christian truth. In the empirical methods and aims of the sciences, we recognize an impulse that is both human and holy, an impulse that, "if it does not stop halfway can bring man to the Word of God."[21] Murray is drawing on John Henry Newman here, but equally he draws on Clement of Alexandria and Origen and the schools of Alexandria, which he claims still represent the Christian ideal of higher learning.[22]

The Christian educator, he says, is the servant of the students, not their master. He is the "midwife" who helps bring to birth the full humanity of the students. He is a tool in the "hand of larger Christian purposes," of a telos leading each student toward intellectual and spiritual wholeness. The faculty member should, therefore, view his work as cooperation with the Spirit of God in building society and the world. The development of "the whole man"—a term in Murray's view synonymous with Christian and Catholic—requires an integration of social, intellectual, moral, and spiritual life. The purpose of higher education then, is to produce the fully developed Christian.[23]

If Murray provides the most articulate theoretical expression of Catholic educational ideals during the period, Roy J. Deferrari (1890–1969) provides a forum for discussing how to implement the ideals in practice. Deferrari, professor of classics and dean of the graduate school at Catholic University of America, organized annual workshops on the topic of integrating Christian principles with academic disciplines, student life, and administration into an organically unified whole. Catholic educators in all fields, says Deferrari, must seek to integrate their disciplines with theology: "Courses in religion or philosophy or Church History alone will not suffice. These subjects, and especially the first two, religion and philosophy, contain the tangible material by which integration in all of the fields may be brought about . . . In addition to their intrinsic value by themselves, they should be made to seep through the teaching of all other subjects."[24]

This idea of theological thinking seeping into other courses illustrates another dimension of integration: the principle of *permeation*. Catholic religious thought should permeate every aspect of the university curriculum and leaven the life of the institution as a whole. The medieval university had achieved such an integration, claims Deferrari, but modern universities had lost it. Even many secular university educators, he says, acknowledge this loss.[25] It is incumbent upon Catholic educators to recover the principle of permeation and make it real and effective in the teaching of other subjects. Unfortunately, Catholic teachers at the time were not well enough prepared to achieve this. The purpose of Deferrari's annual workshops on integration, therefore, was to provide both the theoretical grounding and practical professional development for educators so they could do so. Deferrari urged administrators at Catholic colleges to equip their prospective teachers in the proper methods and techniques for achieving this integration and of reforming the curriculum in accordance with Catholic principles.[26]

During the 1949 annual workshops at Catholic University, participants concluded that the integration of the sciences with philosophy and religion must not be taught as a course in religion or philosophy, but as part of the science class itself. "The instructor should stress the science and bring in essential aspects of religion and philosophy at appropriate times and in such a manner as to demonstrate to the student that Catholic religion, philosophy, and science are all parts of the hierarchy of knowledge and not in opposition to each other." [27] Integration should be carried out, to some extent, in all courses for the science major, at appropriate times and as questions naturally arise. In addition to the individual courses, workshop participants recommended that "an additional course or seminar should be included in the curriculum of the science major to bring about an overall integration of religion and philosophy with the science." This "capstone" course or seminar should be required of all majors.[28]

Many Catholic college educators attempted to realize the goal of integrating all knowledge—spiritual and intellectual. Perhaps the most remarkable thing about this movement toward integration was its aura of newness, or at least of renewal, indicating it had not been the norm prior to this period. Indeed, that was the case. Secular, classical curricula had previously characterized education in Catholic colleges and universities. Theology was not taught at Catholic colleges in America until the first half of the twentieth century, and even then only haltingly and to a few—mostly to students going on to the priesthood. When it began to be taught in colleges more regularly, it was largely a watered-down version of the scholastic manuals used in the seminaries at the time. The manuals presented a highly abstract, arid scholastic theology unrelated to the lives of college students. As a result, there was a vigorous movement among many American Catholic educators to alter the way religion was taught. Instead of scholastic theology, many contended that religion should be taught as "a life to be lived," existentially connected to the lives and the world students would enter upon graduating.[29] For John Courtney Murray, the theology course should focus on "the liveability of the Word of God" and be "wholly orientated toward life."[30] This all had a sense of newness, of innovation, as well as a desire to return to the riches of a forgotten tradition. The revival of Thomas Aquinas's thought was one of the key factors in the renaissance of Catholic intellectual and cultural life during the first half of the twentieth century.

Integration of the Curriculum Illustrated

In this section, I will illustrate how educators attempted to integrate Catholic thought into the curriculum. To do so, I will use three examples or case studies: the social sciences, especially sociology; literature; and the natural sciences, especially biology. I will focus on these representative cases not because I consider them models for how Catholic educators today should integrate religious thought into the curriculum, but because we can learn a good deal from examining the strengths and weaknesses of the curricular reform of an earlier period.

Sociology and "Supernatural Sociology"

The approach of Father Paul Hanly Furfey(1896–1992), a sociologist at the Catholic University of America (CUA), illustrates one educator's attempt to integrate disciplinary and Catholic thought. Furfey holds that his own discipline, sociology, is an amalgamation of different disciplines, especially of sociology and ethics. There is no such thing, he says, as a hermetically sealed discipline. He understands sociology in both the narrow, scientific sense, and the broad, theological sense. Sociology in the "narrow sense" is the study of social life based on inductive methods rather than theology or ethics. In this narrow sense, sociology is neutral and "cannot be either Catholic or non-Catholic."[31] In the "broad sense," sociology relies on values from ethics or moral theology. Both approaches are to be integrated into sociology at Catholic colleges and universities. Furfey draws on Pope Pius XI's letter *Solemnia iubilaria* (1938) to substantiate his claim. "The so-called profane sciences of sociology and economics," writes Pius XI, "cannot be divorced from the philosophical and religious principles which pertain to the origin, nature, and end of man."[32] Furfey interprets this to mean that the church does not condemn sociological investigations that employ inductive reasoning; rather, it insists that Catholic sociologists should not cease their inquiries once they arrive at the limits of inductive reasoning but "should go on to apply to their empirical data the principles of philosophy and religion, thus giving some attention to such areas as social ethics in which ethics overlaps with sociology."[33] This combination of sociology and social ethics produces a "supernatural sociology."

> In this broader field value-judgments enter as premises into chains of rea-soning and yield as conclusions particular value-judgments as to particu-lar social situations—the morality of current race relations in the United States, for example. In this sense there can be, and is, a Catholic sociology. This sociology is not confined to the empirical approach since it draws premises from philosophy and theology.[34]

To fail to integrate this broader philosophical and theological dimension with one's empirical research is to divorce one's study from its proper reli-gious finality. Furfey's thought represents an interesting and potentially fruitful approach to acknowledge and respect value-free, objective methods while still attempting to integrate knowledge gained from these methods into a broader philosophical tradition. He aims to delineate the boundar-ies—permeable boundaries to be sure—of the inductive research methods of sociology as a discipline and the meta-sociological framework in which the sociologist carries out this work. Sociologists should not exclude such meta-sociological frameworks and value judgments by pretending to be objective and value-free; rather, they should make their value commit-ments explicit.[35] Sociologists who wish to focus solely on their empirical research are free to do so, says Furfey, but they also should acknowledge the validity and right of others to go beyond empirical research.[36]

At the same time, Furfey believes sociologists in Catholic universities should fully integrate Catholic perspectives into every course. "The pre-cise purpose of the Catholic college is to interpenetrate every course and the whole life of the institution with the Catholic viewpoint." The very strength of Catholic colleges is that they are not satisfied to merely "give an occasional course on religion but rather that they bring religion into every course."[37] Religious concerns should permeate everything.

Not only does Furfey believe that each course in sociology should incorporate a Christian ethical framework, he also thinks there should be a capstone course that reviews all knowledge in the social sciences in the light of the Christian concept of the "nature and end of man." The course would integrate all the social sciences and "be organized around the theological concept of the Kingdom of God," which is central to Catholic social teachings.[38] Humans achieve their end of the beatific vision in the Kingdom of God socially. Societies are to be judged in accordance with how well they organize themselves to make it possible for all its citizens to achieve the beatific vision. So the integrative course should suggest "techniques of social action for bringing existing societies into conformity with the [Catholic] ideal" of the Kingdom of God.[39] Building the Kingdom of God can be done, though, only with the aid of grace, so the course must stress the importance of taking advantage of the means of grace, especially the Holy Eucharist.[40] Likewise, it must encourage students to live in the world, but not be of the world, to live lives of dedicated service to others and avoid falling into the ways of the world. Furfey's writings gained considerable currency in Catholic circles and exerted a strong influence on Catholic social activists such as Dorothy Day and the Catholic Worker Movement.

Not all Thomists were in agreement with Furfey's principles, however, especially those who focused on the tight distinctions between reason and revelation and, hence, between theology and all other academic disciplines. For example, Franz Mueller of St. Louis University takes exception to some of Furfey's conclusions. St. Thomas, says Mueller, did not confuse his formal categories: he did not "use supernatural categories when dealing with the natural order."[41] To mix them is to confuse them. We must distinguish clearly between the truths of revelation, philosophical speculation, and experimental knowledge, even though we know that the supernatural and the natural orders form a unity. God gave his creatures a degree of freedom and autonomy.

> God does not...direct the activity of His creatures by constantly interfering with them; each creature is really a cause itself, a *causa secunda.* Because of this fact that creatures within their specific order strive autonomously toward their ends the empirical sciences come into being. If we were obliged to refer every mundane thing or act to the first Cause *directly,* then sociology...would be without any subject matter.[42]

Those who want to employ moral theology, philosophy, and ethics synonymously are ignoring "the ordered autonomy which belongs to the different spheres of nature and culture," said Mueller. Sociology is the study of social relations and social structures and how they develop and change, and it is not interested in "the formal cause of these phenomena but in the secondary and material causes of their existence."[43] In other words, it studies societies as they are, as they have developed, as they degenerate or change, but does not make moral judgments about them. It seeks to understand, not to advocate social reform. That is not the role of sociology. Mueller does concede, though, that a "supernatural sociology" is desirable as long as it is kept distinct from empirical or scientific sociology.[44]

Joseph Nuesse of Catholic University shares Mueller's concerns. Sociology may study the same phenomenon as philosophy or theology, that is, the social relations among humans, but it approaches only a specific aspect of it: the proximate causes of social processes that are empirically observable and verifiable. Exploring the meanings and ethical implications belongs to the disciplines of philosophy and theology. "The sociologist *qua* sociologist does not deal with the fact of the immorality or illegality of a human act," only the social context in which an act is considered immoral or illegal.[45] As such, there can be no "Catholic sociology." Nuesse then concedes the necessity of considering the moral implications of social issues, but such considerations must be contributed by other disciplines, that is, philosophy and theology. It is proper that students in the sociology class learn how these issues are related to philosophical and theological concerns. It is vitally important, though, for them to learn what sociology does and attends to as its formal object and what its limits are in relation to other, broader disciplines.[46] Nuesse, like Mueller, insists on these distinctions because too many social science teachers confuse sociology with social philosophy and Catholic social thought. This is as much a disservice to students, they believe, as the tendency of non-Catholic sociologists to insert their own philosophical assumptions into the field.

Furfey readily acknowledges the empirical and experimental dimension of sociology. He insists, however, that there can be no neutral sociology; there is a meta-philosophy—often implicit—underlying any sociological approach. Regarding the blurring of disciplinary boundaries, Furfey argues that one can maintain the distinction between three basic dimensions of sociology—(1) "scientific" sociology, limited to finite social phenomena and data; (2) "theoretical" sociology (social theory); and (3) the larger framework of Catholic social ethics (supernatural sociology)—without confusing students. The teacher merely needs to say: "Thus far I have been presenting scientific facts. Today we shall theorize. Tomorrow I shall give you the Catholic viewpoint which you will not find in the average textbook but which is enormously important."[47] Furfey rejects the position that Catholic social ethics, based on supernatural revelation, should be taught in the religion rather than the sociology course. If one accepts such a position, then many other matters ought to be excluded also: discussion of poverty ought to be excluded because that can be handled by the economist; study of race relations should be taught by the anthropologist or political scientist.

Furfey makes a logical error here; it is not the subject matter (poverty, race relations) that secularists (and strict Thomists) want to exclude—poverty and race relations are valid subject matter for more than one academic discipline. Rather, they want to exclude the theoretical and evaluative framework that is to be brought to bear on the data collected. Secular social scientists want to exclude the *theological* framework, but, as Furfey points out, they do not hesitate to employ their own social philosophies as evaluative criteria. Moreover, Furfey holds that a first-class teacher should have a broad background in other fields, able to relate them to his or her own, unlike narrow academic specialists.[48]

Other Catholic sociologists weighed in on these issues. Notre Dame's Raymond Murray, C.S.C., president of the American Catholic Sociological Society in 1940, said that no sociology is purely inductive but is "inevitably interwoven with the philosophical and religious backgrounds" of each individual sociologist.[49] The research of every sociologist is colored in some way by a social philosophy, whether explicit or implicit. It is appropriate, then, for Catholics to bring their own tradition of social thought to bear on their empirical studies and the interpretation of the data they gather. Catholic sociology "is wedded to a philosophy, to 'preconceived notions,'...which accepts the existence of God, divine revelation, objective morality, conscience, free will, and man's future destiny in a divine order."[50] Other social philosophies might view humans as automatons rather than as free agents or the product of social *mores* only rather than as agents subject to an objective code of morality.[51]

The Catholic sociologist does not thereby neglect to use valid sociological methods, but he will insist on integrating spiritual and ethical values into his work. Catholics, writes Paul J. Mundie, editor of the first issue of the *American Catholic Sociological Review*, "have a body of truths to serve as guides in the study of social theory... Catholics will not be poorer scientists, but rather better scientists for knowing that man has a supernatural destiny and that society has as its goal the organization of social life in such manner as to help man attain this destiny."[52]

The minutes of a 1941 panel of the American Catholic Sociological Society (ACSS) illustrate the thinking of Catholic sociologists on the nature and goals of the introductory course in sociology. Among the recommendations is that the course ensure that " ethical postulates...constitute a foundation for the science of sociology." Yet ethical postulates from other disciplines (philosophy and theology) should take up only a small portion of the time spent on the course. Catholic theology and philosophy should be introduced as the "integrating element in the teaching of sociological material such as social processes and social institutions."[53] Others insist on clear distinctions between sociology as an empirical science and social ethics founded on theology. The panel members believe that readings in "the learned secular magazines of the field" should be avoided except for the most advanced students because of the controversial nature of the material. Use of non-Catholic texts by some Catholic social scientists is evidence of the failure to see the proper finality of the course. Texts written by Catholics are the best to use, but only if the author in question has a strong background in theology and philosophy. Students must be introduced also to the divine dimension of human life—a dimension that is ignored by most secular sociologists, even though they insert their own, often secular, philosophical principles into their teaching.[54]

These minutes from the panel members' discussion illustrate the attempts of Catholic scholars to come to a clear sense of how to relate their specialized discipline to the broader Catholic theological tradition. The strong neo-Thomists among them insist on clear distinctions between empirical sociology and theology; others want to merge them; others to carefully relate them even while keeping proper distinctions between their formal objects. On the whole, they reveal a commitment to somehow integrating and relating knowledge from specialized disciplines into a comprehensive Catholic philosophical framework.

Eva Ross (1903–1970)was one such scholar. Ross taught sociology at Trinity College in Washington, DC, and was the president of the American Catholic Sociological Society in 1943. She held that some sociologists in Catholic colleges can justifiably remain focused solely on inductive methods, but there must be others who know Catholic social thought in detail and who are able to relate sociology to other disciplines such as psychology, anthropology, history, and economics. Teaching these relationships may be only a small part of their teaching compared to foundational empirical studies, but it is of great importance. Students should not have to go to teachers in those other disciplines for an understanding of the broader context of sociology.[55] Why should the desire of the mind for completion in ultimate knowledge be truncated, suppressed, or left unfulfilled? Why must a student be sent elsewhere—to the theology or philosophy departments—for that completion when, in fact, he or she might never go there? Why not at least provide a glimpse of what a Catholic answer might entail to the questions and issues raised in the sociology course? Many Catholic sociologists of the period believed students needed such a perspective.

The Catholic Literary Revival

As noted above, American Catholic educators during the 1920s and 1930s proclaimed a "Catholic Renaissance" in philosophy, literature, and art. The phrase "Catholic literary revival" came to represent this integrative movement in literature.[56] There were two motivating factors in this movement.

The first was to expose students to good Catholic authors as a counter balance to the standard secular writers found in most literature courses (at both secular and Catholic colleges). Philosophy, literature, and culture generally exhibited a moral decadence that was alarming to Christians. Catholic educators believed that Catholic thought, especially that of St. Thomas Aquinas, held the answers to modern problems because it would lead people beyond the values and concerns of this world to the realm of the supernatural, where humans could discover the true meaning of their lives. Modern, naturalistic philosophies confined the mind to the human realm alone, severed from any supernatural moorings or end. Even Romanticism, in rebelling against rationalism, found its moorings in emotion and subjective imagination rather than divine revelation. What was needed was a proper balance between reason, emotion, imagination, and faith in the supernatural. No one better exhibited this fullness and balance than Thomas Aquinas.[57]

A second motivating factor was the acknowledged weakness and poverty of American Catholic literature. Several decades before John Tracy Ellis' 1955 essay criticizing Catholic intellectual life in the United States, Catholic academics were lamenting the poor state of Catholic cultural and artistic contributions to American society. Even though the Catholic Church was the largest denomination in America, with more than twenty million adherents at the time, and Catholics had been gaining considerable economic and political clout, Catholics had produced no great intellectuals or writers of the stature of an Emerson, a Thoreau, or a Whitman. Nor were American Catholics counted among the great scientists of the nineteenth or twentieth centuries. Catholic literature scholars and editors of literary journals bewailed this weakness and sought to foster writers in the mould of European Catholic authors.[58] As things stood, literature professors had three choices: (1) to focus on non-Catholic literature, as was common in most universities; (2) to look to European Catholic literature, or (3) to include second- or third-rate American Catholic literature that displayed more of a pious sentimentality and rigid adherence to clichéd Catholic teachings than true literary excellence. The reality was that most American Catholic authors fell into this latter category, and Catholic intellectuals knew it. Catholic college students also knew it and some even rebelled against having to read such third-rate literature. Arnold Sparr notes how college students at a Catholic Book Club conference protested against pious and childish novels in which the standard plot line was the heroine who, disgusted with the decadence of modern society, "rushed into the convent to save her soul."[59] This trite formula grated on many Catholic intellectuals who wanted a literature rooted in real experience and the existential dilemmas faced by modern men and women.

Secular literature may have been superior from an artistic perspective, but, in general, the Catholic approach to modern, secular literature was confrontational, defensive, and apologetic. John Pick observed that hostility to Catholicism by the dominant Protestant and secular cultural milieus caused Catholics to become defensive and to withdraw from cultural and intellectual developments in America, creating a provincial "ghetto complex" that was foreign to the true Catholic spirit of engagement.[60] Too many Catholic authors, he said, confused polemics, apologetics, and propaganda with true literary creation. As a result, much American Catholic literature of the period degenerated "into shallow religiosity."[61] Nonetheless, some teachers of literature incorporated these inferior works into their courses and believed it was their duty to present such works as examples of good literature. The better literary critics, however, recognized the weakness in these writings, and said so. Such literature resembled propaganda more than literature. It was "preachy," presenting a moralistic Catholic viewpoint rather than subtly presenting religious themes of sin, redemption, and divine love organically into the plot. Pick said it was appropriate for an art form such as the novel to express a worldview—indeed, all literature expresses some philosophy of life, either explicitly or implicitly—but the religious theme in Catholic literature, he said, must become an *organic* part of the whole work, "inextricably welded and fused with the life presented—otherwise the result is mere propaganda and not a work of art."[62] Most American Catholic literature did not meet this standard. As a consequence, Catholic educators and literary critics tried to foster first-rate Catholic literature with American roots. Until such authors emerged, however, they had to rely on the literature of nineteenth and twentieth century Catholic writers from Europe or second-rate American authors.

In the late 1930s a group of literature scholars from Midwestern Catholic colleges began holding annual meetings to discuss the literary revival in Europe and how Catholic literature might be integrated into the curricula of American Catholic colleges.[63] This group eventually coalesced into the Catholic Renascence Society and founded the journal *Renascence: A Critical Journal of Letters*, specifically to stimulate an appreciation of Catholic authors—past and present—and to encourage a critical evaluation of their work. The journal was intended for those "who believe that the constant rebirth of spiritual values in art can give us the light of Spring rather than the dark of Winter."[64] The darkness of winter, it was widely understood, referred to the destructive fruit of materialism, positivism, and naturalism; the light of spring was the cultural heritage of Christian civilization.[65] Courses in Catholic literature began to proliferate at Catholic colleges and universities. Courses on "Modern Catholic Literature" and "The Catholic Literary Revival" became commonplace in the 1930s and 1940s.[66] Educators such as the Franciscan Joachim Daleiden urged the creation of suitable anthologies of the best Catholic writings to be used as college and high school textbooks.[67] Publishers and editors obliged.[68] Daleiden also encouraged Catholic scholars to develop their own reading list as a corrective to Mortimer Adler's "List of Great Books," which omitted many important Catholic authors from its canon. A group of Franciscan literature professors took Adler's list and supplemented it with good Catholic literature and substituted objectionable authors (e.g., Calvin, Spinoza, Locke, Voltaire, Hume, Rousseau, Gibbon, Comte, Darwin, Ibsen, William James, Freud, and Dewey) with acceptable Catholic authors.[69]

One notable characteristic of this literature was how broadly it was conceived. It included a wide range of authors and genres: the novel, poetry, history, the lives of saints, philosophy, criticism, and theology. The canon of great Catholic writers typically included English authors John Henry Newman, poets Gerard Manley Hopkins, Alice Meynell, and Coventry Patmore; essayists and historians such as G.K. Chesterton and Christopher Dawson; and novelists Evelyn Waugh and Graham Greene. French writers included novelists Leon Bloy, Paul Claudel, Charles Peguy, François Mauriac, and Georges Bernanos; historian Etienne Gilson; and philosopher Jacques Maritain. Few American Catholic authors made the canon.

Perhaps the most important aspect of this literary revival was its almost exclusive focus on specifically Catholic literature, treating Catholic literature in isolation from literature generally. Not that there is anything wrong with a college course focusing on Catholic authors. Literature written from a specifically Catholic perspective is as justifiable as literature written from a feminist, a postmodernist, or a romantic perspective. A question then arises: if the focus is to be on Catholic authors, what then of other, non-Catholic literature? Was it to be excluded entirely, or treated separately? Isolating it and treating it separately kept Catholic thought within a separate realm from the rest of literature (broadly conceived), and that is what seems to have been the case. There were exceptions, of course. Some literature professors included both Catholic and non-Catholic authors in their courses, but some of them encountered censure for doing so. For example, in 1958 Sister Kristin Malloy, O.S.B. and Sister Mariella Gable, O.S.B. were dismissed from their teaching positions in the English department at the College of St. Benedict in Minnesota when Sr. Malloy incorporated J.D. Salinger's *The Catcher in the Rye* in a reading list for contemporary American literature. The obscene language in the book was objectionable to the sisters' ecclesiastical superiors.[70]

Some promoters of the Catholic revival drew on the work of John Henry Newman; it would have behooved them to follow his ideas more fully. Newman said that it is not the way to learn to swim not having gone into the water. We must venture into the world of ideas, be what they may, face them and assess them in light of Christian truth, but never censor them outright. During this same time period, John Courtney Murray was saying that scholars and students must enter the stream of contemporary thought and culture and try to influence and guide its course rather than stand athwart the stream and condemn the direction in which it is moving. Unfortunately, few Catholic educators did so.[71] The norm was a confrontational attitude regarding modern literature. Instead of searching out the truth and values within all literature, discerning the errors, and elevating the good within a Catholic vision, they condemned and criticized. In general, the gaze of Catholic literary scholars was inward, to their own literature written by Catholic authors treating explicitly Catholic themes.

The Natural Sciences: Forcing Knowledge into a Neoscholastic Mold

The ideal of the integration of intellectual and spiritual life is attractive to the religious mind and resonates with enduring Catholic educational ideals. Nonetheless, Catholic colleges and universities in America were generally slow to incorporate the newly forming natural and social sciences into their curricula. For centuries Catholic higher education rested on the Renaissance-humanist model of education, with Greek and Latin classics at the center of the curriculum and some version of the trivium and quadrivium making up the remainder. Theology was not taught at all to most college students. Those studying for the priesthood were among the few who actually studied it, and it was offered only after the regular course of studies in the humanities and philosophy. Jesuit colleges and universities, which constituted the most powerful and numerous block of Catholic colleges, had long resisted findings from the sciences. By the late nineteenth and early twentieth centuries, however, Catholic educators began establishing modern departments of science and, later, social sciences. Science course descriptions at many Catholic colleges look much like those at any American college. Some Catholic educators, however, attempted to integrate the hard sciences with philosophy and theology in accord with scholastic principles.

Kenneth Anderson, a biology professor at St. Bonaventure College, attempted to bring all knowledge in the discipline within the scope of a neoscholastic philosophical framework. Anderson was a regular speaker at Roy Deferrari's conferences on integration in Catholic universities.

He demonstrated how biology could be taught so as to point to God and Christian truths. He believed biology should be "taught as ancillary to philosophy and, above all, religion" and that the "Catholic biologist" should have the following objectives in mind when teaching his students:

1. To prove the existence of God and that God is transcendent to the universe of living things.
2. To prove the existence of a soul in all living things and that God is immanent in the universe of living beings.[72]

Biology, says Anderson, has discovered and described the organic processes of cells and living organisms, their complexity of structure and intricacy of design, but it is unable to show evidence that the "vitalism" in these organisms could emerge from chemical processes. The odds of chemicals spontaneously combining to form self-reproducing life forms is so infinitesimal as to be impossible.[73] Hence, one must posit a divine force, a divine spirit that enlivens all beings and moves them toward a purpose. The complexity of structure and intricacy of design demand a creator, so biology is to be integrated with natural theology.

For Anderson, biology must be, in addition to a science, a means of spreading the faith. For the biologist, this means that his science "is not a pursuit divorced from his religion, but becomes for him a means of serving God."[74] The Catholic biologist must not be defensive in the face of modern science, trying to protect students from it. Biology must be integrated with religion in order to "capture it" for Christ; it must "be turned to the service of God." This means that the biologist must be expertly trained not only in his own field but also in philosophy and theology.[75] Biology could then be joined with psychology to demonstrate the existence of a rational, immortal soul in humans, endowed with spiritual faculties and free will, in accord with scholastic philosophy.

Anderson recognizes the divine in the natural world. He acknowledges that pursuit of a scientific discipline could be akin to a religious calling. In his enthusiasm, however, he thoroughly confuses theology, biology, and psychology. His insights into biology become the occasion for imposing a neoscholastic framework on the observation and experience of nature—fitting observations into a preconceived cognitive framework—of forcing the scientific data to "prove" the existence of God. After all, he reasons, if one traces life back far enough, one is forced to ask about its origins and must inevitably arrive at a First Cause, as in Thomas's first proof for the existence of God.[76] Design in nature also supports the teleological proof for the existence of God. Biology therefore supports Thomistic principles.

Anderson also advocates use of biological phenomena as a means of symbolically teaching Catholic doctrine—not in the religion class or from the pulpit, where it would have been appropriate, but in the biology class. For example, he points out how individual cells combine with one another into larger integrated units, working harmoniously together toward some goal. So likewise do individual humans join together in great numbers to form the mystical Body of Christ, a "harmonious organism dedicated to the service of God."[77] He uses other examples, as well. The rise of sap in trees can be compared to the flow of grace in the soul. Biological knowledge is, thus, to be used as a tool for illustrating Catholic doctrine, and this is to be done in the biology class itself.

Though not practiced by all, awkward and procrustean efforts such as these were not uncommon during the period. John Julian Ryan of Boston College, another regular and well-known speaker at conferences on Catholic higher education, says that the purpose of the biology course has several elements, one of which is to purge the student of "evolutionism and mechanism." A second element is to help the student learn the foolishness of attempting to reduce living beings to nonliving principles. Another is to help the student better understand the nature of living cells within an organism, so as to better appreciate what is "meant by calling Grace the *life* of the soul and the Mystical Body a Super-organism." Biology must teach teleology and design in all things and show that all things fit into a hierarchy of being, moving upward from inanimate matter, through a progression of stages to vegetable, animal, and human life, then finally, to the Supernatural.[78] Following up on the biology course is the course in physiology, one goal of which is to show, through the intricacy and functional beauty of the body, that the body must be in-formed by an immortal soul.[79] For Ryan, these ends are the proximate ends of the biology and physiology courses.

The weakness of these approaches to biology is obvious. The subject matter and methods of biology are restricted in scope to a specific area of reality: living organisms. Biological research and findings do elicit questions of broader import, for example, of the origin and purpose of life, and there is no reason the biologist—if he or she has the proper background in philosophy and theology—cannot spend some time explaining how philosophers and theologians have attempted to address the questions raised by biology. But they should not make the methods and findings of biology per se attempt to do that work. Doing so becomes an effort to fit biological data into the procrustean bed of neo-Thomist philosophy.

This facile merging of academic disciplines with Catholic thought was evident in many places during the period from 1920 to 1960. For instance, the College of St. Catherine's in St. Paul, Minnesota, claimed to direct every field of study toward Catholic truth. An article by Sister Jeanne Marie summarizes the religious orientation of academic departments at the college.

> *Physics*: The published statements of such authorities as Millikan, Jeans, Eddington, Compton, and the late Dr. Michelson are welcomed as approaches through experimental physics to evidences of Truth. The wonder of the radio makes spiritual power not easy to deny...
>
> *Chemistry*: The meaning of a universe becomes clearer as the elements are studied in their great variety of combinations. Man's place in this universe becomes sacred when understood to serve the purpose of elevating physical and chemical elements to action on a spiritual plane—glorifying God through the immortal soul of man...
>
> *Mathematics:* By accepting the principles and laws that govern number relationships we pay tribute to a greater intelligence than our own, that of the Creator. Order, precision, and accuracy recommend themselves to spiritual living... 'Mystical Mathematics' our courses have been called.[80]

From a modern scientific and academic perspective, the forced nature of these efforts is obvious. They show no differentiation between the limited scope and methods of the sciences and the broader scope and methods of philosophy and theology. Rather than connecting learning in these areas to a larger Catholic framework in a sophisticated academic way, they collapsed them into one undifferentiated subject.

While it is natural for the theonomous mind to see all things on disciplinary islands in the context of an ultimate horizon, that is, to see all things *sub specie aeternitatis,* there are obvious flaws in the curricular goals of these Catholic educators.

The integration of disciplines must not be forced. The academic must maintain intellectual discipline and not force unity prematurely. As we saw in chapter 2, Thomas Aquinas himself had a more sophisticated sense of integration in the curriculum and the relation of particular subjects to theology and philosophy. Kenneth Anderson and John J. Ryan blurred the distinctions between disciplines to such an extent that they confused them. Though there are not strong boundaries in reality, there are distinctions to be made, and there must be distinctions between academic disciplines. Anderson and Ryan not only collapsed distinctions between biology, psychology, and theology but also blurred the distinction between education and catechism in their zeal to integrate all knowledge in a theological vision. In attempting to follow Thomas and understand that knowledge in all disciplines leads ultimately to God, they failed to make the distinctions that Thomas did. Theology, says Thomas, "does not treat of God and creatures equally, but of God primarily; and of creatures only so far as they are referable to God as their beginning or end."[81] One could reverse Thomas's statement and say that biology does not treat of God and creatures equally, but of creatures primarily, and of God only insofar as questions of God arise naturally when searching for the ultimate causes and meaning of biological phenomena. Anderson and Ryan collapsed the distinction and were, against their own intentions, out of sync with some of the very Thomistic principles they advocated. They tried to make biology a branch of theology—even more, a branch of catechetics, turning the college into more of a seminary than a university.[82]

The integration of disciplines, as difficult as it is, remains a goal that we have an obligation to pursue,[83] but they must be integrated *organically*, allowing each its full development and individuality. Universities must allow for legitimate differentiation and the unique development of disciplinary methods and subject areas.[84] Anderson and Ryan did not do this. Instead, they converted biology (and other academic disciplines) into theology. Not all Catholic educators tried to force a Catholic framework on their disciplines, but it was not uncommon to see such efforts prior to the Second Vatican Council.

Resisting the Research Ideal

The failure of Catholic educators to differentiate between legitimate disciplinary subject matters and methods had another repercussion for Catholic higher education: the failure to appreciate the value of research. After all, the differentiation of the sciences, the process of abstracting subject matters and studying them in detail according to proper methods, implies carrying out original research or at least incorporating the findings of original research into one's courses. Many Catholic colleges, however, to a large extent ignored and even resisted the advancement of knowledge through research.[85] This was not peculiar to American Catholic colleges. Even Newman claimed that research was not the primary function of the university. The research academy, he said, not the university, was the place for research.[86]

Prior to the mid-twentieth century, research had not been a significant component of American Catholic higher education. According to Philip Gleason, "the whole thrust of the old system was toward introducing to students, in inculcating in them, a previously-arrived-at synthesis of secular knowledge, intellectual skills, ethical values, and religious truth. Free investigation or independent research played virtually no role in this process."[87] Moreover, the goal of Catholic colleges had been moral formation and education in the faith, often in opposition to Protestant and, later, secular dominance of American culture. To some extent, this made academic freedom unnecessary, for academic freedom arises from the need to freely conduct research and disseminate the results of new knowledge and to question previously arrived at syntheses. When one already has a fixed system of truth, there is little need to explore new ones. One merely lectures and elaborates on the existing system. The search for new knowledge and truth was perceived as largely antithetical to a traditional education based on transmitting received and unalterable truths. Commitment to traditional educational practices was one of the major reasons for American Catholics' late entry into and resistance to new developments in higher education, including research.

To the extent that a university prohibits the desire of the mind from exploring reality in its breadth and depth, which is to say, to conduct research into the world created by God, it is not truly a university. The quest for holiness and the search for Christian wisdom need not be opposed to the desire of the mind for knowledge and understanding; indeed, they should be part of the same, integrated quest.

Research and inquiry are integral to the telos of the mind in its quest to know reality ever more fully. Legitimate differentiation of research methods and subject matter is necessary to know the world in its full detail. Prior to the Second Vatican Council Catholics were not unanimous in acknowledging this, however, and many rejected research as a proper function of the Catholic university. George Bull, S.J., for example, considers research antithetical to the mission of the Catholic college, even the Catholic graduate school. As we saw earlier, Bull insists on an integrated view of humankind, nature, and God as a basis of the Catholic college curriculum; such an integrated view is one essential characteristic of the "Catholic mind." He agrees with Newman that once you admit a God, then "you introduce among the subjects of your knowledge a fact encompassing, closing in upon, absorbing, every other fact conceivable." This encompassing reality then serves as a boundary and frame within "which all of man's thinking is to be done." We must then penetrate this reality in its depth, but *not in its extension*. We penetrate its depth through contemplation, its extension through research. Contemplation, not research, should be the goal of Catholic education, even at the graduate level.[88] In Bull's view, research is "at war with the whole Catholic life of the mind" and is in "direct and radical conflict with the whole atmosphere of the Catholic life of learning."[89]

Bull's dichotomy between contemplation and research is puzzling because, while the two mental actions are distinct, they have much in common. Research, when viewed rightly, is but an attempt to understand the laws governing God's creation, an attempt to know something of the "mind of God." Contemplation is the sustained appreciation of that creation and of its Creator. It is a long-held Catholic principle that the "book of nature," as well as the book of Scripture, points to God. So it is inexplicable why the further investigation of the book of nature would be considered incompatible with Catholic higher education. Throughout Christian history Catholic thinkers have engaged in the study of the natural world. It was an unfortunate development that some Catholic educators began to place scientific investigation in opposition to love and contemplation. Bull considered research to be the study of passing phenomena, knowledge of which should not be sought for its own sake, but only in proportion to their place in the broader hierarchy of being.[90] He believed that research into the finite and particular constituted, in itself, a refusal to place knowledge in a larger framework. Formation to Christian maturity was the goal of Catholic education, not discovery of new knowledge. Unfortunately, discovery through research and formation in the faith were presented as mutually exclusive alternatives. Not all Catholic educators shared Bull's position, but it was not uncommon either.

In fairness to Bull, it is well to remember that research was equated with specialization, fragmentation, and intellectual secularization, which tend to run counter to integration and unity of knowledge. It was this understanding of research that Bull protested. As we have seen, specialization and fragmentation have indeed created serious problems for the unity of knowledge and for attempts to fashion a coherent curriculum. Many scholars do, in fact, refuse to connect the knowledge in their disciplines to a broader wisdom. But it is not a necessary refusal. It is a mistake to assume that research and contemplation are incompatible simply because some scholars refuse to link them.

The negative attitude toward research reflected, to some extent, the split between analytic reason (*verstand*) and synthetic reason (*vernunft*). Catholics rejected the modern emphasis on analytical reasoning alone, so some of them rejected it altogether in favor of synthetic, integrative reasoning.

The Unfulfilled Promise of Renewal

Catholic colleges and universities during the first half of the twentieth century resisted many of the changes that public and once-Protestant universities had experienced. They clung to traditional educational ideals of

Renaissance humanism, were largely resistant to modern university ideals such as research and academic freedom, and looked on modern philosophical, literary, and cultural developments with suspicion, if not alarm. Even so, Catholic institutions of higher education experienced a widespread renewal during this period, spurred by the Vatican's revitalization of the thought of Thomas Aquinas. This "renaissance" of Catholic life and thought affected most Catholic colleges and universities. It generated a sense of pride and accomplishment in the glories of Catholic thought, and Catholic educators were convinced that Catholicism held the answers to the problems facing the modern world.

The renewal, however, failed to accomplish its goals. Unlike Thomas Aquinas in the thirteenth century, who engaged the conflicting currents of thought in his time, Catholic scholars in the early twentieth century tended to condemn rather than engage modern thought. In trying to integrate Catholic thought with knowledge in other disciplines, they tended to either confuse them or to force knowledge into a narrow neoscholastic mold. Although there were many exceptions, the overall academic quality of Catholic colleges and universities was relatively weak. It was not long before the entire foundation of Catholic higher education was shaken, as we will see in the next chapter.

Chapter 6

The Consequence of Caesar's Gold

In chapters 3 and 4, we discussed how the concept of academic freedom developed in the University of Berlin during the early nineteenth century and was transformed in America during the late nineteenth and early twentieth centuries. It has become, to a large extent, a negative freedom: a freedom *from* external influence rather than a freedom *to* pursue truth in its fullness. The question to be explored in this chapter is what principle of academic freedom did American Catholic colleges and universities adopt after they liberated themselves from heteronomous church control following the Second Vatican Council? Was it merely a freedom *from* external authority, resulting in free inquiry within the confines of narrow disciplinary islands, but not beyond, or was it a freedom to search *both* the depth and extent of Kant's island *and* its relation to the vast sea beyond? This chapter examines their choice and its consequences.

Prior to the Second Vatican Council, American Catholic colleges were mostly insular, holding on to both a classical humanist curriculum that dated from the late Renaissance and a neoscholastic philosophy that was largely out of touch with modern trends in thought. For some time before the Council, many Catholic educators had complained about the poor academic quality of their institutions. Father Virgil Michel charged that the curriculum and methods of teaching in Catholic colleges produced a Catholic "self-satisfied in his internal aloofness" and "egoistic in his self-righteousness," who is "satisfied to believe what he has been authoritatively told to believe."[1] John Tracy Ellis's 1955 article, "American Catholics and the Intellectual Life,"[2] set off a firestorm of controversy and a flurry of publications by Catholics lamenting the failure to develop a strong Catholic intellectual life in America. Catholics had contributed little to American cultural and intellectual life, in spite of their numbers, wealth, and power in American society. Many Catholic educators recognized these weaknesses and were anxious for change.

Everything did change in the 1960s, in American culture, generally, and in the Catholic Church, particularly. It was a time of massive social, political, and religious turmoil. Following the Second Vatican Council, Catholics were confronted with major religious transformations as well as cultural and social disruptions in society at large. In Catholic academic circles, the old heteronomy based on a nature-supernature dualism was starting to crumble. Catholic colleges and universities faced an exciting opportunity to renew and remake their institutions in accordance with fresh guiding principles. The intellectual world was rife with innovative and even radical educational philosophies. The *zeitgeist* called for freedom and openness, often to extremes. In the Catholic realm, scholars had recovered vital aspects of the Catholic tradition long ignored or repressed by the dominance of neoscholasticism. Patristic and medieval attitudes toward higher learning—attitudes of openness and engagement, and of an integrated spiritual and intellectual life—were becoming better known. Teilhard de Chardin had made a significant attempt to integrate Christianity and evolutionary science.[3] John Courtney Murray was beginning a dialogue between Catholic thought and modern, liberal political thought.[4] Dreams of building great Catholic universities, intellectually sound and respectable, no longer constrained by a narrow neoscholastic philosophy and the authoritarian control of the church, abounded and seemed realizable. Catholic academics, for the most part, were anxious to flee the Catholic ghetto and enter mainstream academia in America.

Sociological as well as academic factors played a role in these changes. Catholics, for the most part, had become assimilated into American society and many were becoming economically affluent. A Catholic had been elected president of the United States in 1960. The postwar American economy was booming, and Catholics shared in its prosperity. They wanted their sons and daughters to attend respectable academic institutions on a par with the best secular universities.[5] During the nineteenth century, a majority of Catholic immigrants were from the poorer classes, many of them illiterate or poorly educated. By the turn of the century, however, Catholics were moving upward socially and economically. This upward mobility had an impact on educational aspirations. By the early twentieth century, Catholics were entering colleges and universities in increasing numbers and brought with them higher expectations regarding professional standards and the usefulness of the courses offered. Many Catholic students from the upper-middle class even began entering non-Catholic colleges, where they thought they could receive a better education. Catholics' desire for a first-class education for their children, equal to that at the prestigious secular universities, forced changes in Catholic colleges and universities. As a result, many of them "had to be brought more closely into line with the mainstream of American higher education, their curricula made more flexible and more relevant to the needs of contemporary society, and their facilities enlarged to accommodate a vastly expanded clientele."[6] Academic departments in many of these colleges began to resemble those of non-Catholic colleges.

Social upheaval characterized the mid- and late-1960s. Americans, especially students, agitated and protested for greater freedom and self-determination. Catholic students were no less susceptible to these forces, and many Catholic colleges and universities were in turmoil. Some, such as St. John's University in New York and Catholic University of America, erupted with student protests over perceived violations of academic freedom. Added to this volatile social and political mix, the Second Vatican Council (1961–1965) was a major catalyst for changes in Catholic institutions. *Gaudium et Spes* had called for the opening of the Catholic mind to the modern world, calling for an appreciation of the longings and hopes evident in it and enjoining Catholics to collaborate with their non-Catholic brethren for the betterment of society.

Prior to the Council, Catholic universities in America had been resistant, even dismissive, of the idea of academic freedom, which they associated with secularism. Secularism, in turn, was associated with hostility to religion, generally, and Catholicism, in particular. After the Second Vatican Council, Catholic professors and students demanded academic freedom in line with prevailing practices at other American universities. Catholics, however, did not have their own theological framework for thinking about academic freedom and its meaning within a Catholic university. As Philip Gleason wrote in 1967, "Because the notion of academic freedom is so imperfectly grasped and so little at home in our minds, we have hardly begun to determine its relation to other ideas we possess more familiarly, or to inquire what modifications in our customary thinking its claims might entail."[7] Catholic college leaders had no satisfactory theory of how academic freedom and the research ideal might be related to or founded on Catholic principles.[8] Since Vatican II, academic freedom has become the norm in American Catholic colleges and universities, but the norms are ones developed in secular universities and have not been assessed well in light of Catholic theological principles. They were simply adopted uncritically by Catholic colleges. In part, this was because the demand for academic freedom arose amid confusion and conflict in the church, in American society, and in Catholic universities during the 1960s.

To properly understand the rise of academic freedom, we must understand the historical context in which it arose. In chapter 4, I attempted to do this for the idea of academic freedom in America generally. I now will examine some of the events that led to the adoption of academic freedom in Catholic universities and show the consequences of the decisions that were made.

The fundamental changes in the Catholic Church's self-understanding following Vatican II created an identity crisis for Catholic colleges and universities as well as for the church at large. Previously, the nature and mission of Catholic universities seemed self-evident. They boldly proclaimed their Catholic identity in their mission statements and catalogues, as we saw in chapter 5. Catholics self-assuredly proclaimed that the teachings of the church held the answer to modern problems. Then, in the name of *aggiornamento*, these Catholic colleges and universities were encouraged to open up to modern thought, to appreciate its values, and to enter into dialogue with modern scholars and collaborate with them. Where did Catholic educators go for their ideas of academic freedom? What changes were wrought in their concept of the telos of the Catholic university? On what principles—Catholic, secular, or German idealist—did they found these? As we review Catholic thinking on the issue, we find, not surprisingly, a confused mixture of well-founded developments, on the one hand, and confusion and uncritical acceptance of secular principles, on the other.

The opening up of Catholic institutions to modern thought and the desire for autonomy were not the only factors bearing on the decisions made by Catholic college leaders. The desire for public funds also played a key role in post-Vatican II developments. Beginning in the 1960s, the federal government began providing considerable amounts of money to colleges and universities nationwide, public and private, as long as the funds were used for academic rather than sectarian purposes. Some state governments soon followed, with the same proviso that public funds could not be used for sectarian ends. The desire for public funds led Catholic college leaders to downplay the spiritual dimension of academic life, to sever their colleges' ties with their founding religious orders, and to keep theology as a separate, autonomous discipline rather than incorporate it into the cross-disciplinary dialogues of all disciplines. The religious dimension of academic life was consigned to the margins of campus: —the chapel and campus ministry programs. The curriculum was changed to meet standards of secular academia and of regulations governing federal funding for higher education. Previous mission statements proclaiming the permeation of Catholic thought and life throughout the curriculum were diluted or deleted. Neoscholastic philosophy was scotched as the central, integrative discourse. There were strong pressures on these colleges to conform to secular standards and even to secularize. The trend toward secularization affected even theology in some cases, as Frank Schubert demonstrated.[9] These changes occurred over a short period of no more than 20 years. Here I will focus especially on a series of court cases that had a long-lasting impact on Catholic higher education.

Public funding, as noted, was made available on the condition that it not be used for sectarian purposes. It is well to note that the terms *sectarian* and *religious* are considered synonymous in the American legal system. *Sectarian*, in turn, is associated with "closed-minded," narrow, exclusive, and divisive. The term *sectarian* is applicable—or should be applicable—beyond its association with religion, though. At its root, *sectarianism* refers to an intolerant and exclusive stance toward others who think or believe differently, an unwillingness to even consider the viewpoints of others. Samuel Taylor Coleridge said of sectarianism, "We have imprisoned our own conceptions by the lines, which we have drawn, in order to exclude the conceptions of others."[10] A sect is a group that cuts itself off from the rest of society and is intolerant of other groups and belief systems. It is not that it *distinguishes* itself from other groups—all groups do that to some degree—but rather, that it excludes others; it will not entertain or try to understand their thoughts and will not enter civilly into a dialogue with and debate the beliefs of others. It is a closed-minded, intolerant stance that can pertain to anyone. A Marxist, a feminist, or a postmodernist can be as narrowly sectarian in his or her views as any religious fundamentalist. Secular education, when viewed as limited to Kant's island, is often sectarian in the root meaning of the word. Secular education excludes, and refuses to tolerate, study, and dialogue with anything that is beyond the island, that is, with that which undergirds and permeates the island.

This is not the legal understanding of sectarianism, though. In American jurisprudence, the word *sectarian* is synonymous with *religious* and is considered the opposite of *secular*. That is unfortunate because the opposite of, and cure for, sectarianism is not secularism but "catholicity," meaning universal and comprehensive, free from exclusiveness or narrowness. Secular universities have now become increasingly sectarian in the sense of being dogmatic concerning reigning ideologies, often intolerant of dissent from scientific and progressive orthodoxies, and dismissive of religious perspectives.[11]

Nonetheless, the term *sectarian* came to have its religiously pejorative meaning for justifiable reasons. Religious strife had been a constant cause of war and division in Europe for centuries. In a pluralistic society such as America, with no established religion, sectarian efforts to condemn and exclude the conceptions of others—including scientists, nonbelievers, and believers from other denominations—created strife. Both Catholics and Protestants were guilty of this throughout the nineteenth and first half of the twentieth century. Because of this association, the American legal system tends to associate religion with sectarian strife and to consider them synonymous.

When public funds were made available to colleges with religious affiliations in the 1960s, agencies such as the American Civil Liberties Union (ACLU) quickly brought litigation in an attempt to prohibit them from receiving these funds. They did so on the grounds that the colleges were pervasively sectarian and public support for them constituted an infringement of the separation of church and state. Public support for them, it was claimed, would only lead to further sectarian strife. Most of the religious colleges involved in these cases were Catholic. The most pertinent court cases—which drew the attention and concern of Catholic educators nationwide—are *Horace Mann League v. Board of Public Works of Maryland* (1966), *Tilton v. Richardson* (1972), and *Roemer v. Board of Public Works of Maryland* (1976). The latter two cases were decided by the US Supreme Court. The consequences of these lawsuits, combined with both the dramatic social upheaval of the 1960s and the Second Vatican Council, were far-reaching and profound. Let us now turn to the court cases.

Horace Mann League v. Board of Public Works of Maryland

The plaintiffs in this case—the Horace Mann League of the United States—challenged the constitutionality of grants made by the State of Maryland to four private colleges with denominational affiliations.[12] Two of them were Catholic women's colleges: the College of Notre Dame in Baltimore, operated by the School Sisters of Notre Dame, and St. Joseph's College in Emmitsburg, run by the Sisters of Charity. The complaint alleged that these colleges were "pervasively sectarian" and that religion permeated college life to such an extent that taxpayer funds would be used, for all intents and purposes, to teach the tenets of a particular faith. The state grants were for the construction of buildings, but the plaintiffs argued that religion was so pervasive at these schools that it would "seep into" the secular activities carried out in those buildings. To substantiate these claims, the plaintiffs had only to point to the colleges' own mission statements and other publications—that is, their own claims about themselves—as evidence.

As we saw in the last chapter, most Catholic colleges prior to the Second Vatican Council had proudly and energetically proclaimed that Catholic religious thought and principles permeated every aspect of campus life, including the curriculum. The 1956–1957 catalogue of the College of Notre Dame stated, "The life of a student at Notre Dame is surrounded and permeated with the spirit of faith. Young women are encouraged to grow intimate with their Creator, that they may choose to employ their individual talents in bringing about the world order that He has planned."[13] The court opinion in the *Horace Mann* case cited many such statements from the college's own publications.

> Notre Dame's stated purposes are deeply and intensely religious. The theory of Catholic education is that Prayer, Holy Mass and the Sacraments represent "the Unifying forces," and "the instructional program interlocks with the non-instructional program; objectives with methods and means, and all to an essential, interwoven unity. All of [the College's] objectives are implemented in some degree in every department. The institution's whole life is lived in the Catholic atmosphere, which assumes that earthly life is to be lived…in terms of a preparation for the future life with God," and to that end, it "harmonizes" its entire "program with the philosophy and theology of the Catholic Church." The entire program of the College is so ordered "that [the student's] life and study and the atmosphere of the college are *permeated, motivated, enlarged and integrated by the Catholic way of life* as developed and expressed in the daily prayer, liturgy, Sacraments and Holy Mass of the Church." (Emphasis ours)[14]

These views on Notre Dame's purpose were culled from various published materials of the College and from fund-raising letters to the college's constituents. There is nothing surprising or unusual about the ideas expressed; they accord with the general Catholic view in the first half of the twentieth century that Catholic philosophy and a Catholic way of life should permeate the entire campus. We saw in chapter 5 how pervasive this view was.

The Maryland Court of Appeals ruled that the Catholic colleges were "legally sectarian institutions, rendering the state grants to them invalid and unconstitutional."[15] The following facts were the basis of this decision: "The intensely religious purposes of the colleges; the predominantly Catholic faculty and student body; ownership, control, administration, and governance of the two colleges by Catholic religious orders of nuns; the Catholic design of the curriculum of the colleges; and the religious manifestations of the two campuses such as crucifixes and statues."[16]

Leaders in Catholic higher education nationwide knew that the outcome in the *Horace Mann* case could prove decisive for their ability to receive public funds of any kind, and they followed the case with great interest. According to Joseph Preville, the "ruling in *Horace Mann* stunned the American Catholic higher educational community."[17] Following the court's decision, Francis X. Gallagher, the attorney representing Saint

Joseph College in the case, spoke at a number of meetings of Catholic college educators, including the National Catholic Educational Association and the Jesuit Educational Association, advising them on how they might "guard against future court challenges to their eligibility for direct government assistance."[18] Among the recommendations were the following: to eliminate "excessively sectarian [i.e., religious] language from college catalogues"; to include more laypeople as members of boards, faculty, and administration; to separate college governing boards, legally and financially, from the sponsoring religious order; to rewrite mission and objective statements so as "to eliminate an undue emphasis on the so-called permeation theory"; and to clearly distinguish in official documents the separate roles of the college president and the religious superior of the college community.[19]

Gallagher especially criticized the permeation theory, in both speech and writing, calling it the "Trojan horse" of Catholic higher education.

> May I suggest to you that the term "permeation," as it presently exists, is one of the most mysterious creatures roaming the Catholic academic world...Read the catalogues, the brochures, the literature of our educational world and you will find that, like the poor, "permeation" is always with us. But what is it? Who and what gets permeated? Is it the campus; is it the student; is it the course; is it the teacher; is it the curriculum generally; is it the atmosphere; is it the tone of the college or the continuum or the integrating factor? When I permeate the mathematics course, does a halo surround the equation?...Can church-connected colleges approach a legislative body and assert that a government grant to a church-connected college is but a trifling contribution to religion when we seem to be saying that this "permeation" is our vital distinguishing characteristic, that it has a profound impact at all levels upon all members of the academic community?[20]

Gallagher urged Catholic colleges to eliminate such references. His recommendations and those of other legal experts "received widespread acceptance by the leadership of American Catholic higher education."[21] Catholic Colleges and universities nationwide sought to alter their structures to ensure eligibility for public aid. For example, in the late 1960s, Fordham University commissioned a study to determine what it must do to qualify for New York public funds, which were available to nonsectarian private colleges. The authors of the study, Walter Gellhorn and R. Kent Greenawalt, stated in their report that "belief has grown not only in academic circles but also in ecclesiastical bodies that concern with students' religious activity should be transferred wholly from the universities to the churches."[22] They also speculated that attendance by Protestant,

Jewish, and Muslim students at Fordham was discouraged "by awareness that religiosity intrudes into Fordham's lecture halls." They then asked rhetorically, "How much is gained by routinely mumbling prayers when young men and women have assembled for academic exercise rather than for religious expression" and expressed doubt that "classroom prayers significantly advance either an academic or a religious purpose."[23]

The report's recommendations were almost identical to those of Francis Gallagher, and Fordham readily adopted them in order to qualify for aid from New York State. The Reverend Leo McLaughlin, president of Fordham University, admitted frankly, "one reason that changes are being made in the structure of the boards of trustees is money. These colleges cannot continue to exist without state aid."[24] A national trend had begun.

The *Horace Mann* case applied only to colleges in the State of Maryland, but Catholic educators knew that there would be future challenges elsewhere to their eligibility for public assistance. They quickly sought to restructure their institutions and eliminate evidences of religious influence, such as crucifixes in classroom buildings, religious statues on campus, and mention of Christian principles in their catalogues. They laicized their boards of trustees, which had formerly been in clerical hands; hired non-Catholic faculty; and quickly adopted secular norms of academic freedom.

Tilton v. Richardson

It was only a matter of time before the issue of public aid to religious colleges reached the US Supreme Court. Four Catholic colleges in Connecticut were named in what has become a landmark case, known as *Tilton v. Richardson*.[25] The actions of Fairfield University, a Jesuit school, illustrate the changes made in order to conform to secular academic norms. After the *Tilton* case had been filed, Fairfield began to rapidly change its structure and curriculum in accordance with the legal realities governing sectarian education. The National Catholic Education Association encouraged such changes. Father William C. McInnes, S. J., who was both president of Fairfield and superior of the Jesuits, resigned his office as religious superior. The Department of Theology changed its name to the Department of Religious Studies in 1970 and hired both Protestant and Jewish faculty members.[26]

The school dropped many references to religious permeation in its publications. For decades prior to *Tilton*, Fairfield's catalogue claimed that the university was guided by Pope Pius XI's encyclical *Divini Illius Magistri* ("The Christian Education of Youth").[27] This encyclical proclaims that all education must be "wholly directed to man's last end" and that there can be "no ideally perfect education that is not Christian education."[28] The proper end of Christian education is to cooperate with divine grace in forming the true and perfect Christian, formed in the image of Christ. Christian education encompasses the entirety of human life—physical and spiritual; intellectual and moral; individual, domestic, and social—and to elevate and perfect all these dimensions. The graduate of Christian schools is to be "the supernatural man who thinks, judges and acts constantly and consistently in accordance with right reason illumined by the spirit and teaching of Christ."[29] This reference to *Divini Illius* was eliminated from the college's catalogue in 1968–1969, the same year that the *Tilton* complaint was formally filed in court.

Other references to the permeation theory, however, remained, and attorneys for the ACLU seized on them, arguing that religion pervaded every aspect of the curriculum and life of Fairfield—so much so that students were receiving not a secular, liberal arts education but religious indoctrination. They turned to a number of printed sources to make their case, including Jesuit rules governing education. Such rules were reflected in the 1948 Jesuit document *Instructio Pro Assistentia Americae de Ordinandis Universitatibus, Collegiis, ac Scholis Altis et De Praeparandis Eorundum Magistris*,[30] commonly referred to as the *Instructio*. The language in the *Instructio* claimed the document had a "permanent and mandatory character" for all Jesuit colleges and universities. John B. Janssens, S. J., the general of the Society of Jesus when the *Instructio* was promulgated, wrote in a letter accompanying the *Instructio* that work in the field of education "is primarily a spiritual work." St. Ignatius of Loyola, founder of the Jesuits, had founded colleges to "help youth advance in upright moral conduct as well as knowledge... [Therefore] spiritual direction and instruction in Christian doctrine were of prime importance." The aim was to educate legions of young men who would go into the world and spread knowledge and faith for the "glory of God our Lord." Indeed, said Father Janssens, "if our schools were to graduate men learned in their profession but poorly instructed in their faith and irresolute in its practice and in zeal for its propagation, they would not warrant our present vast expenditure of men and energies."[31] Since this was a "permanent and mandatory" rule for Jesuit higher education, the ACLU attorneys argued that Fairfield University was clearly a pervasively sectarian institution.

That turned out to be a problematic claim, though, because Fairfield could claim that the *Instructio* was now outdated. The Second Vatican Council had altered Catholic life in the intervening years, and Catholic colleges were now open to modern trends in thought. They could claim that academic freedom and autonomy of the sciences were now the rule. There were, however, other documents to which the plaintiffs could point.

The 1968–1969 catalogue for Fairfield's College of Arts and Sciences was dedicated *Ad Maiorem Dei Gloriam*, and had the following to say about its system of education: "Fairfield University is a Catholic and Jesuit university. Its primary objective is the development of the creative intellectual potential of each of its students within a context of religious commitment. It is motivated by the moral and religious inspiration and values of the Judeo-Christian tradition. It is guided in its operation by the spiritual and intellectual ideals of the Society of Jesus."[32] This reference to the educational ideals of the Jesuits enabled the ACLU to link Fairfield to another Jesuit document—*The Decrees of the 31st General Congregation of the Society of Jesus*, promulgated in 1965–1966—which was more recent and therefore not outdated at the time of the *Tilton* trial.[33]

The twenty-eighth article of the *Decrees* dealt with the "Apostolate of Education." This article set forth guidelines for Jesuit colleges and universities in the rapidly changing social environment of modern times. It warned Jesuit educators that new ideas and philosophies, many of them agnostic and atheistic, were becoming prominent in the nation's colleges and universities. Christian scholars must, therefore, be present in academia to help form society and educate the mind "to reverence for God and in the fullness of Christ."[34] Jesuits must continue to operate their own educational institutions to serve as instruments for the "synthesizing of faith and culture... Thus the school becomes an apostolic center within the community."[35] Education is one of the primary ministries of the Jesuits, for "the transmission of human culture and its integration in Christ significantly contribute to realization of the goal set by our Lord 'that God may be all in all things.'"[36] Non-Catholics should also be led "to the knowledge and love of God or at least to the acceptance of moral, and even religious values."[37] Spiritual and moral formation, along with learning in "letters and sciences," were core works of the Jesuit college.[38] Jesuit priest-scholars and lay Catholic scholars are to cooperate "in penetrating the whole human culture with the Christian spirit and better ordering the world to God, its ultimate end."[39] These principles were as old as the Jesuit order itself.

Attorneys for the ACLU and American Jewish Congress (the plaintiffs) fastened onto these guidelines—along with references to *Divini Illius Magistri* and other documents—as proof that religion permeated every aspect of the curriculum and life of Fairfield. The president of Fairfield University, William C. McInnes, S. J., denied that the decree, specifically the "Apostolate of Education," applied to Fairfield. The following exchange during the *Tilton* trial between McInnes and attorneys for the plaintiffs illustrates how the president sought to distance the university from the Jesuit guidelines.

> Q: Do you, as a Jesuit, accept this as a guideline pertaining to the Jesuit role in education?
>
> *McInnes*: Well, as the President of Fairfield University, I do not accept it as a guideline. As an individual religious, yes, I accept it as giving the general spirit in which activities must be carried out; but subject, again, to all of the limitations imposed upon me as the President.
>
> Q: Are you saying that as President of the University, however, you don't recognize this even as a guideline?
>
> *McInnes*: No. I said I recognized it as a guideline, but as an individual— well, yes, you're right. As an individual I recognize it as a guideline. But acting in my official capacity, I have no power to recognize it as controlling the life and activities of Fairfield University.[40]

This disavowal of Catholic principles of higher education was especially surprising coming from a Jesuit educator; the principles, after all, were largely those promulgated by St. Ignatius of Loyola in Part IV of the *Constitutions* of the Society of Jesus (1556) and later the *Ratio Studiorum* of 1599.[41]

The Catholic colleges won the *Tilton* case by a 5–4 majority on the basis that they were not "pervasively sectarian." The Supreme Court established a threefold test to determine whether or not use of public funds for church-related schools was constitutional. First, government aid had to be given for a secular purpose. Second, the primary effect of public aid must neither advance nor hinder religion. Finally, the aid program must not entail "excessive entanglement" of government with church organizations.[42] The effect of this ruling was that Catholic colleges were even more tempted to downplay or sever their ties with the church, to diminish the role of religious life on the campus, and to claim that spiritual life was only secondary to the intellectual aims of the colleges. Fairfield University went so far as to remove the university's patron saint—Saint Robert Bellarmine—from the institution's corporate seal.[43]

Roemer v. Board of Public Works of Maryland

To make matters worse, soon after the decision in the *Tilton* case, several Catholic colleges in Maryland were pulled into yet another court battle challenging their right to accept state money—money that could be used for general purposes, in whatever way the colleges determined. This new case, *Roemer v. Board of Public Works of Maryland,* went to trial in 1972 and was decided by the US Supreme Court in 1976.[44] Attorneys for the plaintiffs once again drew on the published documents and reports of the colleges themselves as evidence of their sectarian nature.

This case reveals the extent to which Catholic college leaders were willing to disavow the religious dimension of academic life on their campuses. In fewer than ten years since the *Horace Mann* decision, the College of Notre Dame had drastically downplayed its references to the permeation of Catholic thought and values in both the academic program and in rules for student life. In its response to the charge that one of its primary goals was to inculcate Catholic values in its students, the college maintained that "religion does not influence the formation of the curriculum, the selection of textbooks, or the mode of teaching courses, except in so far as the Religious Studies Department is necessarily dealing with religion."[45] Concerning faculty hiring, Notre Dame had the following to say: "The faculty is not selected on a religious basis except theoretically if a vacancy involved the Theology Department and a Catholic theology course, in which case the person having the best academic qualifications in this area would probably be a Catholic. Preference may be given to an academically qualified Sister to fill a vacancy, but this is for man-power and economic reasons, not religious reasons."[46]

The strong sense of Notre Dame's Catholic identity as articulated in publications prior to the *Horace Mann* decision was by 1973 severely diminished. College leaders maintained that "the College is often called a Catholic college because of its origin and historic auspices and because it primarily serves Catholic students," not because it taught the Catholic faith or Catholic values.[47] The plaintiff's attorneys countered by presenting evidence from a college report that asserted the college's commitment to the Catholic Church. The College of Notre Dame had this disclaimer: "A reference in [the] report to a commitment of the College to the Catholic Church meant, in the view of the [Notre Dame] President, that the College is committed to one of the traditional general good works of the church which is general education.[48] Kathleen Feeney, SSND, the president of Notre Dame, had the following exchange with the plaintiff's attorney during the trial.

> *Q:* Sister Kathleen, would you agree that the educational process at Notre Dame is designed to teach the woman to develop as a whole; this is [*sic*], her intellectual self as well as her religious self? Isn't that one of the purposes?
> *Feeney:* The education at Notre Dame is an education for freedom, to quote our catalogue. I can say it in those words, because I believe that is what we are all about . . .

Q: Well, let me rephrase my question. What I would like to know, specifically, is whether one of the purposes of Notre Dame is to develop both the intellectual and the religious sides of the individual... Would you answer that question?

Feeney: One of the purposes of Notre Dame is to teach students. I don't think you can divide students into sides... My answer to that question is that Notre Dame education is an education to free the mind. It is an Academic education, which is the freeing—it frees the intellect.

Q: Right. Well, do you, at Notre Dame, believe that Man's relationship to God is the most important relationship in life?...

Feeney: That is a statement I could not make for any person, sir... You are asking me a very personal question, and you are asking me to speak as a College authority, and I am not able to do that. I am not able to speak as a college President, and answer such a question. That is a very personal question, and it would never be answered in an official capacity by a College President.[49]

The College of Notre Dame had, in previous years, strongly emphasized moral formation along with academics. Since the plaintiffs used this as evidence of religious and moral permeation, college leaders now denied moral formation was part of the overall mission of the college. The college's official statement on morality during the *Roemer* case was that "students establish their own code of behavior. They try to create a group mores [sic] which they sometimes call... 'A Christian Conscience,' which the President interprets as simply the standards of honesty and integrity." In order to demonstrate just how far they had distanced themselves from teachings of the church, college officials went on to state that "rules concerning such areas as pre-marital pregnancy and abortion... are obsolete and no longer prevail," and that the administration "feels strongly that a student's personal life is her own affair."[50] The responses reveal a dramatic move away from the previous integral Catholic worldview espoused by the College of Notre Dame.

The responses of Mount St. Mary's College and Loyola College of Baltimore were similar, with both pleading conformance to secular standards as their defense. Mount St. Mary's downplayed its previous emphasis on the "education of the whole man" through which the curriculum leads students to view all aspects of life in relation to all other aspects and encourages the simultaneous development of both the spiritual and the intellectual dimensions of the student. Mount St. Mary's had claimed one of its primary concerns was "imparting to the student the Catholic attitude toward life as a whole... to graduate students so steeped in the Catholic way of life that it colors their every activity, not their religious activity alone."[51] Now, however, college representatives claimed that references to the "whole man" concept was a *philosophical* rather than a Christian concept: "The 'whole man' concept...is a concept that finds expression both in Christian humanism and liberal arts philosophy of education. As an institution, Mount Saint Mary's College adopts that concept as a result of its roots in the liberal arts philosophy and *not* because it finds expression in the theories of Christian humanism."[52]

Maryland's Catholic colleges won the *Roemer* case by a 5–4 margin. Based on the testimony of the colleges' leaders, the US Supreme Court ruled that religion did not permeate the curriculum or campus life and "there was *little risk that religion would seep into the teaching of secular subjects.*"[53] Although campus authorities encouraged spiritual development, it was only "one secondary objective" of each college, and "at none of these institutions does this encouragement go beyond providing the opportunity or occasions for religious experience."[54] It was not essential to the colleges' objectives.[55]

The four dissenting justices were not persuaded by the majority decision; indeed, they were convinced that the prevailing ethos in the colleges did give sufficient evidence of their pervasive religious character. These justices noted that the colleges' "publicity had stressed the permeation of all campus life and study with religious values,"[56] in spite of denials by their leaders. During the trial Loyola College representatives had denied the validity of this evidence, claiming that publications and speeches stressing the permeation of Catholic ideals and teachings represented but "allegorical language and rhetorical imagery" whose aim was "to appeal to a certain audience." (One may infer that the "audience" was devout Catholics who wanted their children to receive a Catholic education.) Loyola's attorney then characterized this as but "the familiar penchant of all Mankind to use or ascribe loftier and commendable attitudes and objectives to one's loyalty, be it Catholic, American, or Democratic."[57] In other words, Loyola was admitting that its language about the permeation of Catholic ideals was nothing more than a public relations tool, and that such publicity-driven images did not necessarily correspond to the reality of Loyola College or any of its actual goals. Nonetheless, Loyola's president, Father Joseph Sellinger, would publicly state that he had not compromised in any way the Catholicity of the college in order to obtain public funds.[58]

Some of the dissenting justices made another pertinent point: receipt of state assistance would undermine the religious dimensions of the colleges in question. Justice William Brennan stated in his dissent, "it is not only the nonbeliever who fears the injection of sectarian doctrines and controversies into the civil polity, but in as high degree it is the devout believer who fears *the secularization of a creed which becomes too deeply involved with and dependent upon the government.*"[59] Justice John Paul Stevens, also dissenting, pointed to "the pernicious tendency of a state subsidy to tempt religious schools to compromise their religious mission without wholly abandoning it."[60] The consequence of Caesar's gold, he was arguing, is a dilution of one's identity and tradition. As a judge in Louisiana once noted, "the consequence of Caesar's gold, is Caesar's control."[61] To see how far this control can extend, let us look briefly at another Maryland college involved in the *Roemer* case.

Western Maryland College in Westminster, affiliated with the Methodist Church, was one of the original defendants in the *Roemer* case. The college had also been a defendant in the *Horace Mann* case a decade earlier and was found to be, along with the two Catholic colleges, legally sectarian. In this new case, the college's administration was determined not to lose its state aid. It agreed to disaffiliate itself from the Methodist Church and to secularize the college in order to be withdrawn from litigation. Specifically, it agreed to the following demands of the plaintiff's attorneys: (1) to "promptly and permanently remove all religious symbols and indicia of church-relatedness, including but not limited to crosses"; (2) to "neither describe itself nor hold itself out as being a church-related college"; (3) to "remain totally neutral as to the spiritual development (in a religious sense) of its students and shall not adopt, maintain, or pursue any objective, policy, or plan of encouraging or discouraging such spiritual development"; (4) to "neither sponsor nor conduct any religious services"; (5) to "require that the baccalaureate services, if any, shall be totally secular in form and substance and shall not include any prayer, religious hymns, or religious sermon"; (6) to refuse to "financially support any religious group or organization including but not limited to the Religious Life Council"; (7) to ensure that "at least 50% of all religion classes" and "50% of all philosophy classes shall be taught by non-Methodists" and no more than 10 percent of the college's board of trustees would be Methodist ministers.[62]

Caesar's gold exacts a heavy price, and Western Maryland College was willing to pay it. The Catholic colleges involved in *Tilton* and *Roemer* did not go this far toward the *legal* renunciation of their religious character, but their leaders' testimonies drew nigh unto it, in spirit if not in law. As a consequence, they developed a new dependence not on church authorities but on public funds.[63] Added later to this dependence came the demands of accrediting agencies and the competitive race to rise in college rankings— rankings, it should be noted, that are based to a considerable extent on the amount of federal research funds a university procures.

The results of these changes were profound. Rather than aiming at the integration of spirituality and intellectual endeavor, Catholic college leaders denied that spirituality played an important role in the academic life of the student. Indeed, they disavowed the importance of what had for centuries been considered a vital unity: the integration of mind and spirit, the "education of the whole person." They disavowed any union with the church other than a historical one. Over a century earlier, Newman stressed the steadying influence of the church in the university's mission and maintained that the church is necessary for the university's overall *integrity*.[64] The Maryland colleges denied there were any links with the church that amounted to anything. We should also note, however, that these colleges were not acting independently. They were supported and encouraged in their actions by the US Catholic Conference, the National Catholic Educational Association, and some of the nation's bishops,[65] though it may be that some of these groups were not completely aware of the precise denials of Catholicity made by the college leaders during the court cases. Nonetheless, a case can be made that the church's leaders failed in their responsibility to "steady" these colleges and help them maintain their integrity.

Repercussions: Negative and Positive

We find in these court cases a tangled mess of confusion, dissimilation, and evasion on the part of Catholic college leaders. This should not surprise us. During transitional periods in which major social, political, and intellectual shifts are occurring, confused and contradictory positions and beliefs often sit side by side, even within the same people. Catholic educational leaders were no exception. They hoped to maintain the religious character of their institutions while simultaneously denying that their religious character amounted to anything. While trying to establish themselves as legitimate academic institutions according to principles of Vatican II, they acceded, without much deliberation or discernment, to secular academic principles in order to be eligible for government funding. They downplayed, and even denied, the spiritual dimension of academic life in Catholic colleges. They readily adopted secular academic norms and concurred with secular thinkers that it is somehow illicit for religion to "seep into" academic coursework.

Catholic colleges and universities during this period, like the church itself, were seeking to find a new ethos for their institutions, new ways of being Catholic academic institutions in the midst of a fluid and chaotic historical period. Without the spur of the court cases, they might have made changes more deliberately and with greater Christian discernment. As it happened, they dove headlong into the secular world, and their responses reveal the confusion and weak foundation on which their Catholic character was constructed. That foundation—a narrow neoscholasticism, clericalism, and authoritarianism—no longer held sway over a majority of Catholic intellectuals. The path toward transformation was entirely new territory, without precedent. The result was that many colleges and universities lost their way and moved down the road toward secularization. Some went all the way, such as Webster College in Missouri and Villa Julie College in Baltimore.[66] This was not the entire story, however, and it would be wrong to judge their actions outside the context of their efforts as a whole. The court cases reveal only one aspect of the transformations that took place following the Second Vatican Council. We now have the advantage of historical hindsight to sort out the truly negative from the beneficial developments.

Some of the changes would have occurred even without the catalyst of the court cases. As early as 1965 members of the International Federation of Catholic Universities began planning meetings to discuss the nature and mission of the Catholic universities in light of the Second Vatican Council, especially *Gaudium et Spes*. Lay participation, autonomy, and academic freedom were all "authorized" by this document. It is well to bear in mind that laicization of boards of trustees, faculty, and administrators is not, in itself, the same as secularization. It was, after all, not lay boards that moved these colleges down the path toward secularization, but the religious and clerics in charge of them.

It is undeniable that many aspects of Catholic colleges and universities have vastly improved since the 1960s. Academic quality has risen considerably. Theology departments are academically strong. Academic freedom is respected and upheld. Campus ministry programs on many campuses are well-funded and vigorous. A spirit of openness to other forms of thought and other religions prevails. The hiring of Protestant and Jewish theologians reflects the growing ecumenism encouraged by Vatican II and does not, as some critics charge, necessarily imply a reduced commitment to Catholic theology. Moreover, to distinguish between the educational function of Catholic colleges, on the one hand, and the church's mission of evangelization and catechesis, on the other, was an appropriate distinction to make, not necessarily a lessening of Catholicity. Many Catholic colleges prior to the Second Vatican Council failed to make this distinction, and the academic quality of their institutions suffered. It is essential, therefore, to distinguish valid changes from secularization.

The Vatican and American Catholic Higher Education

While the court cases were underway, and Catholic college leaders were downplaying and disavowing the relevance of spirituality and Catholic principles in education, another interesting phenomenon was taking place that ran counter to these developments. Most interesting of all is that the counter movement was carried out by many of these same college leaders.

As noted above, members of the International Federation of Catholic Universities (IFCU)—composed of Catholic university presidents and officials worldwide—began meeting to develop a new vision of the nature and mission of the Catholic university in light of the Second Vatican Council. The first major attempt to define the mission of the Catholic university in the post-Vatican II world was the"Land O'Lakes Statement" (1967). The most famous, and controversial, claim made at the Land O'Lakes gathering is that the Catholic university must have "a true autonomy in the face of authority of whatever kind, lay or clerical, external to the academic community itself," if it is to be a true university.[67] This declaration of independence from the institutional church was a nearly revolutionary event. It sparked both praise and condemnation from different quarters, and controversy in all.

It would be wrong, though, to focus only on this push for autonomy from the church. The "Land O'Lakes Statement" also said that the Catholic university is a community of scholars "in which Catholicism is perceptibly present and effectively operative."[68] The Catholic presence occurs, first, through a strong theology department and, consequent to this, an ongoing discussion between theology and all other academic disciplines. Theology enriches itself in this dialogue, brings its own insights to bear on the problems of modern culture, and stimulates "the internal development of the disciplines themselves."[69] A new vision of the relation between theology and other academic disciplines had now arisen. Theology was no longer the "queen" of the sciences, dominating the rest.

> In a Catholic university all recognized university areas of study are frankly and fully accepted and their internal autonomy affirmed and guaranteed. There must be no theological or philosophical imperialism; all scientific and disciplinary methods, and methodologies, must be given due honor and respect. However, there will necessarily result from the interdisciplinary discussions an awareness that *there is a philosophical and theological dimension to most intellectual subjects when they are pursued far enough.*[70]

In this statement we can recognize the idea of a dynamism—a directionality—to inquiry. It does not advocate an imperial dominance of other disciplines by theology. Rather, it focuses on a dialogue leading to ultimate questions. This dialogue between theology and other disciplines can be successful if there is a broad enough range of strong academic disciplines present, and if there are Christian scholars in nontheological areas who are both interested in and able to carry on cross-disciplinary dialogue with theology.[71]

Many critics of developments in Catholic colleges and universities following the Second Vatican Council consider the "Land O'Lakes Statement," along with the court cases discussed above, a beginning point in the transition to secularization.[72] The statement itself does not bear out this criticism. The document calls for a total openness to modern thought—to the religious and intellectual traditions of all humanity. Along with this there should be "a competent presentation of relevant, living, Catholic thought." The Catholic university has the following characteristics: (1) "a concern with ultimate questions; hence a concern with philosophical and theological questions; (2) a concern for the full human and spiritual development of the student"; and (3) "a concern with the particularly pressing problems of our era."[73] Further, the student must not merely be able to study theology but "find himself in a social situation in which he can express his Christianity in a variety of ways and live it experientially and experimentally," where "students and faculty can explore together new forms of Christian living, of Christian witness, and Christian service." An emphasis on the spiritual life will foster "within the Catholic university a self-developing and self-deepening society of students and faculty in which the consequences of Christian truth are taken seriously in person-to-person relationships, where the importance of religious commitment is accepted and constantly witnessed to."[74]

This statement on the spiritual dimension of the Catholic university was almost as strong as any claim of "permeation" in the literature of Catholic colleges and universities prior to the Second Vatican Council. For sure, it describes a different kind of spiritual life (new and experimental), but the emphasis on total religious commitment and permeation remains. Succeeding statements of the IFCU also emphasized the need for the integration of all knowledge in the light of Christian wisdom, the need to make theology relevant to all human knowledge, and affirmed the spiritual dimension of academic life.[75]

However, it was not this emphasis on spiritual and intellectual integration that concerned Vatican officials. The Vatican was concerned about many of the changes taking place in American Catholic higher education, especially their declaration of independence from the institutional church, manifested concretely in the transfer of ownership from the founding religious orders to lay trustees. In response, the Vatican began a dialogue with the leaders of Catholic colleges and universities about the nature and mission of the Catholic university. This dialogue began around 1969 and lasted for over 20 years.[76]

The university leaders continued to insist on autonomy, academic freedom, and a voluntary commitment to the church. The Vatican insisted, for its part, on a juridical and formal relationship through which Catholic institutions of higher education made their commitment to Catholicism explicit in their mission statements. Only the local bishop could determine if a Catholic university, whether founded with ecclesiastical approbation or not, was truly Catholic. The Vatican also wanted rules and norms that would assure the orthodoxy of theologians, making them answerable to the church's Magisterium. These issues created the most pronounced tensions and disagreements between universities and the Vatican. Catholic college leaders were quite aware of the implications of formal ties to Rome for their ability to secure public funds, and they repeatedly referred to them in ongoing correspondence with the head of the Vatican's Congregation for Catholic Education, Gabriel Cardinal Garrone.

Theodore Hesburgh even held forth the threat that American Catholic universities might sever all ties with the church if the Vatican insisted on juridical ties. In a forceful letter to Cardinal Garrone, Hesburgh relayed the consensus position of his fellow American Catholic university presidents.

> [I want] to state as forcefully as possible that general norms and regulations emanating from Rome to govern American Catholic universities would be a disaster at this particular point in our history...Lawyers who are challenging our freedom and autonomy as qualifying us to receive public funds would use the Roman declaration of general norms and regulations to...disqualify all Catholic colleges and universities from receiving state and federal assistance...
>
> If the position of [the Vatican] were to be indicated as fixed norms or principles, all of the major Catholic universities in America would have to simply stop being Catholic to survive...
>
> All our institutions would like to remain Catholic and at the service of the Church, but the price of doing so and still being recognized as American universities is that we also be free and autonomous...
>
> We would like to avoid a confrontation between the Trustees [of the universities] and the Church that would force our lay Trustees to say, "This simply cannot be admitted and, if to admit such regulation is the price of being Catholic, then this institution is no longer officially Catholic."...We think it would be a disaster to the Church to lose the presence and allegiance of the great American Catholic universities.[77]

In spite of persistent tensions such as this, the dialogue continued slowly. In 1972 the members of the IFCU met again to fashion a document on Catholic universities they hoped would be acceptable to the Vatican. The document, "The Catholic University in the Modern World," summarized several previous IFCU documents (Land O'Lakes, Kinshasa, and Rome statements) and incorporated some of the concerns of the Vatican. Among the primary objectives of the Catholic university, they claimed, is the integration of disciplines within a Christian context.

> Every university is intended to be a place where the various branches of human knowledge confront one another for their mutual enrichment. To this task of integration and synthesis, the Catholic university brings the light of the Christian message. This involves a profound conviction that the unity of truth makes necessary the search for a synthesis to determine the place and meaning of the various disciplines within the context of a vision of man and the world that is enlightened by the Gospel.[78]

The document then notes that one of the principal tasks of the Catholic university is "to make theology relevant to all human knowledge, and reciprocally all human knowledge relevant to theology," with each academic discipline remaining respectful of the others. "By insisting on the importance of the Christian message...and by giving expression to this conviction through its academic programs and scholarly research, [the Catholic university] can render eloquent testimony to the truth and undying validity of the Gospel."[79]

As in the previous documents of the IFCU, "The Catholic University in the Modern World" emphasized the spiritual dimension of academic life. It was more open and ecumenical (as opposed to an exclusivist Catholic spirituality), but it was strongly stated. The IFCU leaders promoted the development of a Christian personality that would be able to synthesize intellectual, professional, and religious life in a vital unity.[80] Indeed, in all these documents, one finds strong language regarding the important role of Catholic principles and spiritual life in academics, though the word "permeation" is not used. Ironically, while these college presidents were affirming the spiritual dimension of academic life in these IFCU documents, many of them were simultaneously removing such language from the mission statements of their college catalogues in order to qualify for public funds.

When the Vatican—under the pontificate of John Paul II—proposed a new apostolic constitution on Catholic universities, Catholic college and university leaders were given the opportunity to comment on and critique successive drafts of the developing document. These leaders repeatedly expressed the same theme in their responses: the need for institutional autonomy in order to qualify for public funds. *Tilton* and *Roemer* hovered in the background and were regularly referenced in the responses of American academic leaders.[81] In the disputes between the Vatican and university educators, the tension between autonomy and heteronomy, along with the desire for Caesar's gold, always lurk in the background. Christian theological principles were rarely, if ever, brought in to support the claims of academic freedom. When academic freedom was discussed at length, it was usually in the context of the freedom of theologians. This was natural, since the Vatican was trying to reign in dissenting theologians. But in terms of academic freedom based on the eros of the mind for God, a freedom that belongs to scholars in all disciplines, the many documents and discussions during this extended 20-year period say little, other than to affirm standard secular principles of academic freedom.[82]

John Paul II's apostolic constitution *Ex Corde Ecclesiae* (1990; hereafter ECE) resulted from the discussions between Vatican officials and Catholic college leaders worldwide.[83] *Ex Corde* is not a systematic treatise but a blending of IFCU documents and principles enunciated by the Vatican. It attempts to set forth the principal characteristics of a Catholic university. For John Paul II, a Catholic university is distinguished by its free search for the whole truth about nature, humanity, and God, and the exploration of all aspects of truth in their essential relation to God, from whom all truth flows. This is its telos. All paths to knowledge are considered in the Catholic university because the Logos, or Spirit of intelligence, enables the human mind, made in the image of God, to discover the orderly, divine structure of reality (ECE 4). This enables scholars to move beyond partial or particular truths. Catholic attitudes, principles, and ideals must inform the university's activities and direction (ECE 14), and a Christian spirit must animate the university as a whole, making it a place where the many academic disciplines are brought into dialogue with each other and with Christian truth (ECE 15).

Several key elements must characterize a Catholic university. Among them is *the search for an integration of knowledge*, in accordance with the teaching of Vatican II (ECE 16). *Gaudium et Spes* had called for the opening of the Catholic mind to the modern world and enjoined Catholics to collaborate with their non-Catholic peers for the common good. All scholars working for the common good have dignity in the eyes of God. The scholar who labors "to penetrate the secrets of reality with a humble and steady mind, even though he is unaware of the fact, is nevertheless being led by the hand of God, who holds all things in existence." The council acknowledged the legitimate autonomy of the sciences and their "just liberty" in using their own proper methods, while deploring the habits of mind that deny the rightful independence of science. At the same time, it cautioned against the agnosticism fostered by many of the sciences when their methods of investigation are "wrongly considered as the supreme rule of seeking the whole truth." Further, the council recognized that "by virtue of their methods these sciences cannot penetrate to the intimate notion of things." Because of the limitations inherent in the sciences, there is a need to "harmonize the proliferation of particular branches of study with the necessity of forming a synthesis of them, and of preserving among men the faculties of contemplation and observation which lead to wisdom."[84] The search for integration must involve a continuous dialogue between theology and other academic disciplines. In this dialogue, John Paul II saw theology not so much as the "queen of the sciences" (though he probably would not have rejected that phrase), as their servant, helping them to see beyond what can be seen using disciplinary methods and from within disciplinary boundaries (ECE 19).

Two themes appear in these statements: the freedom and autonomy of the sciences, on the one hand, and the necessity of forming a synthesis of them within an ever-broadening Catholic horizon, on the other. This includes placing each academic discipline in its proper place in a broader Christian philosophical and theological framework. It also means seeking to instill in students an organic vision of reality (ECE 20) and a concern for the ethical and moral implications of the methods and discoveries of research, especially in science and technology (ECE 18).

The process that led to *Ex Corde* was contentious. In the end, though, there was considerable consensus on the part of both the Vatican and university leaders regarding most of the principles just described.[85] The university leaders had promoted the same principles in the various IFCU documents. The disagreements and controversies focused not on these key elements but primarily on the issue of institutional autonomy and the *mandatum* for theologians.[86]

Many Catholic universities have attempted to adopt some of the principles of *Ex Corde*, with uneven results to date. The choices these colleges made following the court cases in the 1960s and 1970s have left them in a quandary. On the one hand, they want to pursue the spiritual and theological dimension of all truth, but, on the other, in order to ensure the flow of public funds, they must claim that spiritual and theological concerns do not enter into the deliberations of "secular" academic disciplines. After all, to foster the theological dimension of knowledge in all disciplines is to allow religion to "seep into" them. Must these colleges, then, forever explore Kant's island in isolation from the vast sea surrounding and undergirding it?

Where We Are Today

In spite of the efforts of the Vatican and the efforts of Catholic colleges and universities to implement aspects of *Ex Corde*, all is not well, as Melanie

Morey and John J. Piderit, S. J., point out in their study of the contemporary Catholic university, *Catholic Higher Education: A Culture in Crisis.*[87] During 2001 and 2002, Morey and Piderit conducted a study of 124 senior administrators (presidents, chief academic officers, vice presidents of student affairs, and executive vice presidents) from 33 Catholic colleges and universities in America. Their goal was to gather data on how these institutions are faring with regard to integrating the Catholic tradition into the academic program and in strengthening their Catholic character. The study's findings demonstrate an inability on the part of these senior administrators to articulate the relationship between the Catholic intellectual tradition and other disciplines, and a failure to develop clear and comprehensive plans for integrating them. The means of such integration continues to elude these institutions. Indeed, Catholic college administrators today seem as confused and uncertain as the leaders during the *Tilton* and *Roemer* trials. Administrators sincerely want to improve the Catholic character of their institutions and to ensure that the Catholic tradition is engaged by students in all disciplines. Faculty resistance and even hostility, however, too often hamper efforts along these lines.[88] Moreover, in spite of the good intentions of administrators, most of them know very little about the Catholic tradition they claim to champion, how it might intersect with the various academic disciplines, and which disciplines "might easily lend themselves to courses or components that explore the tradition." The administrators Morey and Piderit interviewed are often "at a loss about how to make [the Catholic tradition] available to students in the classroom."[89] In fact, most of them admit that their institutions had "rather weak Catholic cultures." As a result, Morey and Piderit conclude that American Catholic higher education is facing a looming crisis.[90]

The study also found that the presidents and senior administrators at Catholic colleges and universities increasingly resemble their peers in non-Catholic institutions, raising questions "about their claims that Catholic colleges and universities are truly distinctive from the rest of American higher education."[91] In fact, these administrators want to resemble as much as possible their secular counterparts, to be seen and respected by their peers at these secular institutions, while also wanting to somehow be distinctively Catholic. They do not know how to bridge these two ideals.[92] Morey and Piderit also found that few of the laypersons who have assumed leadership positions in Catholic colleges and universities "have the depth or breadth of religious formation and education possessed by the religious men and women who preceded them."[93]

I noted earlier that laicization is not the same as secularization, but I must now add a cautionary point. While the laity can be as religious as any ordained priest, monk, or sister, it is also undeniably the case that most laypeople do not receive the extensive and intensive theological and spiritual formation that those in religious orders and the priesthood do. As a result, most laypeople are not well versed in the teachings of the Catholic tradition. Most of them do not know how Catholic theology can intersect with and inform other disciplines. They are not aware of the theological dimension of their own disciplines. To hire them into senior administrative positions on the assumption that, because they are practicing Catholics, they possess expertise in the Catholic tradition is a mistake with major consequences. Only if Catholic institutions are willing to provide these administrators with the kind of extensive training and formation required, will they be able to achieve any kind of integration. This is especially important because the percentage of Catholic faculty members and administrators is diminishing steadily. Of those who are Catholic, even fewer have expertise in the relation between the Catholic tradition and their own discipline.

Today, strong departments of theology sit alongside, though by and large unconnected to, other academic departments.[94] These other departments remain, to this day, confined to Kant's island. Departmental faculty hiring practices, and the profiles and interests of faculty in these departments, largely resemble those at secular universities. While Catholic colleges and universities labored to fully engage modern thought following the Second Vatican Council, they often did so at the expense of retrieving the broader Christian tradition. As a consequence, they still suffer from a sort of dualism between the "religious"—found primarily in separate theology departments and campus ministry programs that are largely insulated from other disciplines—and the "academic," found in all other disciplines, equally insulated from theological thought.

The questions I now raise are these: Can human intelligence, separate from spirituality, come to know truth in its fullness? Can academic pursuits ever be truly competent and satisfactory without the undergirding of a spiritual dimension? If truth is one, as Christians maintain, can any pursuit of truth be adequate if the spiritual dimension of reality is excluded from one's inquiry? Can scholars adequately prescind from consideration of God in order to more thoroughly understand the finite realm in itself, while also ensuring that the theonomous desire of the mind to place all knowledge in theo-philosophical context has a privileged place? Can we foster Catholic rootedness and a catholic openness while avoiding Catholic sectarianism? In the next chapter, I argue that we can.

Chapter 7

"The Direction toward Which Wonder Progresses"

In this chapter, I pose several questions for the Catholic university of the future. Can a coherent Christian vision serve as an organizing tool for the undergraduate curriculum while avoiding the imperialistic tendencies of the encyclopaedists of Berlin[1] and the neo-scholastics of the early twentieth century, or must we accept the current relativism and intellectual equivalence of all viewpoints, simply allowing them to work themselves out through disputation? Must we accept secular approaches to academic inquiry, and later attempt to graft or append religious perspectives onto the various disciplines in some nonorganic way? Or can such differences and disputations take place within a broader Catholic frame of reference that allows the contrary, dissenting, and pluralistic viewpoints of the age a space while simultaneously relating them to a broader Catholic context?

Some would say this is not possible, that the adoption of some overarching tradition will undermine free inquiry. That such a danger exists cannot be denied. It is much too late, however, to maintain that we can do without any overarching frame of reference at all, for if we relinquish an explicitly Catholic framework, some other will take its place. Philosophical assumptions abound in higher education and influence scholarly work, either explicitly or implicitly. For instance, relativism and postmodernism, while denouncing metanarratives, are themselves metanarratives of reality and history based on particular philosophical worldviews, even if those worldviews lack coherence. To speak of a Catholic frame of reference does not mean adopting one philosophical position within the Catholic tradition to the exclusion of any others, as neo-scholastics did. It does mean integrating important Catholic teachings and schools of thought into the curriculum, showing the ways Catholic thinkers have thought about and attempted to apply Christian truth to the issues of their times in a way that is enduringly pertinent.

Another, related question is this: Can we ground academic freedom in the Catholic university on something other than secular American principles, even while adopting and baptizing what is good and true in those principles? I assert that, for the Catholic university, the term "academic freedom" must refer to a specific instance of religious freedom: the freedom to pursue the spiritual dynamism of the mind wherever it will go, as well as the freedom to prescind from going there if one's calling is to focus exclusively on problems within a narrow, limited realm abstracted from the whole. This grounding of the mind's efforts in a spiritual dynamism is what I have called theonomy, or a theo-philosophical approach. If we are not to lose the unique character of Catholic higher education, we must seriously make the attempt to integrate a theonomous approach into the various academic disciplines in Catholic universities. That is the first step.

As noted in chapter 1, a coherent Catholic vision involves much more than adopting a theonomous approach to inquiry. The Catholic intellectual, artistic, and theological tradition, with its extensive body of philosophical, theological, and literary works, must be in continuous dialogue with all academic disciplines. Even more, the overall orientation of the curriculum must lead students to the edge of Kant's island, to the point where they can learn the relationship of the island to the surrounding sea. They do this not through indoctrination or proselytizing, which would make of the Catholic university a sectarian institution, but through academic engagement with relevant aspects of the Catholic tradition.

That tradition is not a narrow one, as was the case with the neo-Thomism of the early twentieth century. After the Second Vatican Council, Thomism almost disappeared from Catholic theology. At the very least, it was relegated to minor status. This had various causes. First, there was the poor application of Thomistic principles by many professors at Catholic colleges and universities, as we saw in chapter 5. Second, the form of Thomism that prevailed during the first half of the twentieth century was a narrow and sectarian—even ideological—version of Thomism whose advocates squelched the thought of those who wished to put forward other legitimate aspects of Thomas's thought,[2] or other legitimate schools of thought in the Catholic tradition. One unfortunate reaction after the Second Vatican Council was to discard Thomas almost entirely, or at least downplay his importance.

A more comprehensive view of Thomas's thought emerged during the twentieth century at the same time that the writings and thought of other medieval scholastics and the church fathers were being recovered, giving Catholic scholars access to the entire tradition. Maurice Blondel, Joseph Marechal, Henri de Lubac, Yves Congar, M.-D. Chenu, and Karl Rahner are just a few of the scholars who helped retrieve that tradition.[3] Together, these historical recoveries helped restore the fullness of the Catholic intellectual and spiritual tradition. This broader Christian patrimony included a theological anthropology that views the human being as fashioned in the image and likeness of God, with a desire for knowledge of God—a desire that orders and fulfills all partial and finite knowledge. The authors on whom this chapter focuses based their work to a large extent on the neglected thought of that broader patrimony, so brief mention of the elements recovered is in order.

Pursuing Truth to Its End

Before the concept of "pure nature" rose to a place of stature in Catholic philosophy, the Catholic tradition held a clear idea of the human being as a desire, or eros, for God. This was a key idea in Thomas's work, as it was in that of Origen, Gregory of Nyssa, and Maximos the Confessor.[4] Augustine wrote of love as the basis of the scholar's desire for knowledge. Love is the dynamism behind academic inquiry.[5] Neither the church fathers nor the medieval scholastics imagined the possibility of a purely *natural* destiny for humankind without reference to its relation to God.[6] God created this world, and the created world is the site of his ongoing action. His grace permeates it and moves it toward himself. He is the engine generating movement and the goal of all desire and striving in the world. This desire, according to Thomas, cannot come to rest in any knowledge of finite things in themselves. The intellect does not reach its ultimate end until its natural desire comes to rest in God.[7] Can we apply this notion to the sciences today? I claim we can.

Scientists first of all focus on the natural world, on proximate causes. They search and examine a defined field of reality, employing a limited portion of their minds (the analytical intelligence) while prescinding from considering the religious foundation of reality and from incorporating religious ways of knowing. But is that the final goal? Should they stop there? Can they arrive at a full understanding of the natural world without going beyond proximate causes to formal and final causes? When human beings encounter and observe the natural world, a sense of wonder arises in their minds, and they desire to know the cause of everything they encounter. The great beauty and intricacy of the created world are so alluring that the human mind is enkindled and drawn to God as the source of that beauty.[8]

We can readily see the application of this movement of the mind in scientific fields. When astrophysicists survey the vastness of the universe, learn of its great age, and decipher its beginnings, they are sometimes led to reflect on the mystery of the universe and are naturally led to think of God[9] (whether or not they allow themselves to carry this reflection to its end depends on various factors: cultural and historical conditioning, their philosophical beliefs, and their degree of open-mindedness). Microbiologists who study the most minute elements of living matter ineluctably come face to face with a mystery that their science cannot answer. They can never quite grasp the full essence of things in a comprehensive way, but their quest reveals an insatiable desire to comprehend the totality of existence in its essence.[10] This desire is present in every human being because the image of God—the Logos—resides at the core of every person, whether or not he or she is aware of it. God's presence also pervades the entire universe, and we discover that presence in exploring the world. The Logos is the principle of order and structure in all reality.

To claim that scientists and other scholars must remain within their specialized domains, in the realm of the finite, is to make a philosophical and epistemological claim about both reality and about the human mind. I challenge this claim from a Christian perspective. According to one major stream of Catholic thought in the twentieth century, there is at the heart of all intellectual inquiry, whether the inquirer is explicitly aware of it or not, a dynamism whose source and goal is the divine.[11] There is an inner teleology driving the mind toward an every greater understanding within an ultimate horizon. Although scientists cannot discover divine reality through their limited tools and methods of investigation, their inquiries—if not truncated—lead up to the limits of scientific knowledge and to larger questions about God. They lead to the edge of Kant's island, where the infinite sea of the divine beckons.

Let us now review in more detail the thought of three of these authors, Henri de Lubac, Karl Rahner and, more recently, Michael Buckley.

Henri de Lubac: Fusing Augustinian and Thomistic Traditions

Henri de Lubac, S.J. (1896–1991), played a principal role in retrieving the richness of patristic and medieval thought on the intimate link between grace and everyday experience and a sense of the presence of God in the natural world. De Lubac believes that "the idea of God is not an idea alongside other ideas" but is the ground that "establishes and permeates all human knowledge." As a foundation for this belief, he draws on theologians throughout the patristic, medieval, and modern traditions, including Thomas Aquinas. As we saw in chapter 2, Thomas says, "All knowers know God implicitly in all that they know."[12] God is constantly at work in the mind, he says, "endowing it with its natural light and giving it direction."[13] In de Lubac's view, the idea of God is "the reality that envelopes, dominates, and measures our thought." Not only is God present as the foundation of our every act of thinking, but God is also present throughout creation. Every living being is a theophany. "Everywhere we find traces, imprints, vestiges, enigmas; and the rays of the divinity pierce through everywhere." It is God who appears to us through the world "to solicit our attention. We ought to be able to meet him anywhere and recognize him everywhere. Whether we consider the 'great world' or the 'little world,' the cosmos that surrounds us or our own spirit, everything real that comes within our orbit is . . . the symbol and sign of God."[14] We need only be attentive to discern God's presence everywhere. For de Lubac, the "secular" or profane is but an abstraction; in reality there is no thing that is purely "in itself." The finite is something only temporary, in flux, and cannot be understood fully and truly except within its divine context. It is but an imaginative concept.

De Lubac brings together both the Augustinian-Bonaventuran and Thomistic traditions, showing that the restless human mind innately longs for the divine and moves toward it, inchoately at first, then explicitly, in all one's inquiries. This sense of the divine is not cognitively grasped or objectifiable, yet it precedes all concrete acts of knowing and judging.

De Lubac attempts to overcome the nature-grace dualism that allowed the diremption of reality into separate orders, secular and divine, and to encourage Christians to find traces of the divine in all things and all human endeavors. This would then be a foundation from which to engage modern thought.

Karl Rahner and the Orientation of the Mind

Karl Rahner, S. J. (1904–1984), did not write a systematic treatise on the nature of higher education, but his thought on the topic can be found in a number of essays spread throughout his *Theological Investigations*. We find that his thought is at times ambiguous but useful nonetheless. Unlike Thomas, Rahner rejects the concept of the architectonic role of theology among the sciences. He says that theology must resist falling into the "trap of claiming a universality of scientific knowledge for itself, or of regarding all other sciences merely as its handmaids or as branches springing from its own roots."[15] Nor should we claim that theology is "a kind of sovereign ruler reducing the other sciences to acting as its instruments and carrying out its plans."[16] He insists on the autonomy of the sciences. The Christian scientist, Rahner says, must be mindful that his life as a whole is *ultimately* oriented to God, but that, *in his scientific work*, he must be "sustained in his work by a spirit of inquiry in the *purely* worldly sense." He must give himself to this scientific task without reserve in hopes of creating "a world that is 'worldly.'"[17]

At times Rahner seems to ridicule those who believe religion should enter "directly and explicitly into everything always and everywhere, and to be 'religious' even in one's approach to the material realities with which one has to cope in the achievement of [one's] aims."[18] This is a striking statement for a theologian who insists that God's grace is offered to everyone, in every aspect of one's life, even the most ordinary activity. Grace, Rahner claims, is a part of human existence whether one accepts or denies it. "It wells up from the depths of man's heart in a thousand secret ways, penetrating into all spheres of his life. It makes him restless; makes him doubt whether existence is really finite and restricted to this present world, fills him with a sense of the immeasurability of that claim which can only be fulfilled by the infinity of God."[19] If, in criticizing those who believe religion should enter into every realm, he meant the kind of undifferentiated merging of theology and science that we saw in chapter 5, then he was right to object.

Rahner is not altogether consistent, though, and various aspects of his thought are in tension with one another. In his essay "Christian Humanism" he writes, "the whole of the human sphere is religious and the whole of the religious sphere is humane."[20] That surely implies that the intellectual dimension, an essential element of the human sphere, also has a religious dimension. He also maintains that academic disciplines must be related to theology and can only find coherence in a broader theological context. Moreover, to say that one's approach to science must be purely worldly, and that it is an error to "let religion enter directly and explicitly into everything," goes against almost two thousand years of Catholic theological thinking, from Origen, Gregory of Nyssa, and Augustine in the patristic period to Thomas Aquinas and Bonaventure in the medieval period. Thomas, while acknowledging that the natural sciences do not have God as their proximate end, believes that they have God as their ultimate end. Moreover, though the things of God must be studied in a separate science called theology, they must also be studied in every particular science.[21] Not only does Rahner's thought sometimes run counter to long tradition, his position in some writings on academic life seems curiously incongruous with his own theological epistemology.

Rahner's Theological Epistemology

Rahner strongly criticizes Kant's restriction of human understanding to the island of phenomena, to what can be known through the senses and human reason alone.[22] As we saw in chapter 3, Schelling and Hegel also criticize Kant on this ground. Rahner, like Aquinas, believes that humans are oriented to God and that the drive of the human mind is toward the infinite.[23] He focuses on the experiencing subject as one whose every act of knowing implies an unthematic ground of experience, which he calls "mystery." In every act of human knowing, humans are obscurely in contact with this mystery. Grace, in Rahner's view, is the communication of God's very self "in a communication whereby God in his own essence...becomes man's innermost authentic principle." The divine self-communication is a consciousness, "the a priori dynamism of man's knowledge toward God's immediacy" and is a "constitutive part of man's existence."[24] There is in the human spirit an a priori capacity to believe, a subjective disposition that is seldom taken into consideration by theologians.

> This *a priori* capacity for revelation and faith must not...be thought of as a localized faculty side by side with others, as a sort of particular sentiment, an intrinsically limited "need." It should be understood as the union of what we have called the transcendental aspect of revelation with the *a priori* capacity (identical with the whole transcendental character of man), for God's self-communication in grace; for it is by these two that God's transcendental revelation is constituted.[25]

Humans are beings with an infinite horizon; they reach beyond their finitude and experience themselves as transcendent, spiritual beings. This infinite horizon evokes wonder and questioning and leads one to investigate and learn, tending always toward knowledge of the divine ground of all being.[26]

In addition to being a constitutive component of all human beings, God's presence is immanent in the world and "is the ultimate future and final cause, which is the true efficient cause operative in all becoming," not a "second" cause side by side with others in the world. God is the "living perpetual transcendent ground of the world's own movement."[27] Rahner maintains, along with Teilhard de Chardin, that the realms of matter and spirit do not merely exist alongside each other; rather, they are intimately related aspects of the self-transcending movement of the world toward God through God's self-communication to the world.[28] This has profound implications for how a scholar goes about his or her inquiries, for truly, from this perspective, God is all in all.

Modern science investigates the natural world, the world of matter and physical forces; for the Christian scientist, that world is imbued with spirit as well and possesses within it a dynamism that moves it toward an end. Moreover, the scientist has an a priori structure of knowing—an orientation toward transcendence—that impels her to explore beyond the limited domain of her scientific discipline (assuming, of course, that exploration is not inhibited or truncated before reaching out beyond the discipline) and to make that implicit, a priori knowledge explicit. If followed in the direction toward which this dynamism tends, the scientist is led inevitably out of the confines of her discipline into interdisciplinary, or cross-disciplinary studies and, ultimately, to the threshold of theology.

Rahner notes that as scholars cross disciplinary boundaries, they often come into cognitive conflict with one another's perspective, with each insisting that his or her own is the most valid point of entry into reality. Scholars in each individual science attempt to monopolize and dominate when engaged in interdisciplinary dialogue because they intuit that their own discipline, if pursued deeply and radically enough, will lead to "the totality of knowledge." He calls this phenomenon "gnoseological concupiscence."[29] For Rahner, this situation reveals a principle that is seldom acknowledged yet is crucial for the soundness of any academic discipline: if we search any dimension of reality deeply enough, we discover that everything is connected to everything else and to the ultimate ground of Being. This principle belongs to each discipline (I would say it belongs to the noetic structure of the mind of each scholar in that discipline and in the nature of reality itself), a principle which is not subject to and cannot be controlled by that discipline.[30] Rahner insists on following the élan of the mind toward transcendence in an attempt to integrate knowledge.

> Every science...can properly sort itself out only...by transcending its own nature; since the individual sciences in each case reach a complete understanding of themselves only when they know more than themselves, the continually fresh...attempt at an integration of the different sciences, including theology, is a task and a moral obligation imposed on man...There must be universities of knowledge which are more than organized collections of different faculties.[31]

The responsibility of the theologian in this interdisciplinary dialogue is to encourage and help scholars in other disciplines cast their gaze beyond the finite realm of proximate causes—beyond Kant's island—toward the divine. This suggests a more appropriate metaphor for theology; rather than "queen of the sciences," we should refer to it as the "servant" or "leaven" of the sciences (discussed later in this chapter).

The Autonomy of the Sciences?: Reprise

There is another angle from which I want to examine Rahner's thought on academic life: his insistence on the autonomy of the sciences. If Rahner acknowledges the necessity of moving beyond limited scientific investigation, why does he sometimes insist on the autonomy of the academic disciplines as if they were self-contained entities? One is tempted to suggest that his writings on academic life do not deliver what his theological epistemology promises, for to claim an absolute autonomy of the secular sciences is based on the dualistic principle that severs the bond between nature and grace, wherein nature is considered a self-sufficient entity in relation to which the supernatural order is extrinsic and in some ways irrelevant. Corollary to this is the strict separation of "natural reason" from revelation. If revelation is viewed as entirely extrinsic to reason, then the desire to keep them separate is understandable. If, however, we adopt a theonomous approach wherein reason operates out of its own spiritual depth, then integration rather than separation becomes the goal.

The concept of the autonomy of the sciences is not problematic in the abstract. In the concrete, however, we must bear in mind that it is not the secular "science" itself that possesses autonomy. The sciences are abstractions conceived by scientists who, in agreement with one another, have decided to focus on, and limit their inquiries to, a restricted dimension of reality, prescinding from all others. The study of that specific aspect of reality—using methods appropriate to the subject matter—is what is called a science or an academic discipline. We cannot claim, however, that "the sciences" are agents in possession of autonomy. They possess no free will, desires, or goals; they make no decisions on which they act. The individual scholars in those sciences are the ones who possess autonomy and who have a right to freedom of inquiry. This means they must be able to investigate the particular area of reality that falls within the scope of their discipline in accordance with the methods agreed on by scholars in the discipline, without external interference. At the same time we must not lose sight of a deeper truth, namely, that these individuals are oriented to God; in them is implanted a natural desire to know reality beyond their limited academic disciplines. The offer of God's self extends to them in their total human existence, not just to some self-enclosed "spiritual" corner of it.

The subject matter they study is connected to the whole of material and divine reality. These scholars therefore must be equally free to explore the relationship of their discipline's subject matter to ever wider and deeper dimensions of reality, and to pursue their inquiries to their ultimate end. This implies asking and exploring larger questions about the relation of a particular realm of reality to the whole. Herein lies the true theological definition of academic freedom: the freedom to explore the truth of the finite in its relation to God. To say, as did Rahner, that the scholar, in his or her *overall* orientation to life must move toward God, but as a scholar he or she must be "worldly," is to separate the human mind and spirit. The solution to overcoming this dualism is to place autonomy and freedom in the human person, not in an abstraction called "the sciences."

I readily concede that scholars must be free to prescind from considering ultimate questions. It is proper to conduct specialized studies of different aspects of reality, employing methods unique to each subject. Even so, reality is one, and all things are interconnected and grounded in a divine reality. Rahner's willingness to assert a strict autonomy is a residue of scholastic dualism and an illustration of the very kind of "separated theology" that de Lubac criticized. It is to claim that there is a self-contained nature that can be understood apart from the divine reality that sustains and encompasses it. It is also to claim that the human mind can work within a purely natural or human frame of understanding without illumination of the divine light. This dualism can no longer be maintained from a Christian perspective. If the autonomy of the sciences is based on this dualistic principle, it must be rejected.

This brings up a number of questions for the Catholic university. Assuming that Catholic scholars were to integrate a theonomous attitude in their studies, how should Catholic universities deal with nonbelieving scientists who humbly and sincerely conduct their investigations in a genuine search for truth? What about the biologist who searches for a cure for malaria, or the chemist who seeks a cure for cancer, but has no interest in exploring the religious dimension of his or her work? Are they not doing enough? Rahner says they are because they implicitly accept the transcendental dimension of their lives and its call to them as a burden and responsibility, even though this is not explicit in their consciousness, or at least not explicitly formulated in religious terms. In this he is certainly right. Such scientists are, in the words of *Gaudium et Spes*, being led by the hand of God, even though they may be unaware of it.[32]

However, what is implicit does seek to become explicit. Those who want to follow their inquiries beyond the normal boundaries of a scientific or humanistic discipline—not merely into the realm of another discipline but into the spiritual and theological dimension of their inquiry—ought to be encouraged. The scientist must be free to pursue a line of inquiry and publish his or her results and be free from having his or her investigations curtailed without warrant. That means freedom from heteronomous interference by religious and political authorities, on the one hand, and freedom from heteronomous interference by secular scholars who have difficulty seeing beyond their limited scientific domains, on the other.

The Catholic university, as a whole, is obligated to foster this dynamism of the mind toward God, even if some scholars in the various departments decline to do so. A Catholic institution must ensure that this possibility is available in all departments, and to those professors and students whom the Spirit calls beyond the small island of purely disciplinary inquiry. Undergraduate students must have the opportunity to explore how this may be done while still maintaining academic rigor. After all, a science is secular only to the extent that scientists close off the larger dimension of their inquiries from the entire continuum of reality and make the restricted knowledge of their limited academic realms an end in itself. The "secular" is but an imaginative concept, with no basis in reality. There is nothing inherently "secular" about the subject matter they study. The role of theology should not be solely as a separate "science of revealed truths" (it is that, but not just that), but also as an aid to understanding all reality through the light of Christian principles. This is not to force or impose theology on other disciplines; it is to encourage theonomous thinking on the part of scholars and to foster engagement of all academic disciplines with relevant theological principles.

Some scholars will want to pursue such engagement because contemporary fields of study can approach but not attain completion through their own methods, as theoretical physicist John Polkinghorne discovered after 25 years as a scientist. He realized that there is something deeper to reality than what could be determined through science. "[Science's] enthralling account is not sufficient by itself to quench our thirst for understanding, for science describes only one dimension of the many-layered reality within which we live...All my life I have been trying to explore reality. That exploration includes science, but it also necessarily takes me beyond it."[33] This inexorably led him toward philosophical and theological questions.

Michael Buckley and the "Direction Toward Which Wonder Progresses"

Michael Buckley, S. J. builds on themes from Aquinas, Bonaventure, and Rahner, but does not share Rahner's neo-scholastic reticence about placing the dynamism of the mind for God at the center of all academic life. For Buckley, the outmoded belief that the "secular" and the "sacred"—and by extension, reason and revelation—are extrinsic to one another issues "from a heritage of the neo-scholastic misunderstanding and miscasting of the relationship between nature and grace."[34] At the end of his *Origins of Modern Atheism*, he writes, "God has emerged again and again in the history of thought as the direction toward which wonder progresses."[35] This profound concept must be explained in some detail.

God, Buckley says, "is given as the orientation of the mind when it moves through nature in its drive for truth—the truth that is the coherence of nature and the satisfaction of the mind."[36] He articulates the relation between spiritual life and academic inquiry in the following way:

> The fundamental proposition that grounds the Catholic university is that the academic and the religious are intrinsically related, that they form an inherent unity, that one is incomplete without the other...Any academic movement toward meaning or coherence or truth, whether in the humanities, the sciences, or the professions, is inchoatively religious. This...obviously does not mean that quantum mechanics or geography is religion or theology. It does mean that the intellectual dynamism inherent in all inquiry initiates processes or habits of questioning that—if not inhibited—inevitably bear upon the ultimate questions that engage religion.[37]

Spiritual life and academic inquiry form an inherent unity; one is, ultimately, incomplete without the other. Religious experience and faith inevitably move toward intellectual understanding of what one experiences and believes. Likewise, intellectual inquiry can only be completed in transcendent truth. Intellectual inquiry seeks satisfaction of the questions it pursues, but satisfaction is never more than temporary. Once knowledge is achieved, new questions arise, which in turn open up further inquiry.[38] Any topic, if pursued long and deeply enough, eventually leads to questions about God, about who or what created the universe and gave it intelligibility, questions that cannot be answered from within the limits of any particular academic discipline.

A critic might contend, as does Rabbi David Novak, that there is nothing in Buckley's conception of the dynamism of the mind that is specifically Catholic. What Buckley has to say about the dynamics of inquiry could be equally said of a Protestant or a Jewish university.[39] That is where Buckley brings in Christ as the paradigm—not just as a model person who possessed virtues that a Catholic scholar might emulate (though that is important)—because it is in Christ that the divine and the human are united. That union is our end, too. The divine becomes incarnate in humanity and is involved in human history. All human undertakings—history, literature, art, culture, and philosophy—can be seen not only in light of the natural or human forces at work in them but in light of the divine presence somehow guiding humanity toward its end. Human history, then, is seen as a history of the human response to God's call, either acceptance or refusal. The reality of Christ is in the union of faith and human culture, united but not identical, distinct but not separated.[40]

This distinction is analogously true in the Catholic university. Faith and culture are united, not identified. Buckley is careful not to merge them to the degree of identification. "It is their unity that constitutes the university. It is their individual integrity that allows for them to be united rather than identified."[41] Note that Buckley says this is *analogously* true in the Catholic university. A caution is therefore in order. We must not place the locus of this union in "the university" itself. It is too easy to say that "the university" must unify faith and culture, that is, that the Catholic university is the place where the human and the divine are united. We must bear in mind that the union of the human and the divine does not occur in an entity called "the university," as if it were a person. That can lead one to assume that if theology and campus ministry programs be but present, all will be well. Real union, however, takes place only in individual human beings within the university, and that means faculty, students, and administrators. It is in these and for these that integrated learning must occur, and that means developing simultaneously their intellectual, moral, and spiritual dimensions, not their intellectual dimension alone. The Catholic university is merely the place within which this union is fostered.

If the disciplines are not integrated in a philosophical and theological vision, such human-divine union will be hindered. The only way to ensure that the movement toward union progresses is to make sure Catholic philosophical and theological principles are integrated into the curriculum of each academic discipline so that the potential for union is available to *every* student. That means the Catholic tradition must inform and relate to each discipline, not be relegated to some separate "religious" corner of the university. In turn, some scholars in each discipline should engage the tradition.

In addition to Buckley's emphasis on the Incarnation, we must draw on the patristic concept of the Cosmic Christ in order to make Christ relevant to the natural sciences. The concept of the Cosmic Christ is based in St. Paul: "All things were created through and for him. He is before all things, and in him all things hold together" (Colossians 1:15–19). Traces of the divine permeate the natural world, as has been professed throughout Christian history.[42] Christ is present in the world and guides it. Christ is the organizing principle of the cosmos, the key to understanding reality and the reason and structure of the cosmos. There are efficient causes, but also a final cause that lures all things, including the human mind, to God. The world is an ordered totality, a cosmos, and Christ is its innermost, ordering, and driving principle.[43]

If this is true, then one "finds God in all things," and no topic is without a religious dimension. Modern science investigates the natural world, the world of matter; for the Christian, that world is imbued with spirit as well and possesses within it a spiritual dynamism. Students at a Catholic university have a right to have this pointed out to them. There must be teacher-guides who can take students to the outer edge of their disciplinary islands and there let them rest in contemplative wonder. Science itself cannot take them further, but subsequent integrative courses that interweave science and theology can. Newman said that theology is pertinent to all other subject matter.

> [God] has relations of his own toward the subject-matter of each particular science which the book of knowledge unfolds; who has with an adorable, never-ceasing energy implicated Himself in all the history of creation, the constitution of nature, the course of the world, the origin of society, the fortunes of nations, the action of the human mind.[44]

God's relations to those other subjects must also be explored, not only in theology departments, but by students in all disciplines, for no subject matter can be understood fully unless its relation to the divine is discerned. Newman says the universe is "so intimately knit together, that we cannot separate off portion from portion... except by a mental abstraction." God, though infinitely transcending the universe, "has so implicated Himself with it... by His presence in it, His providence over it... and His influences through it, that we cannot truly or fully contemplate it without in some main aspects contemplating Him."[45] Unfortunately, the modern secular university—an archipelago of disciplinary islands—interdicts that contemplation. For this reason, Buckley maintains that we must recover the architectonic role of theology in the university curriculum.[46] "Theology integrates the work of the other sciences like a medieval cathedral, not by merging or identifying with these sciences nor by changing them simply into theology, but by giving them coordination or coherence, a context in the radical orientation of the human person toward truth, since it belongs to wisdom to give order and judgment."[47] This will require revising the curriculum of Catholic colleges and universities.[48]

The question then arises:How can this be done without infringing on the methods and conclusions of scholars working within their limited domains? How not impose or coerce? It is my claim that Christian thought must be inculturated theonomously, not imposed heteronomously. This requires a spirituality: the experience that one's entire being—mind and soul—are in movement toward God. It is a consciousness of being drawn toward the divine in a way that is irresistible; one wishes to cooperate in the movement toward it. This experience of being drawn toward God may be strong or weak in one's consciousness, but it is there, always: it affects all one does, how one behaves and lives in accordance with moral principles, and it colors the way one sees and relates to the world. When awareness of this spiritual élan becomes explicit, spirituality and academic inquiry of any kind, though distinct, become unified aspects of the integral movement of the mind's journey to God. They move together in a dialectical interaction.

Theonomy and Inculturation

The theological concept of inculturation can help us understand the relation of spirituality and theology to other academic disciplines. Inculturation, in general, refers to the process by which the Gospel is introduced to cultures in a way that interacts with and leavens the best elements already existing in that culture.[49] It does not destroy or change the culture. Since the time of Justin Martyr, Christianity has held that the *logos spermatikos*—the seeds of the divine Word—are present everywhere in the cosmos. The "ores of divine providence," said Augustine, are "everywhere infused" and can be discovered by anyone.[50] All cultures have developed with some combination of positive and negative elements. Traces of the divine can be found indigenously in every culture. Christianity ideally interacts with the positive, indigenous elements already present, leavens them, and transforms the culture into its full promise. It does not destroy or impose foreign elements on the culture in a nonorganic way, but assists a people in becoming what God calls them to be.[51]

Spirituality and theology enter in an analogous fashion by becoming intimately familiar with the innermost nature and meanings of each academic discipline—its methods, presuppositions, and goals—not to impose, coerce, or censor them, but to discover the "traces of the divine ore" within them. The Christian discerns the positive and negative elements and then enters a dialogue and mutual critique, interactively. Walter Ong, S. J., used the metaphor of yeast (from Matthew 13:33) to illustrate how Catholic thought should be inculturated into other forms of knowledge in the Catholic university.

Yeast is an apt metaphor. In the process of making bread, yeast enters the dough and permeates the entire mass, acting as a catalyst that leavens and elevates it, enabling the dough to reach its full potential. It does not convert the dough into itself but rather enables the dough to achieve a richness and texture that it cannot achieve on its own. The yeast, in turn, is nourished by the dough in which it grows, even as it transforms the dough.

> [The yeast] not only grows in what it feeds on, but it also improves what it feeds on and makes it possible for others to feed on it as well as on itself, the yeast. The Catholic Church is not out to confront and destroy the cultures it is set in or due to encounter, but to interpenetrate these cultures, and not only on its own terms, but interactively. Yeast grows in different sorts of dough—white, whole wheat, rye and so on, not converting one sort of these doughs into any of the others. Moreover, any dough with yeast growing in it can be added to a completely different batch of dough, and the yeast will act on the new batch in accord with the way the new batch is constituted.[52]

Yeast is not added to the dough after it has already been baked. It is first added to a small portion of the flour and other ingredients. Then gradually, the remainder of the flour is added until the entire dough is leavened. This suggests, says Ong, "that the church should build into itself the cultures or mixtures of cultures in which it finds itself."[53] This analogy can be applied to the relation of Christian spirituality to the various academic disciplines. The movement from knowledge acquired within academic disciplines toward matters theological must come about theonomously, from individual scholars within each discipline (those called by the spirit to do so), rather than heteronomously, from the outside. They must move naturally outward from their particular circle toward the all-encompassing whole, even while maintaining their own identities and methods.[54] It is in this sense that Christian spirituality may be said to order and guide the other sciences, as yeast does dough, by serving as a catalyst to their own internal potencies and elements, helping them to rise and become more fulsome. It does not impose on or suppress their natural qualities and virtues; rather, it leavens them. This is a metaphor for theonomy, of reason being moved by its own spiritual depth.[55]

One may argue that the spirituality described here—the eros of the mind for God—is not explicitly Christian. It is founded in the person as an *imago dei* (image of God) and exists in everyone, whether Christian or not. It was present in humans before the Incarnation of Christ, leading people toward the Christ who was to come. This brings up the question of the role of the Catholic tradition, as distinct from spirituality, in academic life. In chapter 1, I said that theonomy in the Catholic tradition differs from theonomy in a Protestant sense. In Protestantism, the individual's experience of and relation to God is primary. It is no less important in Catholicism, but in the latter the divine is also mediated through tradition. This tradition is the ongoing, external expression of the spirituality—or spiritualities—of the entire Catholic community through history.

The writings of the great Catholic thinkers and saints (Clement of Alexandria, Augustine, Bonaventure, Nicholas of Cusa, John Henry Newman, et al.) are externalized expressions of the Spirit. So are doctrines, Scripture, and the entire history of the interpretation of God's revelation in Christ, through the Holy Spirit. As external expressions, they have become phenomena in the objective world, constituting a written tradition. External expressions of the Spirit are also concretized in sacred music and the visual arts, which equally make up the Catholic tradition. This tradition must be an integral component of education in the Catholic university.[56] It has a place with all other scholarly traditions, not as queen or master, but as interlocutor and frame of reference within which inquiry is pursued and scholarly conversation takes place. The various monuments of the tradition—Scripture, doctrines, classic texts—are not allowed to trump or exclude everything else, not even rival worldviews, but they must be allowed to enter into the conversation and to critique all other worldviews.[57] Rival worldviews, of course, in turn critique the Catholic tradition. The teachings of the tradition always have a place at the table as important partners in scholarly conversation.

David Schindler acknowledges that the Christian worldview "cannot function as the premise for argument in any of these disciplines." Christian scholars must respect the internal uniqueness of each discipline. At the same time, no discipline is without some philosophical foundation. Some worldview is implied, tacitly, in the way scholars gather evidence, construct arguments, and form conclusions. That worldview orders knowledge within the discipline along certain lines. The task of the Catholic university, then, is twofold: "to show, from within each discipline and in the terms proper to each discipline, how that discipline is being guided by a worldview...and to show how a Catholic worldview...leads to a more ample understanding of evidence and argument, already within the terms proper to each discipline."[58] Indeed, Schindler maintains that the Catholic university can be "the place where the Church does its thinking" (in Theodore Hesburgh's phrase) only if all aspects of reality are engaged in this way. The assumption that disciplines are separate and autonomous, and must therefore not be asked to seek dialogue and integration, is itself grounded in a particular worldview.[59]

In summary, there are two key elements required of a truly Catholic university. First, there must be a spirituality that catalyzes and leavens academic work, urged on by the dynamic eros of the mind for God.

Spirituality implies an awareness that God dwells in us and in all created things as the Logos, not as a stagnant thing, but as a dynamic élan drawing all things toward the Godhead through the Spirit. This spirituality cannot and must not be imposed on those who do not share or experience it, but it must guide those Catholics who steer the overall direction of the curriculum. Second, the Catholic tradition must be engaged at all levels and with all other disciplines, not merely in a separate theology department. In the final chapter, I offer some practical initiatives Catholic universities can undertake to integrate theology into their research programs and curricula.

Chapter 8

Implications for Faculty
Development and the Curriculum

After the Second Vatican Council, Catholic educational leaders attempted to improve their institutions and build great Catholic universities on the foundation of the modern American university. They and their successors made tremendous progress in improving the academic quality of their institutions and in opening the world of Catholic higher education to the various and divergent streams of modern thought. The principle of academic freedom was officially adopted and Catholic educators radically reoriented the curriculum of Catholic colleges and universities. They became much more ecumenical and free. Their hiring practices became more open to non-Catholic and dissident Catholic scholars. Academic quality improved significantly. Catholic institutions became less sectarian and more catholic.

In spite of these advances, a fundamental flaw remains at the very core of the modern Catholic college and university: spirituality and theology are not well integrated with other academic disciplines because the version of the modern university on which post-Vatican II educators built was neither the integrative model of Berlin nor the medieval vision of a Bonaventure or Thomas Aquinas, but the American research university of the twentieth century. This research university is, as we have seen, narrowly sectarian (in a secular sense) and largely indifferent and even hostile to religious thought. It excludes theological principles from its very core. To begin with such a university and then attempt to add Catholic theological principles makes for a heterogeneous mixture that does not blend well.

This is not a situation that most leaders in Catholic institutions desire. Yet they find themselves in a seemingly irresolvable bind. On the one hand, they sincerely wish to link spirituality and theology with academic life, albeit in some unspecified way. On the other, they want public funds and the esteem of their secular peers. As a result, Catholic universities today stand Janus-faced, looking simultaneously at two worlds: one, that of the secular academy with its norms and seductive prestige; the other, the Catholic realm where spirituality and intellectual life are seamlessly integrated and where Catholic and scientific thought interpenetrate and leaven one another. Catholic college and university leaders do not yet know how to bridge these two worlds.

The mission of the Catholic university must be to provide a haven for the mind and spirit to follow their desire wherever it may lead and in whatever academic discipline a scholar may reside. If the desire calls one to explore some aspect of finite reality, and only that, then that must be protected. Not everyone must follow the mind's desire to God. Not everyone has to explicitly relate knowledge in their disciplines to Christian truth. The university—any university—must protect both those who do and those who do not want to pursue research beyond the confines of their specialization. The Catholic university, however, has an additional obligation: to ensure that there are *some* faculty members in each academic department who not only want to pursue knowledge beyond their disciplines but to actively explore its relation to Christian philosophy and theology.[1] The Catholic university does this by hiring and then fostering the ongoing development of faculty who have this desire.

We can no longer assume that faculty and students in Catholic institutions will be able to connect knowledge in the various academic fields to a broader Christian framework. It must be made explicit for them, and to do so, Christian theological insight must be inculturated across the disciplines. Peter Steinfels writes that the Catholic tradition "must be something that pervades the work and life of a college or university and is not limited to the theology department." Two courses in theology, he says, will not guarantee "any significant grappling with the Catholic heritage if [Catholic theology] is not present elsewhere in the curriculum."[2] Melanie Morey and John Piderit point out that "the Catholic intellectual tradition does not reside solely in the theology and philosophy department, and its vibrancy in any Catholic college or university is dependent on the eagerness of faculty to pursue related academic and intellectual issues that arise within their academic disciplines."[3] This calls for a broader engagement with the Catholic tradition than is currently the case. John Courtney Murray said theology must be integrated with philosophy, literature, history and the social sciences, no matter how difficult the task, and acknowledged that theology's vitality "will always depend both on what it can borrow from these disciplines and on what it can give to them."[4] The mission of the Catholic university is to ensure that the entire continuum of reality is explored in both its full, finite extension and its full spiritual depth. Knowledge of the finite world should be viewed in relation to knowledge of the Infinite, and there should be *as clear an articulation between them as possible*—moving from conceptually separate domains within the continuum of reality to the divine ground of the entire continuum. Not all scholars must follow this directionality, but Catholic universities should ensure that there are *some* faculty members in each academic department who not only want to pursue knowledge beyond their disciplines but to actively explore its relation to Christian philosophy and theology, even while respecting their distinctive methods and subject matters.

I emphasize that this integration and connection must avoid the kind of facile mergence of disciplines with (and procrustean control by) theology that we saw in the latter part of chapter 5. The integrity of and distinctions between disciplinary subject matter and methods must be respected. The goal is to place disciplines in dialogue with theology, and to show that the subject matter in specific disciplines points to larger meanings that cannot be dealt with adequately from within the disciplines themselves.[5] Then we must seek synthesis and integration where possible, humbly aware that it will require difficult and long-term dialogue over many years. I here offer some general principles that should guide faculty and curricular development.

Adopt a New Definition of Academic Freedom

The *sine qua non* of all progress in fulfilling the telos of Catholic higher education is for universities to adopt a theological understanding of academic freedom (the freedom to follow the mind's telos toward an ultimate horizon and the freedom to prescind from going there) and to incorporate it into their mission statements, bylaws, and institutional policies. The promise of the truly Catholic university will be hollow without this as a foundation. Once adopted, Catholic institutions should undertake the following intiatives.

Faculty Hiring and Faculty Development

Fostering the movement beyond finite disciplines to theology will require hiring faculty with expertise in Catholic philosophy or theology as well as their own discipline. This is no different than hiring to fill other kinds of gaps in a department's faculty. Departments routinely hire to fill areas of expertise unrepresented by current faculty. For example, a history department may find it lacks adequate coverage of Middle Eastern or Latin American history, and will open a position for someone trained in those areas. This is the prerogative of the university—to ensure that all relevant areas are covered. In the Catholic university, this means hiring people with expertise in the Catholic intellectual tradition who are also experts in a specific discipline. If the university is unable to recruit scholars with such dual expertise (and there are few today who possess it), then it must dedicate the resources to train and further develop existing faculty who have a desire to expand beyond their disciplinary islands. Morey and Piderit, in fact, found that most faculty do not possess the training to carry out a dialogue between disciplinary knowledge and theological insight.[6] There are a diminishing number of Catholic scholars in Catholic universities, and of these, even fewer actually know enough about the Catholic tradition to be able to place it in conversation with their discipline. Therefore, comprehensive faculty development programs should be established to help faculty gain this expertise. Below are some concrete steps Catholic colleges and universities could take to foster faculty development. (These steps are meant to be suggestive and illustrative, not prescriptive).

a) *Summer and Academic-year Seminars.* Universities should organize summer seminars, modeled on National Endowment for the Humanities (NEH) summer seminars, for 15 to 20 faculty members who are interested in learning about how aspects of the Catholic tradition can inform their own disciplines. The seminars would last from four to six weeks each, and each would have a different topic aimed at introducing faculty to some of the basic literature and issues at the interface of theology and other academic disciplines. Seminar topics could cover areas such as: (1) theology and the natural sciences; (2) Catholic social thought and the social sciences; (3) theological and social science perspectives on personhood; (4) The theological dimension of modern literature; (5) Catholic theology and feminist thought; or (6) the Catholic ideal of liberal learning. The goal of the seminars and institutes would be to present models of how Catholic thought can both inform contemporary issues and fruitfully relate to particular academic disciplines. Senior scholars should, ideally, direct the seminars, and curricular plans aimed at integrating the material into courses should be developed toward the end of the seminars.

In the case of smaller liberal arts colleges where there might not be enough faculty members to constitute a seminar on a given topic, scholars from nearby institutions should be invited to participate in a cooperative venture. If faculty members are unable to dedicate four to six weeks during the summer to these seminars, academic year seminars that meet, say, once or twice a month throughout the academic year, are a possible alternative.

b) *Sabbatical fellowships.* The Catholic intellectual and spiritual tradition cannot be learned and absorbed in a short time. Years of academic study and formation are required. Therefore, some faculty members should receive a sabbatical leave during the academic year dedicated to exploring in depth how the Catholic intellectual tradition can broaden, deepen, and inform their own disciplinary work. For example, a political scientist or economist who studies poverty and third-world development might study basic texts of the Catholic social tradition. A developmental psychologist could focus on narratives of conversion and spiritual development in the Hebrew prophets and in the writings of mystics such as Augustine, Teresa of Avila, Edith Stein, and Thomas Merton, then compare those narratives to models of psychological and moral development expounded by authors such as Erik Erikson, James Fowler, and Lawrence Kohlberg. Sabbaticals would enable faculty to dedicate substantial time to their focused study. In some cases, it might be optimal to have several scholars from different departments study a common theme, such as a theologian, a biologist, and a physicist studying and discussing recent literature at the interface of theology and the natural sciences. The literature in this area is growing rapidly and there would be no shortage of stimulating texts to discuss. Because the Catholic tradition is so rich and extensive, these sabbatical fellowships should be the core and culmination of all faculty development programs. The summer or academic-year seminars should be considered preludes to more extensive study undertaken during the sabbatical.

c) *Course Development.* Faculty should be expected to incorporate what they learn during the seminars and sabbaticals into some of their courses. This will ensure that students, too, have the opportunity to gaze beyond Kant's island toward an ultimate (and luminous) horizon.[7] There are a number of means to do this. The first is for disciplinary scholars to develop introductory and capstone courses in their departments, based on the knowledge gained during seminars and sabbaticals. Another means is to encourage theologians to develop expertise in one of various specialized disciplines, such as psychology, sociology, political science, biology, physics, and literature, and then have students in the majors take courses in the interface between theology and their discipline from them. Yet another alternative is to develop team-taught courses involving theologians and disciplinary experts. Each university must determine which alternative works best for their unique circumstances.

d) *Sharing of Teaching Experiences with Colleagues.* It is vitally important that faculty members who participate in these programs not work in a vacuum. In most cases, they will have to experiment with course materials and teaching methods until they have discovered the most satisfactory means of introducing the material and generating the most fruitful and stimulating conversations among students and faculty colleagues. Scholars who undertake this process should meet regularly with their co-participants, share ideas and experiences, and be in touch with colleagues at other colleges and universities about their experiences. They should convene occasional conferences and develop websites to learn about one another's successes and failures, share syllabi, and discuss innovative teaching methods. The university should also regularly bring in scholars with experience and proven expertise in such integrative courses to give lectures and conduct workshops for faculty.

e) *Spiritual Retreats.* Scholars are, by the very nature of their calling, analytical, critical, argumentative, and rationalistic. These traits make them the astute academics they are. Yet there is another dimension that must also be developed: their spiritual depth and breadth. Theonomous thinking, we will remember, is defined as autonomous reason grounded in its own spiritual depth. That spiritual depth must be evoked, cultivated, and allowed to mature. Catholic universities can aid this process by sponsoring occasional spiritual retreats at a monastery or retreat house for participating faculty members. Chairs of theology departments or directors of campus ministry can work out special arrangements with suitable retreat masters familiar with the academic life. In addition to prayer and silent contemplation, retreats might include talks (by the retreat master) on the spiritual lives and writings of great theologians associated with the academy, such as Thomas Aquinas, John Henry Newman, Simone Weil, or Edith Stein, academics who successfully integrated spiritual and intellectual life. (Again, these recommendations are suggestive, not prescriptive.)

These recommended faculty development efforts are substantially different from and more comprehensive than similar efforts being undertaken by programs such as the Catholic Higher Education Project (CHEP) at Georgetown University's Woodstock Theological Center, and the Catholic Education Institute (CHI) operated by John Piderit, S.J. and Melanie

Morey. The CHEP conducts weekend seminars described as "intimate, two-day conversations in which a group of 12 faculty members from diverse faith traditions and academic disciplines reflect on their scholarly research and aspirations, their scholarship's relationship to their personal religious practices, and the way in which their research is contributing to their university's Catholic mission of advancing human knowledge."[8] The CHI offers workshops and conferences on ways to integrate Catholic theology into curricula.[9] As useful as such seminars are, short term programs touch only the surface of a long and rich tradition.[10] It is my contention that only a long-term, comprehensive faculty development program will truly advance the telos of the Catholic university. The intellectual, spiritual, and theological depths of a religious tradition must be inculturated through lengthy study and participation in its total ethos.

In recent years, centers and institutes for advanced Catholic studies have struggled to emerge, such as the Notre Dame Institute for Advanced Study (NDIAS) and the Institute for Advanced Catholic Studies (IACS) at the University of Southern California. The NDIAS "supports research that is directed toward, or extends inquiry to include, ultimate questions and questions of value, especially as they engage the Catholic intellectual tradition."[11] The Institute offers semester or year long fellowships to a small number of advanced scholars and doctoral students from universities around the world. The IACS sponsors conferences and lectures on how aspects of the Catholic intellectual tradition can be brought to bear on vital issues of the day.[12] The IACS had originally planned to offer fellowships similar to those offered at the NDIAS and the Institute for Avanced Study at Princeton, but has been unable due to lack of funding. These efforts are invaluable and merit support. However, they are quite different from the kind of faculty and curricular development I am advocating in this chapter. Here is why. When scholars from multiple universities gather to discuss "ultimate questions," it benefits their own research agendas and perhaps some of the courses they teach. There are serious limitations, however, on the influence these scholars can have on the culture of their home departments and institutions. They may integrate what they've learned into some of their courses, but what about the rest of the curriculum at that institution? Is it leavened by these scholars' work? Perhaps in some small way, but not to the extent that I am recommending in this chapter. In short, institutes for advanced study are valuable, but insufficient to have an effect on institute fellows' home institutional culture as a whole. Comprehensive programs are necessary to leaven the curriculum and culture of each Catholic institution. A sizeable cadre of Catholic scholars in all disciplines must be formed at each college and university.

Investing in Catholic Scholars with Spiritual Desire

While all faculty members—Catholic and non-Catholic—who are interested in knowing more about the Catholic intellectual tradition should be encouraged to do so, it is vitally important that those sincere in their faith—who experience this work as a spiritual calling—be especially encouraged. Reading the spiritual and theological classics of the tradition is not enough in itself. As Alasdair MacIntyre notes, these texts can be read and interpreted in radically different ways, depending on the particular philosophical and ideological lens a scholar brings to his or her study, be that lens Marxist, Freudian, feminist, postmodern, or Catholic.[13] Interpreting the Catholic tradition through some of these ideological lenses will serve (and has served) to deconstruct and distort the tradition. This is inevitable to some extent, and we cannot censor or ignore these philosophical positions. We must engage them to discover the seeds of truth within them (and who would argue that these positions have not brought some needed correction to distortions within the Catholic tradition?) and also to discern their errors. Catholic universities should be concerned, not to merely attack the errors in these philosophies, but to insist that their critiques of Catholicism be based on a fair understanding of it, not current academic stereotypes.

Scholars who share the faith will be best suited to present the riches of the tradition, its complex and difficult history, and apply its teachings for today. They will also be the ones most willing to undergo the continuous transformation of mind and spirit required to be a Christian mentor to students, to help them develop a strong Catholic sensibility and spirituality, or in a term common during the early twentieth century, a "Catholic mind." Gerald McCool has the following to say:

> The idea of the Catholic mind, even if we grant it only plausibility as an ideal, justifies a number of values in Catholic education which many of us are convinced are sound. Among these are the focus of education on the formation of the total person, the ideal of the integration and distinction of the disciplines, the emphasis on personal influence in teaching and the demands which it places on the teacher, the sacredness of the teacher's work, and the appreciation of the school as a community of personal influence.[14]

John Courtney Murray says the teacher must be the "midwife" of the student's soul.[15] This emphasis on the personal influence of the teacher requires a spirituality that goes beyond the purely cognitive dimension of academic life to the deeply personal. It requires conversion of heart and mind. Teachers who desire to undertake the work of personal transformation are the primary individuals who the university must foster through faculty development programs. Of course, anyone who wishes to learn more about the tradition should be encouraged, but given the constraints of limited resources, those inclining already to full participation in the life of the Word should be afforded highest priority for faculty development resources.

Thinking Outward From Within the Tradition

The standard method for scholars who study religion is to objectify religious phenomena and analyze it from the theoretical framework and methods of their disciplines, usually in a reductionistic fashion (religion is a mere epiphenomenon of psychological, sociological, cultureal, or neurological processes). Such objective analyses are necessary and appropriate, but not sufficient in the Catholic university. Knowledge in all disciplines— the assumptions undergirding disciplinary research methods and scholars' interpretations of the data they collect—must also be studied from a Christian perspective. That is to say that the same kind of scrutiny that disciplinary scholars direct at religious phenomena must be directed by religious thinkers at the assumptions and interpretive findings in the disciplines themselves, as the sociologist Christian Smith has done for the discipline of sociology.[16] Douglas and Rhonda Jacobsen claim that "treating religion as a subject that might appeal to someone's historical or social scientific curiosity is far different from seeing religion as a valid source of human meaning, as a driving fource in scholarly research, or as a core concern for higher education."[17] Even Hegel insisted on approaching academic subjects from a stance in which "spirit" is present,[18] that is, through reason grounded in and informed by inner spiritual illumination. Too often, administrators and scholars in Catholic universities consider the "objective" study of some aspect of religion—for example, the history of Christianity or the sociology of religion—as evidence that the university is fulfilling its Catholic mission. Merely studying religious phenomena from an objective standpoint is not enough; honest, respectful scrutiny must go both ways.

Building Intellectual-Spiritual Communities Outside the Disciplines

The modern university is composed not of a single community of scholar-seekers pursuing truth in its wholeness but a multiplicity of disciplinary and subdisciplinary communities pursuing an understanding of ever-narrower realms of reality. This is both a blessing and a curse; a blessing in that we have experienced a welcome explosion of knowledge in all realms of study; a curse in that knowledge has become fragmented and often unlinked to a moral or theological framework. Disciplinary communities exert a powerful influence over scholars. Mark U. Edwards, Jr. has shown that these communities have considerably more influence on forming and capturing the loyalty of faculty members than do communities with religious foundations.[19] Faculty members undergo many years of intensive formation into their disciplinary cultures. That culture has its own standards, methods, and internal expectations. Its gatekeepers—in the form of academic departments, promotion and tenure committees, editors of journals, organizers of conferences, book reviewers, and reviewers of grant applications—play a key role in determining who is admitted into the community. Those who conform to the discipline's standards have a reasonable chance of gaining full membership, while nonconformists do not.[20] Those who do not meet the expectations of those in the discipline are not likely to receive tenure. After years of formation into these disciplinary cultures, a faculty member's loyalties to the community of scholars in the field are often stronger than loyalty to one's home institution (including its Catholic mission), colleagues in other departments, and one's religious community.

Many scholars, of course, come to the realization that disciplinary cultures and perspectives are too confining. They attempt to expand into the precincts of other disciplines where they may develop new, hybrid forms of community. However, the young, untenured faculty is well-advised not to roam too far afield before gaining tenure because those extradisciplinary communities seldom have a say in promotion decisions. To an even greater extent, if scholars with a spiritual eros roam into the realm of the theological, they may encounter stiff opposition from disciplinary colleagues. Even if they are tenured and determined to forge ahead, they may find themselves somewhat ostracized among their peers and isolated, without collegial support and encouragement (sadly, even at Catholic universities). Therefore, in addition to hiring disciplinary experts with spiritual desire and providing them the time and resources to learn the Catholic tradition in depth, the university must also help foster intellectual-spiritual communities of scholars from various academic disciplines—communities through which these scholars will find mutual encouragement, guidance, and support. Indeed, the Catholic university might even consider using these alternative scholarly communities to assess the work of scholars seeking to stretch themselves beyond Kant's island, especially for purposes of promotion. Disciplinary excellence must be a requirement in tenure and promotion, but movement toward the whole of knowledge must be another important criterion for those scholars who choose to exercise their academic freedom fully and theonomously. The question of justice is relevant here. It would be a grave injustice to hire and develop a scholar with the expectation that he or she will integrate disciplinary and theological insights, only to have them be denied promotion by disciplinary committees with a strong bias against such endeavors. Catholic colleges and universities must, therefore, assess their procedures for promotion and tenure, then develop firm policies that ensure such injustices do not occur.

Forming Intellectually, Morally, and Spiritually Mature Students

Every student in the Catholic university must be able to take courses that connect knowledge in their majors to Catholic philosophy and theology. This is a right that must be protected and ensured. Alasdair MacIntyre says that specialized academic work, though important, should be secondary to the broader goal of helping students place knowledge from their disciplines within an integrated understanding of the whole of reality. He further notes that students in a Catholic university should recognize that learning in the various specialized academic disciplines "remains incomplete until it is to some degree illuminated by philosophical inquiry," which, in turn, is "incomplete until it is illuminated by theologically grounded insight."[21]

MacIntyre seeks to ground the work of the university in a Thomistic framework. First, rational inquiry (reason), *independent of faith and revelation*, integrates the various disciplines into a view of the overall "order of things." This is the task of philosophy. Then, students study theology as a culmination of all other studies.[22] MacIntyre's framework assumes a secular treatment of all subject matter followed by a theological perspective. I am arguing for a more holistic approach. Study of the natural and human sciences should, and must, move toward the edge of Kant's island, to the sea of the divine surrounding and permeating it. At the same time, theonomous thinking must be integrated, as yeast into dough, into the study of the "secular" sciences themselves. This must be done at appropriate times throughout the student's course of studies, not merely at the culmination of those studies (one does not first bake bread and then add the yeast). These sciences maintain their finite boundaries and, for the most part, prescind from synthetic, organic integration with philosophy and theology. Nonetheless, the human mind itself does not have tight compartments; it continually looks beyond the finitude of the disciplines. Students naturally, and regularly, ask questions about the philosophical and theological meaning of concepts they study in their coursework. Their questions about broader philosophical issues must be addressed, to some extent, as they arise in each discipline. This means engaging each academic discipline from a Christian perspective and bringing Christian thought to bear internally on each discipline, as David Schindler says.[23] In the words of the "Land O'Lakes Statement," theology should stimulate the internal development of each discipline[24] such that it moves beyond its inherent limitations and toward the whole. Christian spirituality serves as the catalyst for this overall movement of the mind.

Pursuing the deep truths of each discipline and connecting them to the whole is quite different from merely requiring students to take some courses in theology and philosophy (most Catholic colleges and universities require students to take two or three in each). Such requirements are important, but there is seldom a requirement that the courses in a student's major be related to and informed by relevant aspects of the Catholic tradition.[25] To achieve the latter, there should be a seminar or capstone course of one or two semesters within each major that makes the connections. Introductory courses in each major should introduce students to some of the connections that will be dealt with in more detail in the capstone course. Then, in between the introductory and capstone courses, connections can be made where they naturally arise in the course of individual classes.

Social and cultural realities in the twenty-first century make this integration imperative. During the medieval and early modern periods, one could assume that all academic learning fit readily into a Christian theological worldview. Everyone shared certain background religious assumptions about the truth of Christianity, even when they disagreed about particular religious doctrines. All knowledge would have been assumed to fit within a broader whole, which was a Christian worldview. So Thomas Aquinas's order of the curriculum, and the Jesuit *Ratio Studiorum* based on it, with theology being studied last, made sense. Those who did not go on to study theology or metaphysics would have appropriated a Christian view through enculturation. The teachers would have conveyed Christian thought and assumptions in numerous ways, so students would have absorbed it almost unconsciously. Those common assumptions and worldviews no longer exist in twenty-first-century America, or in the West generally. We can no longer assume students will readily connect knowledge in the various academic fields to a broader Christian framework, or even be able to do this. It must be made explicit for them today.

Individual professors may prescind from broader, integrative studies, but students should be exposed to the entire continuum. One may, of course, argue that students, too, should have the freedom to prescind from exploring beyond Kant's island. While such an argument might seem to have merit, it is unpersuasive. Almost no university allows students to take only courses they want, without an attempt to provide some coherence to their overall plan of study. There are general, core courses that all students must take. Any student who would claim to be liberally educated must take courses in a broad array of subjects. All universities require this, and the Catholic university should ensure that students are exposed to the theological dimension of their chosen fields. The outcome of students' response to theological perspectives cannot, of course, be determined. The Catholic university must make sure that the Catholic tradition is presented fully and accurately. Students will freely examine all aspects of the integrative courses and come to their own conclusions.

Administrative Support

There must be strong and principled administrative support to make sure there are qualified faculty with expertise in both the disciplines and the Catholic tradition. They must ensure that these faculty have the support, time, and resources they require. They must give high priority to transforming the theologically grounded ideal of academic freedom presented in this book into institutional policy.

It bears repeating: the Catholic theological and spiritual tradition cannot be learned and absorbed in a short time. Years of study and formation are required. Scholars with the intellectual and spiritual desire to undertake this study must be supported and rewarded, especially since current, secular academic standards tend to favor those who remain within disciplinary islands. Nor should university administrators be naïve about the extent of resistance to such efforts by many faculty. All of these initiatives will require strong leadership, vision, and commitment (not to mention backbone!) by university administrators, both in terms of rewarding faculty who participate in this long-term effort, and in dedicating sufficient resources.

Further, the university has an obligation to appoint provosts, academic vice presidents, deans, and department chairs who enthusiastically support these initiatives; not those who will look on them merely as more administrative mandates to endure half-heartedly, but those who experience the mission as a spiritual calling and who will use their influence, in a spirit of Christian generosity and understanding toward all, to make appropriate changes in departmental cultures. Administrators must exercise prudent, equable, and thoughtful—though firm—guidance and governance over a long period of time to gradually change attitudes in these cultures. Prudence dictates that radical changes not be forced on faculty abruptly and hastily, engendering strong resistance and diminishing morale (yes, some administrators are wont to do that!). Rather, gradual changes, inspired not by heavy-handed impatience for change but by the Holy Spirit, should guide leaders' decisions so as to inculturate Christian scholarship organically. Catholic leaders should bear in mind the metaphor of yeast discussed in chapter 7. Yeast leavens flour in accordance with the dough's own inherent possibilities; it is a catalyst, not an antagonist. Administrators should be mindful that even Christ did not win disciples to his cause all at once—not even some who later became his ardent followers. Some followed him right away, while others were skeptical. Through the influence of the Holy Spirit, some of the doubters began to ponder his message and, eventually, were able to absorb and accept his teachings. Not until they reached this final step, though, did they come fully on board. It will be no different for many scholars in Catholic colleges and universities. Some will eagerly undertake the effort; others will come around more slowly; some will resist and reject it entirely; and others will remain indifferent or sceptical. Respect must be shown to all, even while the program moves forward with those who experience the work as a spiritual calling.

Finally, administrators should allocate resources for those involved in these faculty development programs: for the senior scholars directing summer or academic-year seminars; sabbatical salaries; seminar books and materials; summer seminar stipends for faculty participants (in line with stipends paid through NEH seminars); retreat expenses; and honoraria for visiting workshop leaders. These constitute serious financial commitments, but they are really no different than supporting sabbaticals for regular disciplinary research, honoraria for outside experts and consultants, and other academic expenses. It may, however, require some redirecting of existing priorities and a long-term commitment to secure endowments for new faculty development programs.

Promoting a Just Legal Framework for Nonsectarian Religious Institutions

Although this recommendation goes well beyond faculty and curricular issues, it is vitally important given the current political and legal context in which Catholic colleges and universities find themselves. We saw in chapter 6 how the American legal system equates the terms "sectarian" and "religious." There was a time in the past when this was an accurate portrayal, a time when denominational rivalries promoted intolerance of ideas different from those of one's own group, leading to social and political conflict. That is far less the case today, when religious universities, including the majority of Catholic institutions, have become remarkably open, tolerant and diverse.

The goal now is to foster a more adequate legal understanding of "sectarianism" in the hope that the legal profession and the courts will disentangle the association between religion and sectarianism. As noted in chapter 6, the opposite of "sectarian" is not "secular" (as some court opinions imply) but "catholic" in the sense of universal, open-minded to all ideas, and tolerant of diverse perspectives. Such openness and tolerance does not require relinquishing one's commitment to a particular tradition. It means engaging other forms of thought from within one's tradition. Catholic legal scholars, therefore, should build a legal theory of sectarianism that is applicable to either secular or religious institutions, based on whether or not they are open or closed to perspectives other than their own. In fact, secular universities have now become increasingly sectarian in the sense of being dogmatic concerning reigning ideologies, intolerant of dissent from scientific and progressive orthodoxies, and dismissive of religious perspectives. If a sizeable cadre of legal scholars, attorneys, and judges were to emerge from Catholic law schools with this rectified and impartial understanding of sectarianism and its legal implications, they might, over time, help inculturate this more just understanding into legal frameworks across the country. If public funds are to be denied to sectarian institutions, that must apply also to *secular* sectarian institutions, Catholic university leaders and legal scholars should not hesitate to correct, in speeches and writings, the currently flawed understanding of sectarianism as synonymous with "religious."

Conclusion

The drive for completeness of meaning is theological, and there is no escaping it if we are not to impede the dynamism inherent in all inquiry. Michael Buckley insists that the Catholic university must not "truncate the dynamism of knowing through interdicting the religious dimension of life or isolating the religious from the academic"; rather, it should seek "to integrate them by allowing each its full development."[26] Karl Rahner maintains that the task of integrating the individual sciences into a unity is a duty placed upon academics. At the same time, he says we must accept the limitation that there will never be a single, all-inclusive, universal formula for expressing that unity. Nonetheless, the quest for integration must be undertaken. Any institution that truncates the dynamism of knowing may be an excellent academic institution within a limited, sectarian framework, but it is not a university in the full meaning of the term. In the Catholic university, a Christian spiritual vision should inform all subject matter.

One major impediment to integration is that both theology and philosophy have ceased being integrative and architectonic disciplines. Theology has become isolated within the academy, and very few people, apart from other theologians, pay attention to the writings of theologians.[27] Theologians and philosophers, therefore, must initiate and foster a deep and ongoing interaction with other disciplines, even to serve as a leaven to the other disciplines. This is a service they must render the academy.

Efforts to inculturate spirituality and theology into the entire curriculum will not fail to make many scholars uneasy. They might fear that the disciplines will be forced into accepting some prior philosophical or theological conceptions that limit inquiry through a sort of "theological imperialism." I do not discount these fears or the real dangers of this happening. The assumption behind this uneasiness, though, is that real universities have no commitments to any philosophical assumptions, that they are neutral places for dispassionate and objective inquiry. That is the Enlightenment version of the university, a version that can no longer be maintained. Every university has a commitment to some worldview or a variety of incompatible worldviews. The typical, secular university is not neutral regarding what knowledge is useful to know and explore, how that exploration ought to proceed, and how information is to be interpreted. Ideological and philosophical commitments, sometimes explicit, more often implicit, underlie every discipline and every university, to some degree (I do not suggest there is unity and coherence to the ideologies). Alasdair MacIntyre reminds us that many rival worldviews have been proposed in the past two centuries as the basis for developing the university curriculum: Hegelian idealism, Enlightenment materialism and its heirs, Marxism, and neo-Kantianism.[28] Today, the curricula of most secular universities are rife with such ideological underpinnings: scientific materialism, relativism, feminism, postmodernism, and the like. Historically, our present-day private, secular universities began as sectarian institutions in the sense that they were denominationally affiliated and tended to exclude other religious perspectives and sometimes scientific perspectives that were not consonant with their denominational beliefs. But gradually the secularist version of sectarianism emerged as the dominant paradigm, to the exclusion of others, eventually pushing religious perspectives to the margin of campus and, in some universities, off campus entirely.[29]

A commitment to some tradition or philosophical view of life cannot be avoided entirely, so it is entirely appropriate for a Catholic university to give a privileged place to the Catholic tradition. Commitment to a tradition does not mean that rival perspectives are excluded—they must not be—or that inquiry does not proceed freely and honestly. It does mean that the knowledge gained through inquiry should be placed in dialogue with theological perspectives in appropriate ways in the curriculum of individual departments and in the curriculum as a whole. The antidote to sectarian education is not secularism, but catholicity—an openness to all ideas and a mutual engagement of them all, including religious ideas.

Contemporary Catholic universities have not done a good job of carrying on that dialogue and ensuring that theology and other disciplines interpenetrate one another, their rhetoric to the contrary notwithstanding. This is not to say that scholars in Catholic universities are not engaged in subject matter appropriate to a Catholic university. Quite the contrary, they are often deeply committed to the urgent issues that face our society and world: human rights and social justice; environmental ethics; globalization and subsidiarity; poverty and third-world development; gender equity; family dynamics and psychosocial development; education reform; democratization; and peace studies. Scholars in any truly Catholic university must engage these issues, and there are few, if any, that do not strive to do so. But this does not distinguish them from secular universities, which are equally concerned with these issues.

What is often missing in the Catholic university is the explicit connection of these issues to the Catholic theological and intellectual tradition. A solid foundation in Catholic thought across the centuries and its relevance to knowledge gained in the disciplines will deepen scholars' exploration and understanding of these contemporary issues. Buckley believes that the "retrieval of a vital contact and interchange between theology and the other disciplines and the rearticulation of the architectonic role of theology becomes a primary task for contemporary theological methodology."[30] In the Catholic university it should also be the task of scientific, social scientific, and humanistic methodologies. A Catholic university must therefore insist that its departments hire faculty who want to make those connections (but must not ask reluctant faculty members to do so).

Since the Second Vatican Council, Catholic universities, on the whole, have become remarkably open to modern thought. Nonbelievers and believers of other faiths have been welcomed into Catholic universities. Scholars who are critical and even hostile to Catholicism reside comfortably, with tenure, in Catholic universities. This open embrace of diverse perspectives and engagement of other viewpoints is no longer an issue for the modern Catholic university. Postmodernism, scientific naturalism, agnosticism, atheism, and a host of other philosophical and ideological perspectives have a home in the Catholic university. The next phase of this engagement is to have scholars in the various disciplines engage *Catholic* thought and engage it deeply—not all scholars, but some in every discipline. Engagement must proceed in both directions, from theology to other disciplines and from other disciplines to theology. The goal can never be to have them simply sit side by side, in isolation from one another.

The Catholic university must ensure that students in the individual disciplines are not confined to Kant's island, even if many of the professors in them confine themselves to it. Students must be free to explore the vast sea beyond the island's borders in order to knit together the perspectives learned on that sea with the knowledge learned on their disciplinary islands.

It will take at least a generation, possibly even longer, for enough changes to be made in Catholic universities along the lines described in this book to come to fruition. But if we begin now in earnest, we may hope that the children and grandchildren of today's students will be able to reap the benefit and promise of truly great Catholic universities.

Notes

1 THE CURRENT STATE OF CATHOLIC HIGHER EDUCATION

1. John Paul II, *Fides et Ratio* (Boston: Pauline Books & Media, 1998).
2. Alice Gallin, O. S. U., ed., *American Catholic Higher Education: The Essential Documents, 1967–1990* (Notre Dame, IN: University of Notre Dame Press, 1992), 7.
3. Edward Manier and John Houck, eds., *Academic Freedom and the Catholic University* (Notre Dame, IN: Fides Publishers, 1967); Neil G. McCluskey, S. J., ed., *The Catholic University: A Modern Appraisal* (Notre Dame, IN: University of Notre Dame Press, 1970); Paul L. Williams, ed., *Catholic Higher Education: Proceedings of the Eleventh Convention of the Fellowship of Catholic Scholars* (Pittston, PA: Northeast Books, 1989); George S. Worgul Jr., *Issues in Academic Freedom* (Pittsburgh, PA: Duquesne University Press, 1992).
4. Recent American historians have documented, from a purely historical perspectives, the severance of academic inquiry from religious belief. See George M. Marsden, *The Soul of the American University: From Protestant Establishment to Established Nonbelief* (New York: Oxford University Press, 1994); James Tunstead Burtchaell, *The Dying of the Light: The Disengagement of Colleges and Universities from Their Christian Churches* (Grand Rapids, MI: Eerdmans, 1998); Julie A. Reuben, *The Making of the Modern University: Intellectual Transformation and the Marginalization of Morality* (Chicago, IL: University of Chicago Press, 1996); Jon Roberts and James Turner, *The Sacred and the Secular University* (Princeton, NJ: Princeton University Press, 2000); David J. O'Brien, *From the Heart of the American Church: Catholic Higher Education and American Culture* (Maryknoll, NY: Orbis Books, 1994); and Philip Gleason, *Contending with Modernity: Catholic Higher Education in the Twentieth Century* (New York: Oxford University Press, 1995). None of these historians address the topic of the relation of spirituality to theology and other academic disciplines in Catholic universities. As historians, they do not draw on theological anthropology or theological epistemology to contextualize and inform their work.
5. John Henry Newman, *The Idea of a University* (Notre Dame, IN: University of Notre Dame Press, 1982).

6. Theodore M. Hesburgh, C. S. C., ed., "The Challenge and Promise of a Catholic University," in *The Challenge and Promise of a Catholic University* (Notre Dame, IN: University of Notre Dame Press, 1994), 4.

7. Ibid.

8. Mark U. Edwards Jr., *Religion on Our Campuses: A Professor's Guide to Communities, Conflicts, and Promising Conversations* (New York: Palgrave MacMillan, 2006), vii.

9. Douglas Jacobsen and Rhonda Hustedt Jacobsen, eds., *The American University in a Postsecular Age* (New York: Oxford, 2008), 7.

10. David Schindler, *Heart of the World, Center of the Church: Communion Ecclesiology, Liberalism, and Liberation* (Grand Rapids, MI: Eerdmans; Edinburgh: T & T Clark, 1996), 143–76.

11. Hesburgh, "The Challenge and Promise," 7.

12. Ibid., 6.

13. Melanie M. Morey and John J. Piderit, S. J., *Catholic Higher Education: A Culture in Crisis* (Oxford: Oxford University Press 2006), 105–9.

14. See also Christian Smith, "Secularizing American Higher Education: The Case of Early American Sociology," in Christian Smith, ed., *The Secular Revolution: Power, Interests, and Conflict in the Secularization of American Public Life* (Berkely, CA: University of California Press, 2003), 97–159.

15. Ibid., 9, 56–59.

16. Immanuel Kant, *The Critique of Pure Reason*, trans. Norman Kemp Smith (London: Macmillan, 1933), 257.

17. Timothy Healy, S. J., "Belief and Teaching," *Georgetown Magazine* (Jan.–Feb. 1982): 3–5, quoted in Michael J. Buckley, S. J., *The Catholic University as Promise and Project: Reflections in a Jesuit Idiom* (Washington, DC: Georgetown University Press, 1998), 11–12.

18. John Haughey, S. J. also refers to the university as "necessarily a secular operation." John C. Haughey, S. J., *Where is Knowing Going?: The Horizons of the Knowing Subject* (Washington, DC: Georgetown University Press, 2009), 91.

19. John Henry Newman, "Intellect, the Instrument of Religious Training," in *Sermons on Various Occasions* (London: Longmans, Green, 1921), 6–7.

20. Ibid., 12–13.

21. Ibid., 13.

22. Karl Rahner, *Foundations of Christian Faith: An Introduction to the Idea of Christianity*, trans. William V. Dych (New York: Seabury Press, 1978), 22.

23. Christopher F. Schiavone, *Rationality and Revelation in Rahner: The Contemplative Dimension* (New York: Peter Lang, 1994), 169, 170–71. I am indebted to Schiavone's account of Rahner's view on revelation and rationality.

24. Paul Tillich, *History of Christian Thought: From Its Judaic Origins to Existentialism* (New York: Simon and Schuster, 1967), 362, 365.

25. St. Augustine, *Soliloquies* I: 12, trans. Kim Paffenroth (Hyde Park, New York: New City Press, 2000), 32.; St. Augustine, *The Trinity XII: 24,* trans. Edmund Hill, O. P. (Brooklyn, New York: New City Press, 1991), 336.

26. There has been a welcome proliferation of studies on spirituality in recent decades. Along with this has come a proliferation of definitions of spirituality. Lawrence Cunningham and Keith Egan have included a sampling of 23

separate definitions of spirituality in their introduction to spirituality. See Lawrence S. Cunningham and Keith J. Egan, *Christian Spirituality: Themes from the Tradition* (New York: Paulist Press, 1996), 21–28; Walter Principe, "Toward Defining Spirituality," *Sciences Religieuses/Studies in Religion* 12 (Spring 1983): 127–41; Kees Waaijman, *Spirituality: Forms, Foundations, Methods* (Leuven: Peeters, 2002), 305–66.

27. Paul Tillich, drawing on Augustinian thought, distinguished "theonomy" (law or rule by God) from both "autonomy" (self-rule or law) and "heteronomy" (strange or foreign rule, imposed externally). See Tillich, *A History of Christian Thought*, 184–85, 188; see also his *Reason and Revelation; Being and God*, vol. 1, *Systematic Theology* (Chicago, IL: University of Chicago Press, 1951), 84–85.

28. The understanding of *tradition* that I use in this book is considerably broader than, say, that of David Schindler and Alasdair MacIntyre. For Schindler, there is a "mutual relation between fidelity to conciliar-magisterial teaching, participation in the sacramental life of the church, prayer, and social service, on the one hand, and the formation of a truly Catholic mind on the other" (see Schindler, *Heart of the World, 147*). Where I deviate from Schindler is that my understanding of tradition is broader than "fidelity to conciliar-magisterial teachings," and encompasses the entire Great Tradition of the church that, of course, includes conciliar-magisterial teachings. MacIntyre's perspective on tradition, while broader than that of Schindler, is based primarily on the thought of Thomas Aquinas, who attempted to synthesize the conflicting strains of Catholic thought, both Augustinian (in its variant forms) and Aristotelianism. (See Alasdair MacIntyre, *Three Rival Versions of Moral Inquiry: Encyclopaedia, Genealogy, and Tradition* (Notre Dame, IN: University of Notre Dame Press, 1990), 58–148). While I draw on Thomas, I also draw on a wide range of other thinkers, past and present, to frame my arguments.

29. This understanding of spirituality does not exclude external practices and rituals; rather, it isolates a basic aspect of the spiritual experience that is prior to outward expressions of the spiritual life.

30. Michael J. Buckley, S. J., *At the Origins of Modern Atheism* (New Haven, CT: Yale University Press, 1987), 360.

31. More recently, John Haughey has written about the dynamism of the mind and unity of knowledge it seeks. See John C. Haughey, S. J., *Where is Knowing Going?: The Horizons of the Knowing Subject* (Washington, DC: Georgetown University Press, 2003).

32. Justin Martyr, *The First Apology*, in *The Writings of Justin Martyr and Athenagoras*, trans. Marcus Dos, D. D., George Reith, D. D., and Rev. B. P. Pratten (Edunburgh: T. & T. Clark, 1909), 46–47.

33. Bernard McGinn, *The Foundations of Mysticism: Origins to the Fifth Century* (New York: Crossroads, 1994), 114.

34. Origen, Prologue to the *Commentary on the Song of Songs*, in *Origen*, trans. Rowan Greer (New York: Paulist Press, 1979), 224–31; McGinn, *Foundations*, 119–20.

35. Gregory of Nyssa, *The Life of Moses*, trans. Abraham Malherbe and Everett Ferguson (New York: Paulist Press, 1978), 31.

36. This does not negate or undermine the importance of pursuing an explicit focus on the kind of revealed knowledge characteristic of the science of theology.
37. Thomas Aquinas, *Summa Contra Gentiles*, 4 vols., trans. Anton C. Pegis et al. (Notre Dame, IN: University of Notre Dame Press, 1975), vol. 3, 50 and 62:3.
38. Thomas Aquinas, *The Disputed Questions on Truth*, vol. 3, Library of Living Catholic Thought, trans. Robert W. Schmidt, S. J. (Chicago, IL: Henry Regnery, 1954), q. 22, a. 2, ad. 1.
39. See footnote 25 above.
40. I am mindful of the qualms many scholars will have about the introduction of spirituality into the discussion of how theology might stimulate other academic disciplines. There has been considerable debate over the past two and a half decades over whether spiritually should be integrated even into theology programs, let alone other academic disciplines. Some of these articles have been collected in Elizabeth A. Dreyer and Mark S. Burrows, eds, *Minding the Spirit: The Study of Christian Spirituality* (Baltimore: Johns Hopkins, 2005). My reasons for including spirituality in this discussion will become apparent in the course of this book.
41. Joseph Pieper, *Leisure: The Basis of Culture* (Indianapolis: Liberty Fund, n. d.), 9, 12, 50, 69, 75–76.
42. Gerald A. McCool, "Spirituality and Philosophy: The Ideal of the Catholic Mind," in *Examining the Catholic Intellectual Tradition,* ed. Anthony J. Cernera and Oliver J. Morgan (Fairfield, CT: Sacred Heart University Press, 2000), 42–43.
43. John Courtney Murray notes that such an effort "involves a theory of knowledge and knowing...a metaphysics of cognition—the question of the dynamic structure of intelligence itself and of the processes whereby intellectual consciousness moves from the moment of wonder to the moment of attainment of truth." See John Courtney Murray, "The Future of Humanistic Education," in *Bridging the Sacred and the Secular: Selected Writings of John Courtney Murray,* ed. J. Leon Hooper, S. J. (Washington, DC: Georgetown University Press, 1994), 167.
44. Roberts and Turner, *The Sacred and Secular University,* 19–41, 83–93.
45. Morey and Piderit, *Catholic Higher Education,* 108–9.
46. Ibid., 62–63.
47. Ibid., 55, 63–64.
48. Ibid., 97–100, 107, 347–50.

2   The Medieval Liberal Arts and the Journey of the Mind to God

1. Theodore M. Hesburgh, C. S. C., "The Challenge and Promise of a Catholic University," in *The Challenge and Promise of a Catholic University* (Notre Dame, IN: University of Notre Dame Press, 1994), 4.

2. Michael J. Buckley, S. J., *The Catholic University as Promise and Project: Reflections in a Jesuit Idiom* (Washington, DC: Georgetown University Press, 1998), 55–56.

3. Nor can we attempt to reestablish the traditional trivium and quadrivium or the Jesuit *Ratio Studiorum*. These curricular forms may have served Catholic higher education well in the past, but neither can accommodate modern currents of knowledge.

4. Buckley, *The Catholic University*, 56.

5. I am referring to intellectual and spiritual ideals of the telos of the mind not particular curricular forms from the medieval period.

6. St. Augustine, *Teaching Christianity:De Doctrina Christiana*, trans. Edmund Hill, O. P. (Hyde Park, New York: New City Press, 1996) I, 12, 13. This theme of God externalizing himself in the world, through his Word, was common in the Middle Ages; cf. Hugh of St. Victor, *The Didascalicon: A Medieval Guide to the Liberal Arts*, trans. Jerome Taylor (New York: Columbia University Press, 1991), 156; Bonaventure, *De Reductione Artium ad Theologiam*, trans. Sister Emma Therese Healy (Saint Bonaventure, NY: Franciscan Institute 1955), 16.

7. Augustine, *Confessions*, trans. Maria Boulding, O. S. B. (New York: Vintage, 1998), X: 8, 9, 10; Augustine, *The Trinity*, trans. Edmund Hill, O. P. (Brooklyn: New City Press, 1991), VIII: 4, 9. In *City of God*, Augustine praises the Neoplatonists, who declared that "God himself, the creator of all things, is the light of the mind, which makes possible every acquisition of knowledge." Augustine, *City of God*, trans. Henry Bettenson (London: Penguin, 1972), VIII: 7.

8. Robert E. Cushman, "Faith and Reason," in *A Companion to the Study of St. Augustine*, ed. Roy W. Battenhouse (New York: Oxford University Press, 1955), 295.

9. Ibid.

10. Augustine, *Teaching Christianity*, II: 60.

11. Ronald H. Nash, *The Light of the Mind: St. Augustine's Theory of Knowledge* (Lima, Ohio: Academic Renewal Press, 2003), 1.

12. Ibid., 7–8.

13. Edmund Hill, O. P., "Introduction," in Augustine, *The Trinity* (Brooklyn: New City Press, 1991), 22.

14. Augustine, *The Trinity*, XII: 1, 3.

15. Cushman, "Faith and Reason," 292.

16. Ibid.; Augustine, *Soliloquies*, trans. Kim Paffenroth (Hyde Park, NY: New City Press, 2000), I: 12.

17. Cushman, "Faith and Reason," 295.

18. Ibid., 301–2; Augustine, *City of God*, VIII: 10.

19. Cushman, "Faith and Reason," 297.

20. Ibid., 302–3. According to Cushman, Aristotle's intellectualism undermined the Platonic concept of *sophia*, and Thomas Aquinas, adopting Aristotle's thought, was unable to revive wisdom as superior to *scientia*, and "himself conduced to the ascendancy of science over wisdom in modern times." I question Cushman's conclusion, as will be seen later, though there are aspects of

Thomas's thought that, if taken in isolation from his thought as a whole, can lead one to that interpretation.

21. Ewert Cousins, "Introduction," in *Bonaventure, The Soul's Journey into God* (New York: Paulist Press, 1978), 21.

22. Bonaventure, *Journey of the Mind into God*, trans. Philotheus Boehner, O.F.M. (Indianapolis: Hackett, 1993), prologue 4. Where Boehner translates the Latin *industria* as "industry," I have translated it as "intelligent work" because the Latin here refers more to the virtue of diligent study than to "hard and diligent work" in the American understanding of the term "industry." See http://www.oed.com/view/Entry/94859?redirectedFrom=industry.

23. Bonaventure, *De Reductione artium ad theologiam*, trans. Sister Emma Therese Healy (Saint Bonaventure, NY: Franciscan Institute, 1955), 26.

24. Ibid., III: 6, 7.

25. Bonaventure, *Journey*, II: 12.

26. Thomas Aquinas, *Summa Contra Gentiles*, vol. 3, trans. Anton C. Pegis et al. (Notre Dame, IN: University of Notre Dame Press, 1975), 50: 3, 5; cf. Thomas Aquinas, *Summa Theologica*, vol. 1, trans. Fathers of the English Dominican Province (Allen, TX: Christian Classics, 1948), q. 12, a. 1.

27. Aquinas, *Summa Contra Gentiles*, vol. 3, 50, 62: 3.

28. Aquinas, *Summa Theologica*, I–II: q. 3, a. 8.

29. Aquinas, *Summa Contra Gentiles*, vol. 3, 17; see also St. Thomas Aquinas, *Faith, Reason and Theology: Questions I–IV of His Commentary on the De Trinitate of Boethius* (hereafter, Commentary on *De Trinitate*), Mediaeval Sources in Translation 32, trans. Armand Maurer (Toronto: Pontifical Institute of Mediaeval Studies, 1987), q. 5, a. 3: "When that which constitutes the intelligibility (ratio) of a nature and through which the nature itself is understood, has a relation to, and a dependence on something else, clearly we cannot know the nature without that other thing."

30. Jean-Pierre Torrell, *Spiritual Master*, vol. 2 of *St. Thomas Aquinas*, trans. Robert Royal (Washington, DC: Catholic University of America Press, 2003), 346; See Aquinas, *Summa Theologica*, vol. 1, q. 93, a. 4.

31. Torrell, *Spiritual Master*, 81–82.

32. Aquinas, *Summa Contra Gentiles*, vol. 3, 25, 9; vol. 1, 1.; Aquinas, *Summa Theologica*, vol. 1, q. 1, a. 5.

33. Thomas, *Commentary on De Trinitate*, q. 1, a. 1, ad. 6.

34. Thomas, *Disputed Questions on Truth*, Vol. 3, Library of Living Catholic Thought, trans. Robert W. Schmidt S. J. (Chicago: Henry Regnery, 1954), q. 22, a. 2, ad. 1.

35. Cushman, "Faith and Reason," 292. See St. Augustine, *De Trinitate*, VIII: 4; *City of God*, VIII: 7; *Soliloquies*, I: 12. For St. Augustine, this light was the *uncreated* light of God not merely a natural, created light as in Thomas.

36. Thomas Aquinas, *Commentary on De Trinitate*, q. I, a. 1, ad. 6.

37. Ibid., ad. 8.

38. Ibid., q. 5, a. 3.

39. Ralph McInerny, "Introduction" in St. Thomas Aquinas, *Commentary on Aristotle's De Anima*, trans. Kenelm Foster, O. P., and Silvester Humphries, O. P. (Notre Dame, IN: Dumb Ox Books, 1994), xvii.

40. Thomas Aquinas, "Prologue," in the *Commentary on Aristotle's Metaphysics*, trans. Richard J. Blackwell, Richard J. Spath, and W. Edmund Thirlkel (Notre Dame, IN: Dumb Ox Books, 1995), xxix–xxx (emphasis added).
41. Aquinas, *Commentary on De Trinitate*, q. 2, a. 3, ad. 5.
42. Aquinas, *Summa Contra Gentiles*, vol. 1, 9, 4; cf. Armand Maurer, "Introduction," in *Faith, Reason and Theology*, trans. Armand Maurer (Toronto: Pontifical Institute of Mediaeval Studies, 1987), xv; Torrell, *Spiritual Master*, 53–100.
43. In Thomas's time there were, of course, no social sciences or humanities disciplines as we know them today.
44. One may discern an isomorphism with the thought of Hegel in this Trinitarian structure of Thomas's thought: God, or the Absolute, considered in and for itself; of the going forth of God into otherness, that is, into nature as the self-objectification of God; and of the return of God to himself through the Spirit (see chapter 3 below). Note that I say *isomorphism* not *identity*. Gerald McCool also noted the similarities between Hegel and Thomas. See Gerald A. McCool, S. J., "Twentieth-Century Scholasticism," in "Celebrating the Medieval Heritage," ed. David Tracy, supplement, *Journal of Religion* 58 (1978): S218–S220.
45. To speak of an academic discipline as having autonomy is an example of what Alfred North Whitehead referred to as a "fallacy of misplaced concreteness." See A. N. Whitehead, *Science and the Modern World* (New York: Free Press, 1967), 51, 58.
46. Whenever the Catholic Church has closed itself to new ideas, it has been disastrous for the church and for learning as a whole.
47. David Schindler, "Catholicism and the Liberal Model of the Academy in America; Theodore Hesburgh's Idea of a Catholic University," in David Schindler, *Heart of the World, Center of the Church: Communion Ecclesiology, Liberalism, and Liberation* (Grand Rapids, MI: Eerdmans; Edinburgh: T & T Clark, 1996), 143–76 passim.

3   Berlin: The Prototype of the Modern University

1. Johann Gottlieb Fichte, *Deduced Scheme for an Academy to be Established in Berlin*, in G. H. Turnbull, *The Educational Theory of J. G. Fichte* (London: University Press of Liverpool, 1926); F. W. J. Schelling, *On University Studies*, trans. E. S. Morgan, ed. Norbert Guterman (Athens: Ohio University Press, 1966); Friedrich Schleiermacher, *Occasional Thoughts on Universities in the German Sense, with an Appendix Regarding a University Soon to Be Established*, trans. Terrence Tice and Edwina Lawler (San Francisco, CA: Edwin Mellen Press, 1991).
2. It is not my intention to idealize the German university model as did many Americans in the nineteenth century. Nonetheless, in spite of many substantive

flaws in German Idealist philosophy, it has valuable insights and lessons we can learn and appropriate.

3. Daniel Fallon, *The German University: A Heroic Ideal in Conflict with the Modern World* (Boulder: Colorado Associated University Press, 1980), 28–29.

4. Prior to the establishment of the University of Berlin, the Schools of Theology, Law, and Medicine dominated the universities of Europe, while Philosophy, which included most of the arts and sciences at that time, was subordinate to them.

5. G. Felicitas Munzel, "Kant, Hegel, and the Rise of Pedagogical Science," in *A Companion to the Philosophy of Education,* ed. Randall Curren (Malden, MA: Blackwell, 2003): 113–29.

6. In 1807 Johann Gottlieb Fichte (1762–1814) was invited by Wilhelm von Humboldt to submit a blueprint for the new University of Berlin. See footnote 1 above. His blueprint was not ultimately the one selected (Schleiermacher's was—see footnote 27 below).

7. Johann Gottlieb Fichte, "Ueber die einzig mögliche Störung der akademischen Freiheit," in *Sämtliche Werke* 6 (Berlin: Verlag von Veit und Comp, 1845), 451–76.

8. The nineteenth-century concept of the encyclopedia contrasts markedly with the idea of encyclopedia we know today, as a vast assemblage of information ordered alphabetically, but without a coherent unity of perspective.

9. Fichte, *Deduced Scheme,* 192–93.

10. Ibid., 198.

11. Richard Hofstadter and Walter P. Metzger, *The Development of Academic Freedom in the United States* (New York: Columbia University Press, 1955), 373.

12. Ibid., 381.

13. Ibid., 382.

14. Alan White, *Schelling: An Introduction to the System of Freedom* (New Haven, CT: Yale University Press, 1983), 8–9. For references to Augustine's theory of knowledge, see chapter 2, footnotes 7 and 8.

15. Schelling, *On University Studies,* 10.

16. Ibid., 11.

17. Ibid., 116.

18. Ibid., 117.

19. Ibid., 122.

20. Ibid., 123 *(emphasis added).*

21. Ibid., 103.

22. Ibid., 106.

23. Ibid., 104.

24. Ibid., 107.

25. Ibid., 109.

26. Ibid., 111.

27. A year after Fichte was invited to submit his scheme for the new university, Friedrich Schleiermacher (1776–1834) submitted his own unsolicited thoughts on how the university at Berlin should be organized, along with an

exposition of its guiding principles. This work ultimately became one of the guiding documents for the university. Schleiermacher also served on many of the planning committees for the university over a period of years and, in the view of Terrence Tice, can be regarded as a cofounder the university, along with Wilhelm von Humboldt. Schleiermacher's vision for the university's design has made a significant impact on subsequent definitions of the modern university. This is true not only in his advocacy of autonomy from the state and academic freedom for university scholars, but also in the relation of theology to other academic disciplines, for better or worse, at least in Protestant universities. See Friedrich Schleiermacher, *Occasional Thoughts*, 11.

28. Ibid., 3.
29. Ibid., 9.
30. Ibid., 9–10.
31. Ibid., 14.
32. Immanuel Kant, *The Conflict of the Faculties*, trans. Mary J. Gregor (Lincoln: University of Nebraska Press, 1979).
33. Schleiermacher, *Occasional Thoughts*, 14.
34. Ibid., 24.
35. Ibid., 37.
36. Ibid., 38.
37. G. W. F. Hegel, *Encyclopedia of the Philosophical Sciences in Outline and Critical Writings*, ed. Ernst Behler (New York: Continuum, 1990).
38. Ibid., 54.
39. George Wilhelm Friedrich Hegel, *Hegel: The Letters*, trans. Clark Butler and Christiane Seiler (Bloomington: Indiana University Press, 1984), 341.
40. Hegel, *Encyclopedia*, 139.
41. Ibid., 140.
42. George Wilhelm Friedrich Hegel, *Lectures on the Philosophy of Religion* (Berkeley: University of California Press, 1988), 415–16.
43. Ibid., 101, 141.
44. Nicholas of Cusa, *On Learned Ignorance*, trans. Jasper Hopkins (Minneapolis, MN: A. J. Banning Press, 1990).
45. One would need to distinguish Hegel's view from a Catholic view of the Trinity. This is not the place to do that, but it must be pointed out that, although there is a certain isomorphism between them, there are crucial differences also. For both Hegel and Schelling, the Absolute, or *Geist*, is identical with the human mind. Christianity teaches that humans are made in the image and likeness of God, that we participate in the life and mind of God, but our mind is not God's mind thinking through the particular subjectivity of the individual human being. Rather, we *participate* in God's thought and creativity.
46. George Wilhelm Friedrich Hegel, foreword to Hinrich's *Religion in Its Inner Relation to Science*, in *Miscellaneous Writings of G. W. F. Hegel*, ed. Jon Stewart, SPEP Studies in Historical Philosophy (Evanston, IL: Northwestern University Press, 2002), 337–53, at 345.
47. Ibid., 344–45. Hegel, like Schelling, explicitly ties this thought to Kant's island, the land of finite human understanding.

48. The similarity of Hegel's distinction between understanding and reason to Thomas Aquinas's distinction between (analytical) reason and (synthetic) intellect is a topic that I cannot undertake in this work, but one worth exploring. See Thomas Aquinas, *Faith, Reason and Theology: Questions I–IV of His Commentary on the De Trinitate of Boethius*, Mediaeval Sources in Translation 32, trans. Armand Maurer (Toronto: Pontifical Institute of Mediaeval Studies, 1987), q. 5, a. 3. See also chapter 2 above.
49. Hegel, *Philosophy of Religion*, 406.
50. Ibid., 434.
51. Ibid., 406.
52. George Wilhelm Friedrich Hegel, *Phenomenology of Spirit*, trans. A. V. Miller (Oxford: Oxford University Press, 1977), 11.
53. Hegel, *Philosophy of Religion*, 432.
54. Fichte, *Deduced Scheme*, 198–99, 203.
55. Ibid., 188–89.
56. Schleiermacher, *Occasional Thoughts*, 35.
57. Ibid., 37–38.
58. Ibid., 36. In the medieval and early modern periods, the faculty of arts (which included philosophy) was always subordinate to the faculties of theology, medicine, and law. Kant had earlier argued against this subordinate role of philosophy and the arts. See Kant, *The Conflict of the Faculties*.
59. Friedrich Schleiermacher, *On Religion: Speeches to Its Cultured Despisers,* trans. and ed. Richard Crouter, Cambridge Texts in the History of Philosophy (New York: Cambridge University Press, 1996), 22.
60. Ibid., 23.
61. Ibid., 23n4.
62. Ibid., 23.
63. Ibid., 25.
64. Ibid.
65. Ibid., 36–37.
66. Ibid., 70.
67. Schelling, *On University Studies,* 82.
68. Ibid., 83.
69. Ibid., 94.
70. Ibid., 158n.
71. Hegel, *Lectures on the Philosophy of Religion,* 77–80.
72. Ibid., 113.
73. Ibid., 79–81.
74. G. F. Munzel, "Kant, Hegel, and the Rise of Pedagogical Science," 124–26.
75. Fichte, *Deduced Scheme,* 194–95.
76. This tendency was not unique to the German idealists. According to Alasdair MacIntyre, the ninth edition of the *Encyclopedia Britannica* exhibits this same tendency: it began with an overarching philosophical worldview; authors who shared that worldview were then chosen to write articles on particular topics. This way, knowledge within the various subject matters were made a "fit" with the whole. See Alasdair MacIntyre, *Three Rival Versions of Moral*

Inquiry: Encyclopedia, Genealogy, Tradition (Notre Dame, IN: University of Notre Dame Press, 1990), 18–25.

77. Fichte, *Deduced Scheme*, 193.

78. John Henry Newman, *Historical Sketches* (London: Basil Montagu Pickering, 1872), 16.

79. See chapter 4, note 31, below.

80. George Wilhelm Friedrich Hegel, *Philosophy of Nature*, 2 vols., ed. and trans. Michael J. Petry (London: Allen and Unwin, 1970), 1:197.

81. Terry Pinkard, *Hegel: A Biography* (Cambridge: Cambridge University Press, 2000), 575.

82. Hegel, *Encyclopedia*, 140.

83. Hegel, *Philosophy of Nature*, 2:17–18; cf. Hegel, *Encyclopedia*, 160–62.

84. Ibid., 17.

85. Ibid., 21.

86. Pinkard, *Hegel*, 569.

87. Ibid., 571.

88. John Henry Newman, *The Idea of a University* (Notre Dame, IN: University of Notre Dame Press, 1960), 14–32.

89. Ibid., 441–42, 445–46.

90. Some Thomists today continue to insist on a secular program of studies followed by philosophy and theology rather than an integration of philosophy and theology with other studies. See, for example, Alasdair MacIntyre, "Catholic Universities: Dangers, Hopes, Choices," in *Higher Learning and Catholic Traditions*, ed. Robert E. Sullivan, (Notre Dame, IN: University of Notre Dame Press, 2001), 4–5.

91. See, for example, Hesburgh, *The Challenge and Promise*, 6; John Paul II, *Ex Corde Ecclesiae*, 6.

4 Academic Freedom and Religion in America

1. There are a number of excellent studies of the transformations of both Catholic and non-Catholic universities during the late nineteenth and early twentieth centuries. See George M. Marsden, *The Soul of the American University: From Protestant Establishment to Established Nonbelief* (New York: Oxford University Press, 1994); George Marsden and Bradley J. Longfield, eds., *The Secularization of the Academy* (New York: Oxford University Press, 1992); Philip Gleason, *Contending with Modernity: Catholic Higher Education in the Twentieth Century* (New York: Oxford University Press, 1995); James Turner, *Language, Religion, Knowledge* (Notre Dame, IN: University of Notre Dame Press, 2003); Jon H. Roberts and James Turner, *The Sacred and the Secular University* (Princeton, NJ: Princeton University Press, 2000); Julie Reuben, *The Making of the Modern University: Intellectual Transformation and*

the Marginalization of Morality (Chicago, IL: University of Chicago Press, 1996).

2. C. Joseph Nuesse, *The Catholic University of America: A Centennial History* (Washington, DC: Catholic University of America Press, 1990).

3. The first section of this chapter is indebted to James Turner and Jon Roberts, who have done invaluable work on the history of institutional and intellectual secularization in American universities during the late nineteenth and early twentieth centuries. See Roberts and Turner, *Sacred and the Secular University*.

4. Thomas Aquinas, *Summa Theologica*, 5 vols., trans. Fathers of the English Dominican Province (Allen, TX: Christian Classics, 1948), vol. 1, q. 2, a. 3 and a. 3; Thomas Aquinas, *Summa Contra Gentiles*, 4 vols., trans. Anton C. Pegis et al. (Notre Dame, IN: University of Notre Dame Press, 1975), vol. 1, 13.

5. Kennneth J. Howell, *God's Two Books: Copernican Cosmology and Biblical Interpretation in Early Modern Science* (Notre Dame, IN: University of Notre Dame Press, 2002); M. D. Chenu, *Nature, Man and Society in the Twelfth Century: Essays on New Theological Perspectives in the Latin West*, ed. and trans. Jerome Taylor and Lester K. Little (Chicago, IL: University of Chicago Press, 1968), 1–48.

6. William Paley, *Natural Theology* (Oxford: Oxford University Press, 2006).

7. Roberts and Turner, *The Sacred and Secular University*, 23.

8. Ibid.

9. Ibid.

10. Marsden, *The Soul of the American University*, 157.

11. Roberts and Turner, *Sacred and Secular University*, 27.

12. Ibid., 28.

13. Paul Tillich, *A History of Christian Thought: From Its Judaic and Hellenistic Origins to Existentialism* (New York: Simon and Schuster, 1967), 362–66, 511.

14. Roberts and Turner, *Sacred and Secular University*, 29–30.

15. Ibid., 30–31.

16. Walter P. Metzger, "The Age of the University," in *The Development of Academic Freedom in the United States,* ed. Richard Hofstadter and Walter P. Metzger (New York: Columbia University Press, 1955), 367–412.

17. Roberts and Turner, *Sacred and Secular University*, 85.

18. Ibid., 86.

19. Ibid.

20. Ibid., 86–87.

21. John Dewey, "Academic Freedom," *Educational Review* 47 (January 1902): 1–14.

22. Roberts and Turner, *Sacred and Secular University,* 63.

23. Thomas Aquinas, *Summa Theologica*, vol. 1, q. 1, a. 1.

24. Cajetan, *In Primam*, q. 12, a. 1, n. 10, quoted in Henri de Lubac, *The Mystery of the Supernatural*, trans. Rosemary Sheed (New York: Herder and Herder, 1967), 181.

25. Michael J. Baxter and Frederick Bauerschmidt, "*Eruditio* without *Religio*?: The Dilemma of Catholics in the Academy," *Communio* 22 (Summer 1995): 291–93; cf. Kallistos Ware, "Scholasticism and Orthodoxy: Theological Method as a Factor in the Schism," *Eastern Churches Review* 5 (1973): 23.

26. Immanuel Kant, *The Critique of Pure Reason*, trans. Norman Kemp Smith (London: Macmillan, 1933), 257.

27. Tillich, *A History of Christian Thought*, 188–89.

28. In the late nineteenth century, Nietzsche proclaimed this process of secularization complete when he wrote that we have killed God, we have wiped him from the heavens. By this he meant that the separate realm of the supernatural no longer had cogency as a concept. Moreover, he concluded, without the values given by the supernatural, there remained no values except what humans create for themselves.

29. Henri de Lubac, S. J., *Catholicism: A Study of Dogma in Relation to the Corporate Destiny of Mankind* (London: Burns, Oates & Washbourne, 1950), 166–67. See Joseph A. Komonchak, "Theology and Culture at Mid-Century: The Example of Henri de Lubac," *Theological Studies* 51 (1990): 592. Komonchak's article is an excellent summary of de Lubac's thought and achievement.

30. Charles W. Eliot, "Academic Freedom," *Science* 26 (1907): 2.

31. For excellent studies of disputes over religious education and separation of church and state, see John McGreevy, *Catholicism and American Freedom: A History* (New York: W.W. Norton, 2003); Philip Hamburger, *Separation of Church and State* (Cambridge, MA: Harvard University Press, 2002).

32. Pope Leo XIII, *Aeterni Patris* (Boston: Pauline Books & Media, n.d.). (Numbers in the in-text citations refer to paragraphs in the document.

33. This was not something entirely new. The Jesuit *Ratio Studiorum* of 1599 already prescribed Aristotle for philosophy and Thomas's *Summa Theologica* for theology, to the exclusion of almost all other Christian writers and non-Christian philosophers. See *The Jesuit Ratio Studiorum of 1599*, trans. Allan P. Farrell, S. J. (Washington, DC: Conference of Major Superiors of Jesuits, 1970).

34. Pope Pius X, *Pascendi Domenici Gregis* (Boston: Pauline Books & Media, n.d.). Numbers in the in-text citations refer to paragraphs in the document.

35. Philip Gleason, *Contending with Modernity: Catholic Higher Education in the Twentieth Century* (New York: Oxford University Press, 1995), 16.

36. This kind of censorship was not new in Catholic universities. The Jesuit *Ratio Studiorum* also forbade the use of questionable (especially modern) material and prohibited any criticism of the thought of St. Thomas. See Farrell, *Ratio Studiorum*, 26, 30–37, 66, 80.

37. See note 13 above.

38. Autonomy from God is, of course, different from autonomy from other humans. The act of independent thought and decision making, of becoming a mature adult able to think and act on one's own, does not imply autonomy and independence from God, only from the control of other people.

39. Pope Pius XII, *Humani Generis* (Boston: Pauline Books & Media, n.d.). Numbers in the in-text citations refer to paragraphs in the document.

40. Hunter Guthrie, S. J., *Tradition and Prospect: The Inauguration of the Very Reverend Hunter Guthrie, S. J.* (Washington, DC: Georgetown University Press, 1949), 71–72.

41. Hunter Guthrie, S. J., *Georgetown Journal* 79 (October 1950): 32, quoted in Robert MacIver, *Academic Freedom in Our Time* (New York: Columbia University Press, 1955), 135.

42. Guthrie, *Tradition and Prospect*, 73.

43. Yves M.-J. Congar, O. P., *Tradition and Traditions: An Historical and a Theological Essay*, trans. Michael Naseby and Thomas Rainborough (New York: Macmillan, 1967), 122.

44. Ibid., 119–37.

45. Edward B. Rooney, S. J., "The Philosophy of Academic Freedom," in *A Philosophical Symposium on American Catholic Education*, ed. Hunter Guthrie, S. J. and Gerald G. Walsh, S. J. (New York: Fordham University Press, 1941), 126.

46. Fairfield University, *Catalogue of the College of Arts and Sciences* 13, no. 1 (1959–1960).

47. We must also bear in mind that modern universities often systematically excluded Catholic faculty and Catholic theological perspectives from their institutions. See Alasdair MacIntyre, *Three Rival Versions of Moral Enquiry: Encyclopaedia, Genealogy, and Tradition* (Notre Dame, IN: University of Notre Dame Press, 1990), 224.

48. Thomas T. McAvoy, *Father O'Hara of Notre Dame: The Cardinal Archbishop of Philadelphia* (Notre Dame, IN: University of Notre Dame Press, 1967), 102.

49. Cited in McAvoy, *Father O'Hara*, 115.

50. *Bulletin of the University of Notre Dame, 1919–1922* (Notre Dame, IN: University of Notre Dame, 1920), 36.

51. John Courtney Murray, "Reversing the Secularist Drift," *Thought* 24 (March 1949): 36.

52. Ibid., 38.

53. Ibid., 39.

54. Jacque Maritain, "Thomist Views on Education," in *Modern Philosophies and Education: The 54th Yearbook of the National Society for the Study of Education*, Part I, ed. Nelson B. Henry (Chicago, IL: National Society for the Study of Education, 1955), 78–79.

55. John Henry Newman, *Historical Sketches* (London: Basil Montagu Pickering, 1872), 16.

56. John Henry Newman, *Idea of a University* (Notre Dame, IN: University of Notre Dame Press, 1982), 178.

57. Ibid, 358–59.

58. John Henry Newman, *Apologia Pro Vita Sua*, ed. A. Dwight Culler (Boston: Houghton Mifflin, 1956), 249–52.

59. There has always been a counter tradition that surfaces regularly in Christian thought. Etienne Gilson referred to this tradition as the "Tertullian school," after the late-second- and early-third-century author who rhetorically asked,

"What has Athens to do with Jerusalem?" In the long run, the Catholic Church has insisted that Athens has a great deal to do with Jerusalem, but this has not been evident in Catholic education in all periods. See Etienne Gilson, *Reason and Revelation in the Middle Ages* (New York: Charles Scribner's Sons, 1948), 3–33.

60. American Association of University Professors, "General Report of the Committee on Academic Freedom and Academic Tenure," *Bulletin of the American Association of University Professors* 1 (1915): 20.

61. Ibid., 29.

62. Ibid., 33–35.

63. Ibid., 27–28.

64. Arthur O. Lovejoy, "Academic Freedom," in *Encyclopaedia of the Social Sciences*, 15 vols., ed. Edwin R. A. Seligman et al. (New York: Macmillan, 1930), 1: 384.

65. Roberts and Turner, *Sacred and Secular University*, 88.

66. American Association of University Professors, "Statement of Principles on Academic Freedom and Tenure," in *Academic Freedom and Tenure*, ed. Louis Joughin (Madison: University of Wisconsin Press, 1967), 34, 35.

67. MacIver, *Academic Freedom in Our Time*; Russell Kirk, *Academic Freedom: An Essay in Definition* (Chicago, IL: Henry Regnery, 1955); Sidney Hook, *Heresy, Yes—Conspiracy No!* (New York: John Day, 1953); Hofstadter and Metzger, *The Development of Academic Freedom*; Robert Maynard Hutchins, *The University of Utopia* (Chicago, IL: University of Chicago Press, 1953).

68. Hook, *Heresy, Yes—Conspiracy, No!* 154 *(emphasis added)*.

69. MacIver, *Academic Freedom*, 4, 285.

70. Ibid., 6.

71. Ibid., 9.

72. See chapter 7 below.

73. MacIver, *Academic Freedom*, 135.

74. Ibid., 260.

75. First Global Colloquium of University Presidents, "Statement on Academic Freedom," in *Report of the First Global Colloquium of University Presidents*, ed. Johanna Fine and Matthew Moneyhon, January 18–19, 2005, available from Columbia University website: http://www.columbia.edu/cu/president /communications%20files/globalcolloquium.htm; accessed January 8, 2008 (emphasis added).

76. Most academics would not dispute the appropriateness of the phrase, "wherever it may lead," but they think of this as applying to situations where the scholar pursues lines of inquiry that make religious believers anxious and uncomfortable. The "wherever" is the point at which students begin to question, and perhaps reject, their inherited beliefs. The same academics rarely advocate the freedom to pursue lines of inquiry that make disciplinary specialists and secularists anxious and uncomfortable about their learned (and inherited) assumptions about the world and their disciplines. Students do, after all, have religious experiences as well as inherited beliefs, experiences that sometimes conflict with the teachings and assumptions of the various social and natural sciences.

They, too, must be allowed to have these perspectives fully understood and fairly placed in dialectical conversation with the findings and philosophical assumptions arising from the various secular sciences.

77. Ibid., *emphasis added*.
78. Ibid.
79. Philip Gleason, "Academic Freedom and the Crisis in Catholic Universities," in *Academic Freedom and the Catholic University*, ed. Edward Manier and John Houck (Notre Dame, Ind.: Fides Publishers, 1967), 48.

5   The Pursuit of Intellectual and Spiritual Wholeness, 1920–1960

1. Andrew M. Greeley, *From Backwater to Mainstream: A Profile of Catholic Higher Education*, Carnegie Commission Studies (New York: McGraw-Hill, 1969).
2. Pope Pius XI, *Divini Illius Magistri* (Washington, DC: National Catholic Welfare Conference, 1936). Numbers in in-text citations refer to paragraphs in the document.
3. Philip Gleason, *Keeping the Faith: American Catholicism, Past and Present* (Notre Dame, IN: Notre Dame University Press, 1987), 139. A spate of books, articles, and pamphlets on the philosophy and ideals of Catholic higher education was published in the 1940s and 1950s. See Leo R. Ward, *Blueprint for a Catholic University* (St. Louis, MO: B. Herder, 1949); John D. Redden and Francis A. Ryan, *A Catholic Philosophy of Education* (Milwaukee, WI: Bruce Publishing, 1955); Roy J. Deferrari, ed., *The Philosophy of Catholic Higher Education* (Washington, DC: Catholic University of America Press, 1948); William F. Cunningham, C.S.C., *General Education and the Liberal College* (St. Louis, MO: B. Herder, 1953); John Julian Ryan, *The Idea of a Catholic College* (New York: Sheed & Ward, 1945); John Julian Ryan, *Beyond Humanism: Towards a Philosophy of Catholic Education* (New York: Sheed & Ward, 1950); William McGucken, S.J., "The Philosophy of Catholic Education," in *Philosophies of Education: The Forty-first Yearbook of the National Society for the Study of Education*, ed. Nelson B. Henry (Chicago, IL: National Society for the Study of Education, 1942), 251–88.
4. John Henry Newman, *The Idea of a University* (Notre Dame, IN: University of Notre Dame Press, 1982), 38.
5. George Bull, *The Function of the Catholic College* (New York: America Press, 1933), 10.
6. Ibid., 3–4.
7. Ibid., 5.
8. Ibid.
9. Mount St. Mary's College, *Catalogue, 1949–50*, 11 (Archives of Mount St. Mary's University, Emmistburg, Maryland).

10. The Catholic University of America, *Catalogue, 1940–41*, 24 (Archives of the Catholic University of America).

11. College of St. Thomas, *Bulletin, 1939–1940*, 19 (Archives of the University of St. Thomas, St. Paul, Minnesota).

12. College of St. Thomas, *Bulletin, 1949–1950*, 26 (Archives of the University of St. Thomas, St. Paul Minnesota).

13. Virgil Michel, "The Basic Need of Christian Education Today," *Catholic Educational Review* 28 (1930): 10, 11.

14. Ibid., 11–12.

15. Fulton J. Sheen, "Organic Fields of Study," *Catholic Educational Review* 28 (1930): 203–4.

16. Fulton J. Sheen, "Education for a Catholic Renaissance," NCEA *Bulletin* 26 (1929): 47.

17. See for example, Charles Curran's attempt to apply Murray's political thought to Catholic university education. Charles E. Curran, *Catholic Higher Education, Theology, and Academic Freedom* (Notre Dame, IN: University of Notre Dame Press, 1990), 160–62. David Schindler takes this as a legitimate interpretation of Murray's position and attempts to refute its implications. See David L. Schindler, *Heart of the World, Center of the Church: Communio Ecclesiology, Liberalism, and Liberation* (Grand Rapids, MI: Eerdmans; Edinburgh: T & T Clark, 1996), 155–59.

18. John Courtney Murray, S.J., "Towards a Christian Humanism: Aspects of the Theology of Education," in *Bridging the Sacred and the Secular: Selected Writings of John Courtney Murray, S.J.*, ed. J. Leon Hooper, S.J.(Washington, DC: Georgetown University Press, 1994), 124.

19. Ibid., 127.

20. Ibid., 128.

21. Ibid., 127–28.

22. John Courtney Murray, S.J., "The Christian Idea of Education," in *Bridging the Sacred and Secular*, 141.

23. Murray, "Towards a Christian Humanism," 125.

24. Roy J. Deferrari, ed., "The General Interest in, and Need for, Integration," in *Integration in Catholic Colleges and Universities*(Washington, DC: Catholic University of America Press, 1950), 5.

25. Ibid, 6–7.

26. Ibid., 7–8.

27. Kenneth E. Anderson, "On Integrating the Sciences," in Deferrari, *Integration in Catholic Colleges*, 394.

28. Ibid., 395.

29. John Montgomery Cooper, "Catholic Education and Theology," in *Vital Problems of Catholic Education in the United States*, ed. Roy J. Deferrari (Washington, DC: Catholic University of America Press, 1939), 127–29.

30. John Courtney Murray, S.J., "Necessary Adjustments to Overcome Practical Difficulties," in *Man and Modern Secularism: Essays on the Conflict of the Two Cultures*, ed. National Catholic Alumni Federation (New York: National Catholic Alumni Federation, 1940), 154.

31. Paul Hanly Furfey, "Value-Judgments in Sociology," *American Catholic Sociological Review* 7 (1946): 83–86, 89.
32. Quoted in ibid., 87.
33. Ibid., 87.
34. Ibid., 89.
35. Ibid., 91.
36. Ibid., 94.
37. Paul Hanly Furfey, "Why a Supernatural Sociology?" *American Catholic Sociological Review* 1 (1940): 168.
38. Paul Hanly Furfey, "The Integration of the Social Sciences," in Deferrari, *Integration in Catholic Colleges and Universities*, 219.
39. Ibid, 222–23.
40. Ibid, 229.
41. Franz Mueller, "The Formal Object of Sociology," *American Catholic Sociological Review* 1 (1940): 56.
42. Ibid.
43. Ibid., 59.
44. Franz Mueller, "The Possibility of a Supernatural Sociology," *American Catholic Sociological Review* 1 (1940): 146.
45. C. J. Nuesse, "The Sociologist as Teacher," *American Catholic Sociological Review* 5 (1944): 215.
46. Ibid., 216–17.
47. Furfey, "Why a Supernatural Sociology?," 168.
48. Ibid., 170–71.
49. Raymond W. Murray, C.S.C., "Presidential Address, 1939," *American Catholic Sociological Review* 1 (1940): 39.
50. Ibid., 41.
51. Ibid.
52. Paul J. Mundie, "Introductory Comments," *American Catholic Sociological Review* 1 (1940): 5.
53. "The Introductory Course in Sociology," *American Catholic Sociological Review* 2 (1941): 122, 124.
54. Ibid., 123, 124.
55. Eva J. Ross, "Sociology and the Catholic," *American Catholic Sociological Review* 1 (1940): 6–9.
56. Arnold Sparr, *To Promote, Defend, and Redeem: The Catholic Literary Revival and the Cultural Transformation of American Catholicism, 1920–1960* (Westport, CT: Greenwood Press, 1990).
57. Calvert Alexander, S.J., *The Catholic Literary Revival* (Milwaukee, Wisconsin: Bruce Publishing Company, 1935), 4. Alexander explicitly tied the literary revival to the renewal of scholastic philosophy, and acknowledged that the revival was a protest against modern trends in thought and culture.
58. John Pick, "The Renascence in American Catholic Letters," in *The Catholic Renascence in a Disintegrating World*, ed. Norman Wey and, S. J.(Chicago, IL: Loyola University Press, 1951), 157–182.
59. Sparr, *Promote, Defend, and Redeem*, 13.

60. Pick, *Renascence*, 173.
61. Ibid., 168.
62. Ibid., 173.
63. Mother Grace, O.S.U., "The Catholic Renascence Society: Its Past and Present," in *Renascence: A Critical Journal of Letters*, Vol. 1 (1948–1949), 3–6, 39.
64. John Pick, "Editorial: Here and Now,"*Renascence: A Critical Journal of Letters*, Vol 1 (1948–1949), 2.
65. Mother Grace, "Catholic Renascence," 3.
66. Sparr, *Promote, Defend, and Redeem*, 100–104.
67. Fr. Joachim Daleiden, O.F.M., Response to Victor Herman, O.F.M., "Literature from the Catholic Viewpoint," in Franciscan Educational Conference, *Report of the Twenty-Second Annual Meeting* (December 1940):176.
68. Sr. Mary Louise, S.L., ed., *Over the Bent World* (New York: Sheed and Ward, 1939); Charles Brady, ed., *A Catholic Reader* (Buffalo, NY: Desmond and Stapleton, 1947); Francis B. Thornton, ed., *Return to Tradition: A Directive Anthology* (Milwaukee, WI: Bruce Publishing Company, 1948).
69. Fr. Joachim Daleiden, O.F.M., "Mortimer Adler's 'List of the Great Books': Additions and Substitutes," in Franciscan Educational Conference, *Report*, 403–414. One will immediately notice how broadly these educators conceived the term "literature": Most of these authors were philosophers; a few were scientists.
70. See Nancy Hynes, O.S.B., "Introduction" to Mariella Gable, O.S.B., *The Literature of Spiritual Values and Catholic Fiction*, ed. Nancy Hynes, O.S.B. (Lanham, MD: University Press of America, Inc.), xvii.
71. Frank O'Malley, professor of English at the University of Notre Dame from 1934 to 1974, was one exception. He included non-Catholic as well as Catholic writers in his courses, and analyzed them from the perspectives of philosophers such as Aristotle, Thomas Aquinas, and Henri Bergson. See John W. Meaney, *O'Malley of Notre Dame* (Notre Dame, IN: University of Notre Dame Press, 1991); also Arnold Sparr, *Frank O'Malley: Thinker, Critic, Revivalist* (Notre Dame, IN: University of Notre Dame Press, 1983).
72. Kenneth E. Anderson, "Biology as Speculative, Practical, and Contemplative," in Deferrari, *Integration in Catholic Colleges and Universities*, 199.
73. Here Anderson makes a logical error of mistaking temporary difficulty (of discovering a mechanism for how life arises) for a permanent impossibility. As science advances, it steadily eliminates those temporary difficulties with valid scientific explanations.
74. Kenneth E. Anderson, "On Integrating Biology, Psychology, Natural Theology, and Liturgy," in *Discipline and Integration in the Catholic College*, ed. Roy J. Deferrari (Washington, DC: Catholic University of America Press, 1951), 164.
75. Ibid., 165.
76. Anderson, "Biology as Speculative," 201; cf. Thomas Aquinas, *Summa Theologica*, 5 vols., trans. Fathers of the English Dominican Province (Allen, TX: Christian Classics, 1948), vol. 1, q. 2, a. 3.

77. Anderson, "On Integrating Biology," 168; "Biology as Speculative," 211–18.
78. John Julian Ryan, *The Idea of a Catholic College* (New York: Sheed & Ward, 1945), 47.
79. Ibid., 51.
80. Sr. Jeanne Marie, "The Religious Development of Women at the College of St. Catherine," *Journal of Religious Instruction* 3 (1933): 874–78.
81. Thomas Aquinas, *Summa Theologica*, 5 vols., trans. Fathers of the English Dominican Province (Allen, Tex.: Christian Classics, 1948), vol. 1, q. 1, a. 3.
82. I do not want to belittle the value of the seminary aspect of college education. Any institution created for the education and training of youth is a seminary in the broad meaning of the word: a seedbed where youth are temporarily removed from the concerns of daily life and allowed to grow into knowledgeable and, one hopes, virtuous citizens before being transplanted into society. If religion is not allowed to be part of their formation, some form of ideology will rush in to fulfill that role.
83. *Gaudium et Spes,* 56, 61.
84. Colleges and universities, while allowing for differentiation of the sciences, must also ensure unity and coherence lest we end up with an incoherent assemblage of unrelated, mutually exclusive, and sometimes even hostile academic departments. As we will see in chapters 6 and 7, one flaw in Catholic higher education today is that the centrifugal tendency is threatening the center. In allowing the free growth and development of the academic disciplines, Catholic universities have done a poor job of maintaining connection to a broader theological and philosophical vision. Catholic educational leaders *desire* to do that but have no mechanism for ensuring it. Catholic colleges offer, even require, theology and philosophy courses, but these are studied as subjects largely unrelated to the students' own disciplines. They sit side by side with other disciplines without any organic connections. The connections may occur by happenstance through the efforts of individual faculty members, but it does not occur as a result of and within the context of a coherent, guiding curricular framework.
85. Philip Gleason, "Academic Freedom and the Crisis in Catholic Universities," in *Academic Freedom and the Catholic University*, ed. Edward Manier and John Houck (Notre Dame, IN: Fides Publishers, Inc., 1967), 45–46.
86. Newman, *Idea*, xxxvii. Michael Buckley points out that, in spite of Newman's insistence on teaching as the primary function of the university, he nonetheless wanted his faculty members to have time for writing and research, and "he established a university journal that would twice a year present the research of the faculty in arts and sciences." See Michael J. Buckley, S.J., "Newman and the Restoration of the Interpersonal in Higher Education," in *The Santa Clara Lectures*, vol. 13 (Santa Clara, CA: Ignatian Center for Jesuit Education, Santa Clara University, 2006), 3.
87. Gleason, "Academic Freedom," 46.
88. George Bull, S.J., "The Function of the Catholic Graduate School," *Thought* 13 (1938): 364–80.
89. Ibid., 380, 371.
90. Ibid., 370.

6 THE CONSEQUENCE OF CAESAR'S GOLD

1. Virgil Michel, "The Basic Need of Christian Education Today," *Catholic Educational Review* 28 (1930): 6–8.
2. John Tracy Ellis, "American Catholics and the Intellectual Life," *Thought* 30 (1955–1956): 351–88.
3. Pierre Teilhard de Chardin, *The Phenomenon of Man* (London: Collins, 1955).
4. John Courtney Murray, S. J., *We Hold These Truths: Catholic Reflections on the American Proposition* (Kansas City, MO: Sheed & Ward, 1960).
5. Philip Gleason, *Keeping the Faith: American Catholicism Past and Present* (Notre Dame, IN: University of Notre Dame Press, 1987), 58–81.
6. Philip Gleason, "American Catholic Higher Education: A Historical Perspective," in *The Shape of Catholic Higher Education*, ed. Robert Hassenger (Chicago, IL: University of Chicago Press, 1967), 27–28.
7. Philip Gleason, "Academic Freedom and the Crisis in Catholic Universities," in *Academic Freedom and the Catholic University*, ed. Edward Manier and John W. Houck(Notre Dame, IN: Fides Publishers, 1967), 34.
8. Ibid., 47. Charles Curran and James Annarelli have both written works on academic freedom and Catholic higher education, but the academic freedom they treat pertains primarily to theologians in the context of commitment to Christian doctrine and responsible exercise of church authority. Both Curran and Annarelli base the freedom of the theologian on American, secular principles of academic freedom. See Charles E. Curran, *Catholic Higher Education, Theology, and Academic Freedom* (Notre Dame, IN: University of Notre Dame Press, 1990); James John Annarelli, *Academic Freedom and Catholic Higher Education* (Westport, CT: Greenwood Press, 1987).
9. Frank D. Schubert, *A Sociological Study of Secularization in the American Catholic University: DeCatholicizing the Catholic Religious Curriculum* (Lewiston, ME: Edwin Mellen Press, 1990). Prior to the Second Vatican Council, Catholic theology was essentially the dogmatic theology of the church. Following the Council (1965–1975), theology was transformed into a more general, ecumenical Christian theology. In some universities, it eventually devolved into a general "religious studies" curriculum on many Catholic campuses (1975–1985). It should be noted that adoption of the "religious studies" label does not necessarily imply a secularization of the theology curriculum. Some colleges and universities that adopted that title continued to teach Catholic theology from the perspective of faith. See Sandra Yocum Mize, *Joining the Revolution in Theology: The College Theology Society, 1954–2004* (Lanham, MD: Rowman& Littlefield, 2007).
10. *Oxford English Dictionary*, s. v. "Sectarianism."
11. For a discussion of the effect of secular orthodoxies on faculty, See Mark U. Edwards, Jr., *Religion on Our Campuses: A Professor's Guide to Communities, Conflicts, and Promising Conversations* (New York: Palgrave MacMillan, 2006), 117. For a discussion of faculty reticence to discuss religion seriously, see Mark

U. Edwards, Jr. "Why Faculty Find it Difficult to Talk about Religion," in *The American University in a Postsecular Age*, ed. Douglas Jacobsen and Rhonda Hustedt Jacobsen (New York: Oxford, 2008), 82–88.

12. *Horace Mann League v. Board of Public Works of Maryland*, 242 Md. 672 (1966).

13. College of Note Dame, *Catalogue, 1956–1957*, 20–21., Archives of College of Notre Dame, Baltimore, Maryland.

14. *Horace Mann v. Board of Public Works*, 679–80.

15. Joseph R. Preville, "Catholic Colleges, the Courts, and the Constitution: A Tale of Two Cases," *Church History* 58 (June 1989): 200.

16. Ibid., 200–1.

17. Ibid., 201.

18. Ibid.

19. Ibid., 201–2.

20. Francis X. Gallagher, "The Maryland College Aid Case," *Ave Maria* (July 9, 1966): 9.

21. Preville, "Catholic Colleges," 202.

22. Walter Gellhorn and R. Kent Greenawalt, *The Sectarian College and the Public Purse* (Dobbs Ferry, NY: Oceana Publications, 1970), 103.

23. Ibid.,108–9.

24. Preville, "Catholic Colleges," 203.

25. *Tilton v. Richardson*, 403 US 672 (1971). The colleges were Fairfield University, Albertus Magnus College, Annhurst College, and Sacred Heart University.

26. Trial Transcript, Second Day of Trial, *Tilton v. Richardson* Collection, 578–80., Nysellius Library, Fairfield University, Fairfield, Connecticut.

27. Fairfield University, *Catalogue of the College of Arts and Sciences, 1959–1960*, 17.

28. *Divini Illius Magistri*, 6, 7.

29. Ibid., 96.

30. The *Instructio* can be found in the *Jesuit Educational Quarterly* 11, no. 2 (October 1948): 69–83.

31. John B. Janssens, S. J., "Letter to the Fathers and Scholastics of the American Assistancy," in ibid., 69, 70.

32. Fairfield University, *Catalogue of the College of Arts and Sciences, 1968–1969*, 27.

33. Jesuit Conference, *Documents of the 31st and 32nd General Congregations of the Society of Jesus,* ed. John W. Padberg, S. J.(Saint Louis, MO: The Institute of Jesuit Sources, 1977).

34. Ibid., 228.

35. Ibid., 229–30.

36. Ibid., 230.

37. Ibid.

38. Ibid., 232.

39. Ibid., 242.

40. Trial Transcript, *Tilton v. Richardson* Collection, 383–84., Nysellius Library, Fairfield University, Fairfield, Connecticut.

41. Saint Ignatius of Loyola, *The Constitutions of the Society of Jesus*, trans. George E. Ganss, S. J. (St. Louis, MO: The Institute of Jesuit Sources, 1970). Part 4 of the *Constitutions* covers education in Jesuit universities. For a translation of the Jesuit *Ratio Studiorum,* see *The Jesuit Ratio Studiorum of 1599*, trans. Allan P. Farrell, S. J. (Washington, DC: Conference of Major Superiors of Jesuits, 1970).

42. *Tilton v. Richardson*, 684–89.

43. Preville, "Catholic Colleges," 306.

44. *Roemer v. Board of Public Works of Maryland*, 426 US 736 (1976). The Catholic colleges were Mount St. Mary's College and St. Joseph College in Emmitsburg; the College of Notre Dame in Baltimore; and Loyola College of Baltimore. Another college with religious affiliations—Western Maryland College—was withdrawn from the case after it agreed to disaffiliate itself from its founding religious body (the Methodist Church) and to accede to the demands of the ACLU attorneys to hire a certain percentage of non-Methodist faculty members, even in its theology department.

45. George W. Constable, "Findings of Fact Proposed by the Defendant, College of Notre Dame," in the United States District Court for the District of Maryland, August 31, 1973, 17, ACLU Deposition File, Archives of Mount St. Mary's University, Emmitsburg, Maryland.

46. Ibid., 18.

47. Ibid.

48. Ibid, 19.

49. Trial Transcript, *Roemer v. Board of Public Works*, questioning of Sr. Kathleen Feeley, SSND, President of College of Notre Dame, 482–86.

50. Constable, "Findings of Fact Proposed by the Defendant," 8.

51. Mount St. Mary's College, *Catalogue, 1949–1950*, 11.

52. "Mount St. Mary's College," ACLU Deposition File, Mount St. Mary's University Archives, Emmitsburg, Maryland (emphasis added).

53. *Roemer v. Board of Public Works*, 751 (emphasis added).

54. Ibid., 755.

55. Deposition of John J. Dillon Jr., February 12, 1973, 126–30, ACLU Deposition File, Mount St. Mary's College Archives, Emmitsburg, Maryland.

56. Nicholas Varga, *Baltimore's Loyola, Loyola's Baltimore, 1851–1986* (Baltimore: Maryland Historical Society, 1990), 509.

57. Ibid., 509–10.

58. Ibid., 510.

59. *Roemer v. Board of Public Works*, 772. (emphasis added).

60. Ibid., 775.

61. Meyer Eisenberg et al., "The Dissenting Report," Commission to Study State Aid to Nonpublic Education, *Report to the Governor and General Assembly of Maryland* (January 1971): 69.

62. Lawrence S. Greenwald, "Stipulation Between Appellants and Western Maryland College, Appellee," March 17, 1975, Archives of the National Catholic Education Association/Association of Catholic Colleges and Universities, Box 61; Folder: Court Cases, Archives of the Catholic University of America, Washington, DC.

63. To point out how Catholic colleges and universities downplayed the religious dimension of learning in order to secure public funds is not to assert that they should not seek public funds at all. Their goal should be to make the case for funds not on the basis of conformity to secular academic principles but on the basis that they are no longer sectarian in the true sense of the word, that is, they no longer exclude and display hostility to non-Catholic thought.

64. John Henry Newman, *The Idea of a University* (Notre Dame, IN: University of Notre Dame Press, 1982), xxxvii.

65. Preville, "Catholic Colleges,," 203–4, 208. See also Joseph R. Preville, "Catholic Colleges and the Supreme Court: The Case of Tilton vs. Richardson," *Journal of Church and State* 30 (Spring 1988): 295, 302–3.

66. James Tunstead Burtchaell, *The Dying of the Light: The Disengagement of Colleges and Universities from Their Christian Churches* (Grand Rapids, MI: Eerdmans, 1998), 593, 717.

67. "Land O'Lakes Statement," in *American Catholic Higher Education: Essential Documents, 1967–1990*, ed. Alice Gallin, O. S. B. (Notre Dame, IN: University of Notre Dame Press, 1992), 7.

68. Ibid., 7.

69. Ibid., 8.

70. Ibid. (emphasis added).

71. Ibid., 8–9.

72. See Burtchaell, *Dying of the Light*, 595, 715.

73. "Land O'Lakes Statement," 10.

74. Ibid., 10–11.

75. "Kinshasa Statement: The Catholic University in the Modern World" (1970), in Gallin, *American Catholic Higher Education*, 14; and "The Catholic University in the Modern World" (1972), in Gallin, *American Catholic Higher Education*, 37–57.

76. The various documents of the IFCU and some of the correspondence with the Vatican have been collected in Gallin, *American Catholic Higher Education*. Additional correspondence can be found in the IFCU file in the Archives of the Catholic University of America, and in the IFCU boxes of the Theodore Hesburgh files in the Archives of the University of Notre Dame.

77. Rev. Theodore M. Hesburgh, C. S. C., to His Eminence Gabriel Cardinal Garrone, March 30, 1970, Hesburgh Files 97/06 [IFCU], Archives of the University of Notre Dame.

78. Gallin, *American Catholic Higher Education*, 38.

79. Ibid.

80. Ibid., 50–51.

81. "Synthesis of Responses Received from US Catholic College and University Presidents to the Pontifical Document on Catholic Universities," in Gallin, *American Catholic Higher Education*, 262–63, 270, 280.

82. See note 8 above.

83. John Paul II, *Ex Corde Ecclesiae* (Washington, DC: United States Catholic Conference, 1990). Numbers in in-text citations refer to paragraphs in the document.

84. *Gaudium et Spes*, 36, 56, 57, 59, 62, 63.

85. Gallin notes that college and university leaders appreciated the extensive consultation process established by the Vatican, giving Catholic educators ample time to comment on various drafts of the document. See Gallin, *American Catholic Higher Education*, 190. I also note the irenic tone of *Ex Corde* in contrast to encyclicals of the first half of the twentieth century, such as *Pascendi* and *Humani Generis*.

86. *Ex Corde* also insists that Catholic colleges and universities are parts of the church and important elements in its evangelization efforts.

87. Melanie M. Morey and John J. Piderit, S. J., *Catholic Higher Education: A Culture in Crisis* (New York: Oxford University Press, 2006).

88. Ibid., 99. Ironically, the senior administrators who would like to ensure that the Catholic tradition is engaged are often the ones who have hired and promoted many of the indifferent and hostile faculty at their institutions.

89. Ibid., 347–48.

90. Ibid., 3, 5.

91. Ibid., 15.

92. Ibid., 349–50.

93. Ibid., 3.

94. Michael J. Buckley, S. J., *The Catholic University as Promise and Project: Reflections in a Jesuit Idiom* (Washington, DC: Georgetown University Press, 1998), 176–77. Morey and Piderit, *Catholic Higher Education*, 105–9; Alasdair MacIntyre, "Catholic Universities: Dangers, Hopes, Choices," in *Higher Learning and Catholic Traditions*, ed. Robert E. Sullivan (Notre Dame, IN: University of Notre Dame Press, 2001), 7–9.

7 "The Direction toward Which Wonder Progresses"

1. See chapter 3 above.

2. Joseph A. Komonchak, "Thomism and the Second Vatican Council," in *Continuity and Plurality in Catholic Theology: Essays in Honor of Gerald A. McCool, S. J.*, ed. Anthony J. Cernera (Fairfield, CT: Sacred Heart University Press, 1998), 62–73.

3. I do not claim that these authors had no differences; they did. I am drawing on their commonalities, which are far more extensive and important than their differences, to frame the argument for this book.

4. See chapter 1, page 13–14.

5. St. Augustine, *The Trinity*, trans. Edmund Hill, O. P. (Brooklyn: New City Press, 2000), X, 1–4.

6. Joseph A. Komonchak, "Theology and Culture at Mid-Century: The Example of Henri de Lubac," *Theological Studies* 51 (1990): 585.

7. Thomas Aquinas, *Summa Contra Gentiles*, 4 vols., trans. Anton C. Pegis et al. (Notre Dame, IN: University of Notre Dame Press, 1975), vol. 3, 50 and 62:3; *SCG*, vol. 2, 4 (hereafter *SCG*); Thomas Aquinas, *Faith, Reason and*

Theology: Questions I-IV of His Commentary on the De Trinitate of Boethius, Mediaeval Sources in Translation 32, trans. Armand Maurer (Toronto: Pontifical Institute of Mediaeval Studies, 1987), q. 6, a. 1.

8. *SCG,* vol. 2, 2.

9. See, for example, Stephen W. Hawking, *A Brief History of Time: From the Big Bang to Black Holes* (New York: Bantam Books, 1988), 131; Paul Davies, *Cosmic Jackpot: Why Our Universe Is Just Right for Life* (Boston: Houghton Mifflin, 2007), 6, 204.

10. I am here describing an academic ideal that *should* characterize intellectual life in a Catholic university.

11. David L. Schindler, "Religious Freedom, Truth, and American Liberalism: Another Look at John Courtney Murray," *Communio* 21 (Winter 1994): passim. Cf. Stephen J. Duffy, *The Graced Horizon: Nature and Grace in Modern Catholic Thought* (Collegeville, MN: Liturgical Press, 1992), 8.

12. Henri de Lubac, *The Discovery of God* (Grand Rapids, MI: Eerdmans, 1996), 35, 39. See also Thomas Aquinas, *The Disputed Questions on Truth,* vol. 3, Library of Living Catholic Thought, trans. Robert W. Schmidt, S. J. (Chicago, IL: Henry Regnery, 1954), q. 22, a. 2.

13. Thomas, *Commentary on De Trinitate,* q. 1, a. 1, ad. 6.

14. De Lubac, *Discovery of God,* 38, 88. Cf. Bonaventure's *Itinerarium Mentis in Deum,* trans. Philotheus Boehner, O. F. M. (Indianapolis: Hackett, 1990). According to Bonaventure, the vestiges of God are found everywhere in the universe. Through contemplation of these vestiges we are led to God.

15. Karl Rahner, "Theology as Engaged in an Interdisciplinary Dialogue with the Sciences," *Theological Investigations,* 23 vols. (New York: Crossroads, 1983), 13:90.

16. Karl Rahner, "On the Relationship Between Natural Science and Theology," *Theological Investigations,* 23 vols. (New York: Crossroads, 1983), 19:19.

17. Karl Rahner, "On the Situation of the Catholic Intellectual," *Theological Investigations,* vols. (New York: Herder and Herder, 1971), 8:104–5 (emphasis added).

18. Ibid., 105.

19. Karl Rahner, "The Task of the Writer in Relation to Christian Living," *Theological Investigations,* 23vols. (New York: Herder and Herder, 1971), 8:114.

20. Karl Rahner, "Christian Humanism," *Theological Investigations,* 23vols.(New York: Seabury, 1976), 9:189.

21. Thomas Aquinas, Prologue to the *Commentary on Aristotle's Metaphysics,* trans. Richard J. Blackwell, Richard J. Spath, and W. Edmund Thirlkel (Notre Dame, IN: Dumb Ox Books, 1995), xxix–xxx.

22. See chapter 1, note 19.

23. Karl Rahner, *Foundations of Christian Faith* (New York: Crossroads, 1984), 53.

24. Karl Rahner, "Reflections on the *Foundations of Christian Faith,*" *Theology Today* 28, no. 3 (Fall 1980): 210–11.

25. Karl Rahner, "Revelation," in *Sacramentum Mundi: An Encyclopedia of Theology,* 6 vols., ed. Karl Rahner et al. (New York: Herder and Herder, 1970), 5:352.

26. Rahner, *Foundations*, 32.

27. Rahner, "Revelation," 348, 352.

28. Rahner, *Foundations*, 181–82.

29. Rahner, "Theology as Engaged in Interdisciplinary Dialogue," 90.

30. Ibid., 83–84.

31. Karl Rahner, "Natural Science and Theology," 20–21.

32. *Gaudium et Spes*, 36.

33. John Polkinghorne, *Exploring Reality: The Intertwining of Science and Religion* (New Haven, CT: Yale University Press, 2005), ix.

34. Michael J. Buckley, S. J., "The Catholic University and the Promise Inherent in Its Identity," in *Catholic Universities in Church and Society: A Dialogue on Ex Corde Ecclesiae*, ed. John P. Langan, S. J. (Washington, DC: Georgetown University Press, 1993), 80.

35. Michael J. Buckley, S. J., *At the Origins of Modern Atheism* (New Haven, CT: Yale University Press, 1987), 360.

36. Michael J. Buckley, "Within the Holy Mystery," in *A World of Grace: An Introduction to the Themes and Foundations of Karl Rahner's Theology*, ed. Leo J. O'Donovan (New York: Crossroad, 1984), 35.

37. Michael J. Buckley, S. J., *The Catholic University as Promise and Project: Reflections in a Jesuit Idiom* (Washington, DC: Georgetown University Press, 1998), 15.

38. Michael J. Buckley, S. J., "Transcendence, Truth, and Faith: The Ascending Experience of God in all Human Inquiry," *Theological Studies* 39 (1978): 633–55.

39. Rabbi David Novak, "Commentary," in Langan, *Catholic Universities in Church and Society*, 99.

40. Buckley, *Catholic University as Promise*, 17–20.

41. Ibid., 18.

42. Gregory of Nyssa, *The Life of Moses*, trans. Abraham J. Malherbe and Everett Ferguson (New York: Paulist Press, 1978); cf. St. Augustine, *Teaching Christianity: De Doctrina Christiana*, trans. Edmund Hill, O. P. (Hyde Park, New York: New City Press, 1997), II, 60; Bonaventure, *Itinerarium Mentis in Deum*, I, II.

43. Louis Dupré, *Passage to Modernity: An Essay in the Hermeneutics of Nature and Culture* (New Haven, CT: Yale University Press, 1993), 15–18.

44. John Henry Newman, The *Idea of a University* (Notre Dame, IN: University of Notre Dame Press, 1982), 27.

45. Ibid., 38.

46. Buckley, *Catholic University as Promise*, 172–82.

47. Ibid., 176.

48. Integrating theology and other disciplines, or at least carrying on a fruitful dialogue between them, can be accomplished in some academic disciplines more easily than in others. It is difficult to see how a dialogue can take place between theology and say, chemistry, engineering, or mathematics, for example, but difficulty should not rule out the attempt.

49. For treatments of theological inculturation, see Aylward Shorter, *Towards a Theology of Inculturation* (Maryknoll, NY: Orbis Books, 1994); Peter

Schineller, S. J., *A Handbook of Inculturation* (New York: Paulist Press, 1990).

50. St. Augustine, *De Doctrina Christiana*, II, 60.

51. I am speaking here of the ideal of theological inculturation, not the way Christianity has historically interacted with various cultures, which can, as often as not, be described as *imposition on* cultures rather than true inculturation.

52. Walter J. Ong, "Yeast: A Parable for Catholic Higher Education," *America* (April 7, 1990): 348.

53. Ibid.

54. As we saw in chapter 2, that is how St. Thomas conceived of the relation between theology and other disciplines; it fulfills and transforms them even while they inform the work of theology. See chapter 2, footnotes 41 and 42.

55. John Haughey also draws on Ong's metaphor of yeast. See John C. Haughey, S. J., *Where is Knowing Going?: The Horizons of the Knowing Subject* (Washington, DC: Georgetown University Press, 2009), 93–96.

56. The tradition includes, of course, the Magisterium, and its teachings also have a place at the table.

57. David Schindler, *Heart of the World, Center of the Church: Communion Ecclesiology, Liberalism, and Liberation* (Grand Rapids, MI: Eerdmans; Edinburgh: T & T Clark, 1996), 170–71.

58. Ibid.

59. Ibid., 175–76.

8   IMPLICATIONS FOR FACULTY DEVELOPMENT AND THE CURRICULUM

1. John Haughey, drawing on the epistemology of Bernard Lonergan, has recently shown how the dynamism of knowing and inquiring tends beyond finite categories toward self-transcendence in a process very similar to the one described in this book. Yet Haughey is surprisingly ambiguous regarding whether scholars in the Catholic university—once they've transcended the categorical—should engage the Catholic intellectual tradition specifically. In fact, he seems to hold it is not necessary, which raises an obvious question: if the self-transcending movement beyond categorical knowledge is sufficient without also engaging a particular tradition, then why have Catholic universities at all? What does the specifically Catholic university add? Haughey is silent on this. Regardless, Haughey's fine book is must reading for anyone interested in this topic. John C. Haughey, S. J., *Where is Knowing Going?: The Horizons of the Knowing Subject* (Washington, DC: Georgetown University Press, 2009), 89, 91, 102.

2. Peter Steinfels, "Catholic Identity: Emerging Consensus," *Origins* (August 24, 1995): 175.

3. Melanie M. Morey and John J. Piderit, S. J., *Catholic Higher Education: A Culture in Crisis* (New York: Oxford University Press, 2006), 105.

4. John Courtney Murray, S. J., "On the Idea of a College Religion Course," in *Jesuit Educational Quarterly* 12 (October, 1949): 80.

5. Haughey, *Where is Knowing Going?*,, 56.

6. Morey and Piderit, *Catholic Higher Education*, ibid., 107.

7. A scholar at the beginning stages of course development would do well to read John Piderit and Melanie Morey's edited volume of essays, *Teaching the Tradition*. The essays are aimed at assisting faculty to more fully integrate Catholic themes in their course work. The volume features articles by disciplinary specialists from the natural sciences, mathematics, the social sciences, and the humanities. See John J. Piderit, S. J. and Melanie M. Morey, eds., *Teaching the Tradition: Catholic Themes in Academic Disciplines* (New York: Oxford University Press, 2012).

8. See http://woodstock.georgetown.edu/programs/Catholic-Higher-Education .html.

9. See http://www.catholicexcellence.org/.

10. With sufficient funding, the CHEP and CHI programs would no doubt do much more than they now do.

11. See http://ndias.nd.edu/about-us/.

12. See http://www.ifacs.com/.

13. Alasdair MacIntyre, *Three Rival Versions of Moral Inquiry: Encyclopaedia, Geneaology, and Tradition* (Notre Dame, IN: University of Notre Dame Press, 1990), 228–236.

14. Gerald A. McCool, "Spirituality and Philosophy: The Ideal of the Catholic Mind," in *Examining the Catholic Intellectual Tradition*, ed. Anthony J. Cernera and Oliver J. Morgan (Fairfield, CT: Sacred Heart University Press, 2000), 49.

15. John Courtney Murray, S. J., "Towards a Christian Humanism: Aspects of the Theology of Education," in *Bridging the Sacred and the Secular: Selected Writings of John Courtney Murray, S.J.* ed. J. Leon Hooper, S. J. (Washington, DC: Georgetown, 1994), 128.

16. Christian Smith, "Secularizing American Higher Education: The Case of Early American Sociology," in Christian Smith, ed., *The Secular Revolution: Power, Interests, and Conflict in the Secularization of American Public Life* (Berkeley, CA: University of California Press, 2003), 97–159.

17. Douglas Jacobsen and Rhonda Hustedt Jacobsen, *The Americ an University in a Postsecular Age* (Oxford, New York: Oxford University Press, 2008), 14.

18. G. W. F. Hegel, "Foreword to Hinrich's *Religion in Its Inner Relation to Science*," in *Miscellaneous Writings of G. W. F. Hegel*, ed. Jon Stewart (Evanston, IL: Northwestern University Press, 2002), 345–46.

19. Mark U. Edwards, Jr., *Religion on Our Campuses: A Professor's Guide to Communities, Conflicts, and Promising Conversations* (Palgrave MacMillian, 2006).

20. Ibid, 103–104.

21. Alasdair MacIntyre, "Catholic Universities: Dangers, Hopes, Choices," in *Higher Learning and Catholic Traditions*, ed. Robert E. Sullivan (Notre Dame, IN: University of Notre Dame Press, 2001), 8.
22. Ibid., 4–5.
23. Schindler, *Heart of the World, Center of the Church*, 171.
24. "Land O'Lakes Statement," in *American Catholic Higher Education: Essential Documents, 1967–1990*, ed. Alice Gallin, O. S. B. (Notre Dame, IN: University of Notre Dame Press, 1992), 8.
25. Piderit and Morey, eds., *Teaching the Tradition*, 6.
26. Buckley, *The Catholic University*, 85.
27. Buckley, *The Catholic University*, 176–77.
28. MacIntyre, "Catholic Universities," 5.
29. George M. Marsden, *The Soul of the American University: From Protestant Establishment to Established Nonbelief* (New York: Oxford University Press, 1994).
30. Buckley, *The Catholic University*, 177.

Selected Bibliography

Alexander, Calvert S. J., *The Catholic Literary Revival*. Milwaukee, WI: Bruce Publishing Company, 1935.

American Association of University Professors. "General Report of the Committee on Academic Freedom and Academic Tenure." *Bulletin of the American Association of University Professors* I (1915).

Anderson, Kenneth E. "Biology as Speculative, Practical, and Contemplative." In *Integration in Catholic Colleges and Universities*. Edited by Roy J. Deferrari, 198–218. Washington, DC: Catholic University of America Press, 1950.

———. "On Integrating Biology, Psychology, Natural Theology, and Liturgy." In *Discipline and Integration in the Catholic College*. Edited by Roy J. Deferrari, 164–68. Washington, DC: Catholic University of America Press, 1951.

Annarelli, James John. *Academic Freedom and Catholic Higher Education*. Westport, CT: Greenwood Press, 1987.

Aquinas, Thomas. *Commentary on Aristotle's "Metaphysics."* Translated by Richard J. Blackwell, Richard J. Spath, and W. Edmund Thirlkel. Notre Dame, IN: Dumb Ox Books, 1995.

———. *Commentary on Aristotle's "De Anima."* Translated by Keelm Foster, O. P., and Silvester Humphries, O. P. Notre Dame, IN: Dumb Ox Books, 1994.

———. *The Disputed Questions on Truth*. Vol. 3. Library of Living Catholic Thought. Translated by Robert W. Schmidt, S.J. Chicago, IL: Henry Regnery, 1954.

———. *Faith, Reason and Theology: Questions I–IV of His Commentary on the De Trinitate of Boethius*. MediaevalSourcesinTranslation32. Translated by Armand Maurer. Toronto: Pontifical Institute of Mediaeval Studies, 1987.

———. *Summa Contra Gentiles*. 4 vols. Translated by Anton C. Pegis, James F. Anderson, Vernon J. Bourke, and Charles J. O'Neil. Notre Dame, IN: University of Notre Dame Press, 1975.

———. *Summa Theologica*. 5 vols. Translated by the Fathers of the English Dominican Province. Allen, TX: Christian Classics, 1948.

Baxter, Michael J., and Frederick Bauerschmidt. "*Eruditio* without *Religio*? The Dilemma of Catholics in the Academy." *Communio* 22 (Summer 1995): 284–302.

Benne, Robert. *Quality with Soul: How Six Premier Colleges and Universities Keep Faith with Their Religions Traditions*. Grand Rapids, MI: Eerdmans, 2001.

Bonaventure. *De Reductione artium ad theologiam*. Translated by Sister Emma Therese Healy. Saint Bonaventure, NY: Franciscan Institute, 1955.

———. *Itinerarium Mentis in Deum*. Translated by Philotheus Boehner, O. F. M. (Indianapolis: Hackett, 1990).

———. *Journey of the Mind into God*. Translated by Philotheus Boehner, O. F. M. Indianapolis: Hackett, 1990.

Brady, Charles ed., *A Catholic Reader*. Buffalo, New York: Desmond and Stapleton, 1947.

Buckley, Michael J., S.J. *At the Origins of Modern Atheism*. New Haven, CT: Yale University Press, 1987.

———. *The Catholic University as Promise and Project: Reflections in a Jesuit Idiom*. Washington, DC: Georgetown University Press, 1998.

———. "The Catholic University and the Promise Inherent in Its Identity." In *Catholic Universities in Church and Society: A Dialogue on Ex Corde Ecclesiae*. Edited by John P. Langan, S. J. Washington, DC: Georgetown University Press, 1993.

———. "Newman and the Restoration of the Interpersonal in Higher Education." In *The Santa Clara Lectures*, vol. 13. Santa Clara, CA: Ignatian Center for Jesuit Education, Santa Clara University, 2006.

———. "Transcendence, Truth and Faith: The Ascending Experience of God in all Human Inquiry." *Theological Studies* 39 (1978): 633–55.

———. "Within the Holy Mystery." In *A World of Grace: An Introduction to the Themes and Foundations of Karl Rahner's Theology*. Edited by Leo J. O'Donovan, 31–49. New York: Seabury, 1980.

Bull, George, S.J. *The Function of the Catholic College*. New York: America Press, 1933.

———. "The Function of the Catholic Graduate School." *Thought* 13 (1938): 364–80.

Burtchaell, James Tunstead. *The Dying of the Light: The Disengagement of Colleges and Universities from Their Christian Churches*. Grand Rapids, MI: Eerdmans, 1998.

Cere, Daniel. "Newman, God, and the Academy." *Theological Studies* 55 (1994): 3–23.

Chenu, M.D. *Nature, Man and Society in the Twelfth Century*. Chicago, IL: University of Chicago Press, 1957.

Congar, Yves M.-J., O.P. *Tradition and Traditions: An Historical and a Theological Essay*. Translated by Michael Naseby and Thomas Rainborough. New York: Macmillan, 1967.

Cooper, John Montgomery. *Religion Outlines for Colleges*, 4 vols. Washington, DC: Catholic Education Press, 1928–1934.

———. "Catholic Education and Theology." In *Vital Problems of Catholic Education in the United States*. Edited by Roy J. Deferrari., 127–43. Washington, DC: Catholic University of America Press, 1939.

Cunningham, Lawrence S., and Keith J. Egan. *Christian Spirituality: Themes from the Tradition*. New York: Paulist Press, 1996.

Cunningham, William F., C.S.C. *General Education and the Liberal College.* St. Louis, MO: B. Herder, 1953.

Curran, Charles E. *Catholic Higher Education, Theology, and Academic Freedom.* Notre Dame, IN: University of Notre Dame Press, 1990.

Cushman, Robert E. "Faith and Reason." In *A Companion to the Study of St. Augustine.*Edited by Roy W. Battenhouse, 287–314. New York: Oxford University Press, 1955.

D'Costa, Gavin. *Theology in the Public Square: Church, Academy, and Nation.* Malden, MA and Oxford: Blackwell, 2005.

Davies, Paul. *Cosmic Jackpot: Why Our Universe Is Just Right for Life.* Boston: Houghton Mifflin, 2007.

Deferrari, Roy J., ed. *Integration in Catholic Colleges and Universities.* Washington, DC: Catholic University of America Press, 1950.

———, ed. *Theology, Philosophy, and History as Integrating Disciplines in the Catholic College.* Washington, DC: Catholic University of America Press, 1953.

———, ed. *The Philosophy of Catholic Higher Education.* Washington, DC: Catholic University of America Press, 1948.

———, ed. *Vital Problems of Catholic Education in the United States.* Washington, DC: Catholic University of America Press, 1939.

de Lubac, Henri. *Catholicism: A Study of Dogma in Relation to the Corporate Destiny of Mankind.* London: Burns, Oates & Washbourne, 1950.

———. *The Discovery of God.* Translated by Alexander Dru. Grand Rapids, MI: Eerdmans, 1996.

———. *The Mystery of the Supernatural.* Translated by Rosemary Sheed. New York: Herder and Herder, 1967.

Dewey, John. "Academic Freedom." *Educational Review* 47 (January 1902): 1–14.

Dreyer, Elizabeth A., and Mark S. Burrows, ed. *Minding the Spirit: The Study of Christian Spirituality.* Baltimore, MD: Johns Hopkins, 2005.

Dupré, Louis. *Passage to Modernity: An Essay in the Hermeneutics of Nature and Culture.* New Haven, CT: Yale University Press, 1993.

Edwards, Mark U., Jr. *Religion on Our Campuses: A Professor's Guide to Communities, Conflicts, and Promising Conversations.* New York: Palgrave MacMillan, 2006.

———. "Why Faculty Find it Difficult to Talk about Religion." In *The American University in a Postsecular Age,* 82–88.Edited by Douglas Jacobsen and Rhonda Hustedt Jacobsen (New York: Oxford, 2008).

Eliot, Charles W. "Academic Freedom," *Science* 26 (1907): 2.

Ellis, John Tracy. "American Catholics and the Intellectual Life." *Thought* 30 (1955–1956): 351–88.

Evans, John Whitney. *The Newman Movement: Roman Catholics in American Higher Education, 1883–1971.* Notre Dame, IN: University of Notre Dame Press, 1980.

Fallon, Daniel. *The German University: A Heroic Ideal in Conflict with the Modern World.* Boulder: Colorado Associated University Press, 1980.

Farrell, Allan P., S.J., trans. *The Jesuit Ratio Studiorum of 1599*. Washington, DC: Conference of Major Superiors of Jesuits, 1970.

Farrell, Walter, O.P. "Argument for Teaching Theology in Catholic Colleges." *NCEA Bulletin* 43 (1946–1947): 239–44.

Fichte, Johann Gottlieb. *Deduced Scheme for an Academy to be Established in Berlin*. In *The Educational Theory of J. G. Fichte*. Edited by G. H. Turnbull. London: University Press of Liverpool, 1926.

———. "Ueber die einzig mögliche Störung der akademischen Freiheit." In *Sämtliche Werke*, vol. 6, 451–76. Berlin: Verlag von Veit und Comp, 1845.

First Global Colloquium of University Presidents. "Statement on Academic Freedom." In *Report of the First Global Colloquium of University Presidents*, January 18–19, 2005. Edited by Johanna Fine and Matthew Moneyhon.http://www.columbia. edu/cu/president/communications%20files/globalcolloquium.htm.

Furfey, Paul Hanly. "Value-Judgments in Sociology." *The American Catholic Sociological Review* 7 (1946): 83–95.

———. "Why a Supernatural Sociology?" *The American Catholic Sociological Review* 1 (1940): 167–71.

———. "The Integration of the Social Sciences." In *Integration in Catholic Colleges and Universities*. Edited by Roy J. Deferrari, 219–30. Washington, DC: Catholic University of America Press, 1950.

Gallagher, Francis X. "The Maryland College Aid Case." *Ave Maria* (July 9, 1966): 8–11.

Gallin, Alice, O.S.U., ed. *American Catholic Higher Education: The Essential Documents, 1967–1990*. Notre Dame, IN: University of Notre Dame Press, 1990.

———. *Ex Corde Ecclesiae: Documents Concerning Reception and Implementation*. Notre Dame, IN: University of Notre Dame Press, 2006.

Garcia, Kenneth N. "Academic Freedom and the Service Theologians Must Render the Academy." *Horizons: Journal of the College Theology Society* (July, 2011): 75–103.

Gellhorn, Walter, and R. Kent Greenawalt. *The Sectarian College and the Public Purse*. Dobbs Ferry, NY: Oceana Publications, 1970.

Gilson, Etienne. *Reason and Revelation in the Middle Ages*. New York: Charles Scribner's Sons, 1948.

Gleason, Philip. "Academic Freedom and the Crisis in Catholic Universities." In *Academic Freedom and the Catholic University*. Edited by Edward Manier and John Houck, 33–56. Notre Dame, IN: Fides Publishers, 1967.

———. "The American Background of *Ex Corde Ecclesiae*: A Historical Perspective." In *Catholic Universities in Church and Society: A Dialogue on Ex Corde Ecclesiae*. Edited by John P. Langan, S.J., 1–19. Washington, DC: Georgetown University Press, 1993.

———. "American Catholic Higher Education: A Historical Perspective." In *The Shape of Catholic Higher Education*. Edited by Robert Hassenger. Chicago, IL: University of Chicago Press, 1967.

———. *Contending with Modernity: Catholic Higher Education in the Twentieth Century*. New York: Oxford University Press, 1995.

———. *Keeping the Faith: American Catholicism, Past and Present*. Notre Dame, IN: Notre Dame University Press, 1987.

Greeley, Andrew M. *From Backwater to Mainstream: A Profile of Catholic Higher Education*. Carnegie Commission Studies. New York: McGraw-Hill, 1969.

Gregory of Nyssa. *The Life of Moses*. Translated by Abraham Malherbe and Everett Ferguson. New York: Paulist Press, 1978.

Guthrie, Hunter, S.J. *Tradition and Prospect: The Inauguration of the Very Reverend Hunter Guthrie, S.J.* Washington, DC: Georgetown University Press, 1949.

Hamburger, Philip. *Separation of Church and State*. Cambridge, MA: Harvard University Press, 2002.

Haughey, John C., S. J., *Where is Knowing Going?: The Horizons of the Knowing Subject*. Washington, DC: Georgetown University Press, 2009.

Hawking, Stephen W. *A Brief History of Time: From the Big Bang to Black Holes*. New York: Bantam Books, 1988.

Hegel, G. W. F. *Encyclopedia of the Philosophical Sciences in Outline* and *Critical Writings*. Edited by Ernst Behler. Translated by Steven A. Taubeneck. New York: Continuum, 1990.

———. "Foreword to Hinrich's *Religion in its Inner Relation to Science*."In *G.W. F. Hegel, Miscellaneous Writings*. Edited by Jon Stewart, 337–353. Evanston, IL: Northwestern University Press, 2002.

———. *Hegel: The Letters*. Translated by Clark Butler and Christiane Seiler. Bloomington: Indiana University Press, 1984.

———. *Lectures on the Philosophy of Religion*. Edited by Peter C. Hodgson. Translated by R. F. Brown, P. C. Hodgson, and J. M. Stewart. Berkeley: University of California Press, 1988.

———. *Phenomenology of Spirit*. Translated by A. V. Miller. Oxford: Oxford University Press, 1977.

———. *Philosophy of Nature*. 3 vols. Edited and translated by Michael J. Petry. London: Allen and Unwin, 1970.

Henry, Douglas V., and Michael D. Beaty, eds. *Christianity and the Soul of the University: Faith as a Foundation for Intellectual Community*. Grand Rapids, MI: Baker Academic, 2006.

Hesburgh, Father Theodore M., C.S.C., ed. *The Challenge and Promise of a Catholic University*. Notre Dame, IN: University of Notre Dame Press, 1994.

———. *The Hesburgh Papers: Higher Values in Higher Education*. Kansas City, MO: Andrews and McMeel, 1979.

Hofstadter, Richard, and Walter P. Metzger. *The Development of Academic Freedom in the United States*. New York: Columbia University Press, 1955.

Hook, Sidney. *Heresy, Yes—Conspiracy No!* New York: John Day, 1953.

Horace Mann League v. Board of Public Works, 242 Md. 679–80 (1966).

Howell, Kennneth J. *God's Two Books: Copernican Cosmology and Biblical Interpretation in Early Modern Science*. Notre Dame, IN: University of Notre Dame Press, 2002.

Hugh of St. Victor, *The Didascalicon: A Medieval Guide to the Liberal Arts*. Translated by Jerome Taylor. New York: Columbia University Press, 1991.

Hutchins, Robert Maynard. *The University of Utopia*. Chicago, IL: University of Chicago Press, 1953.

Ignatius of Loyola. *The Constitutions of the Society of Jesus*. Translated by George E. Ganss, S.J. St. Louis, MO: Institute of Jesuit Sources, 1970.

International Federation of Catholic Universities (IFCU). Correspondence between Vatican officials and leaders of American Catholic college leaders (1969–1990). Archives of Catholic University of America, Washington, DC.

Jacobsen, Douglas, and Jacobsen, Rhonda Hustedt, eds. *The American University in a Postsecular Age*. Oxford and New York: Oxford, 2008.

Jaspers, Karl. *The Idea of the University*. Translated by A.T. Reiche and H.F. Vanderschmidt. London: Peter Owen, 1960.

Jeanne Marie, Sr. "The Religious Development of Women at the College of St. Catherine." *Journal of Religious Instruction* 3 (1933): 874–78.

John Paul II. *Ex Corde Ecclesiae*. Washington, DC: United States Catholic Conference, 1990.

———. *Fides et Ratio*. Boston: Pauline Books and Media,1998.

Justin Martyr. *The First Apology*. In *The Writings of Justin Martyr and Athenagoras*. Translated by Marcus Dods, D.D., George Reith, D.D., and Rev. B. P. Pratten. Edinburgh: T & T Clark, 1909.

Kant, Immanuel. *The Conflict of the Faculties*. Translated by Mary J. Gregor. Lincoln: University of Nebraska Press, 1979.

———. *The Critique of Pure Reason*. Translated by Norman Kemp Smith. London: Macmillan, 1933.

Kirk, Russell. *Academic Freedom: An Essay in Definition*. Chicago, IL: Henry Regnery, 1955.

Komonchak, Joseph A. "Theology and Culture at Mid-Century: The Example of Henri de Lubac." *Theological Studies* 51 (1990).

———. "Thomism and the Second Vatican Council." In *Continuity and Plurality in Catholic Theology: Essays in Honor of Gerald A. McCool, S. J.*, edited by Anthony J. Cernera, 62–73. Fairfield, CT: Sacred Heart University Press, 1998.

Landy, Tom. "Catholic Studies at Catholic Colleges and Universities." *America* (January 3, 1998): 12–17.

Leo XIII. *Aeterni Patris* (1879). Boston: Pauline Books & Media, n.d.

Lovejoy, Arthur O. "Academic Freedom." In *Encyclopaedia of the Social Sciences*, 15 vols.Edited by Edwin R. A. Seligman et al., vol. 1, 384–88. New York: Macmillan, 1930.

McAvoy, Thomas T. *Father O'Hara of Notre Dame: the Cardinal Archbishop of Philadelphia*. Notre Dame, IN. University of Notre Dame Press, 1967.

MacIntyre, Alasdair. "Catholic Universities: Dangers, Hopes, Choices." In *Higher Learning and Catholic Traditions*. Edited by Robert E. Sullivan, 1–21.Notre Dame, IN: University of Notre Dame Press, 2001.

———. *Three Rival Versions of Moral Enquiry: Encyclopaedia, Genealogy, and Tradition*. Notre Dame, IN: University of Notre Dame Press, 1990.

———. *God, Philosophy, Universities: A Selective History of the Catholic Philosophical Tradition*. Lanham, MD: Rowman & Littlefield, 2009.

MacIver, Robert M. *Academic Freedom in Our Time*. New York: Columbia University Press, 1955.

Mahoney, Kathleen A. *Catholic Higher Education in Protestant America: The Jesuits and Harvard in the Age of the University*. Baltimore, MD: Johns Hopkins University Press, 2003.

Manier, Edward, and John Houck, eds. *Academic Freedom and the Catholic University*. Notre Dame, IN: Fides Publishers, 1967.

Maritain, Jacques. *Education at the Crossroads*. New Haven, CT: Yale University Press, 1943.

————. "Thomist Views on Education." In *Modern Philosophies and Education, The 54th Yearbook of the National Society for the Study of Education*. Edited by Nelson B. Henry. Chicago: National Society for the Study of Education, 1955.

Marsden, George. *The Soul of the American University: From Protestant Establishment to Established Nonbelief*. Oxford: Oxford University Press, 1994.

Marsden, George, and Bradley J. Longfield, eds. *The Secularization of the Academy*. Oxford: Oxford University Press, 1992.

Martyr, Justin. *The First Apology*. In *The Writings of Justin Martyr and Athenagoras*. Translated by Marcus Dods, D.D., George Reith, D.D., and Rev. B. P. Pratten. Edinburgh: T & T Clark, 1909.

Maurer, Armand."Introduction."In *Faith, Reason and Theology*. Translated by Armand Maurer. Toronto: Pontifical Institute of Mediaeval Studies, 1987.

McCluskey, Neil G., S.J., ed. *The Catholic University: A Modern Appraisal*. Notre Dame, IN: University of Notre Dame Press, 1970.

McCool, Gerald A., S.J. *From Unity to Pluralism: The Internal Evolution of Thomism*. New York: Fordham University Press, 1989.

————. "Spirituality and Philosophy: The Ideal of the Catholic Mind," in *Examining the Catholic Intellectual Tradition*. Edited by Anthony J. Cernera and Oliver J. Morgan (Fairfield, CT: Sacred Heart University Press, 2000)

McGinn, Bernard. *The Foundations of Mysticism: Origins to the Fifth Century*. New York: Crossroads, 1994.

McGreevy, John. *Catholicism and American Freedom: A History*. New York: W. W. Norton, 2003.

McGucken, William S.J., "The Philosophy of Catholic Education." In *Philosophies of Education: The Forty-first Yearbook of the National Society for the Study of Education*. Edited by Nelson B. Henry. Chicago, IL: National Society for the Study of Education, 1942.

McInerny, Ralph. Introduction to St. Thomas Aquinas, *Commentary on Aristotle's De Anima*. Translated by Kenelm Foster, O.P., and Silvester Humphries, O.P. Notre Dame, IN: Dumb Ox Books, 1994.

Meaney, John W. *O'Malley of Notre Dame* (Notre Dame, IN: University of Notre Dame Press, 1991).

Metzger, Walter P. "The Age of the University." In *The Development of Academic Freedom in the United States*. Edited by Richard Hofstadter and Walter P. Metzger(New York: Columbia University Press, 1955), 367–412.

Michel, Virgil. "The Basic Need of Christian Education Today." *Catholic Educational Review* 28 (1930): 3–12.

Milbank, John. *Theology and Social Theory: Beyond Secular Reason*. Oxford and Cambridge, MA: Blackwell, 1990.

Mize, Sandra Yocum. *Joining the Revolution in Theology: The College Theology Society, 1954–2004*. Lanham, MD: Rowman & Littlefield, 2007.

Morey, Melanie M., and John J. Piderit, S.J. *Catholic Higher Education: A Culture in Crisis*. Oxford: Oxford University Press, 2006.

Mueller, Franz. "The Formal Object of Sociology." *American Catholic Sociological Review* 1 (1940): 55–61.

———. "Person and Society According to Thomas Aquinas." In *Thomistic Principles in a Catholic School*. Edited by Theodore Brauer et al., 184–263. St. Louis, MO: B. Herder, 1943.

———. "The Possibility of a Supernatural Sociology." *American Catholic Sociological Review* 1 (1940): 141–46.

Mundie, Paul J. "Introductory Comments," *American Catholic Sociological Review* 1 (1940).

Munzel,G. Felicitas. "Kant, Hegel, and the Rise of Pedagogical Science." In *A Companion to the Philosophy of Education*.Edited by Randall Curren (Malden, MA: Blackwell, 2003): 113–29.

Murray, John Courtney, S.J. "Necessary Adjustments to Overcome Practical Difficulties." In *Man and Modern Secularism: Essays on the Conflict of the Two Cultures*. Edited by National Catholic Alumni Federation, 152–57. New York: National Catholic Alumni Federation, 1940.

———. "Reversing the Secularist Drift." *Thought* 24 (March 1949): 36–46.

———. Courtney, S. J. "Towards a Christian Humanism: Aspects of the Theology of Education."In *Bridging the Sacred and the Secular: Selected Writings of John Courtney Murray, S. J.* Edited by J. Leon Hooper, S.J.(Washington, DC: Georgetown, 1994),

———. "Towards a Theology for the Layman." *Theological Studies* 5 (1944): 43–75; 340–78.

———. *Bridging the Sacred and the Secular: Selected Writings of John Courtney Murray, S. J.* Edited by J. Leon Hooper. Washington, DC: Georgetown University Press, 1994.

———. *We Hold These Truths: Catholic Reflections on the American Proposition*. Kansas City, MO: Sheed & Ward, 1988.

Murray, Raymond W., C.S.C. "Presidential Address, 1939." *American Catholic Sociological Review* 1 (1940): 39–42.

Nash, Ronald H. *The Light of the Mind: St. Augustine's Theory of Knowledge*. Lima, OH: Academic Renewal Press, 2003.

National Catholic Education Association (NCEA). Correspondence between Vatican officials and leaders of American Catholic college leaders (1969–1990). Washington, DC: Archives of Catholic University of America.

Newman, John Henry. *Apologia Pro Vita Sua*. Edited by A. Dwight Culler. Boston: Houghton Mifflin, 1956.

———. *Historical Sketches*. London: Basil Montagu Pickering, 1872.

———. *The Idea of a University*. Notre Dame, IN: University of Notre Dame Press, 1982.

———. "Intellect, the Instrument of Religious Training." In *Sermons on Various Occasions,* 1–14.London: Longmans, Green, 1921.

———. *Rise and Progress of Universities.* With an Introduction and Notes by Mary Katherine Tillman. Notre Dame, IN: University of Notre Dame Press, 2001.

Nicholas of Cusa, *On Learned Ignorance.* Translated by Jasper Hopkins (Minneapolis, MN: A. J. Banning Press, 1990).

Nuesse, Joseph C. *The Catholic University of America: A Centennial History.* Washington, DC: Catholic University of America Press, 1990.

———. "The Sociologist as Teacher." *American Catholic Sociological Review* 5 (1944): 215–20.

O'Brien, David J. *From the Heart of the American Church: Catholic Higher Education and American Culture.* Maryknoll, NY: Orbis, 1994.

Ong, Walter J., S. J. "Yeast: A Parable for Catholic Higher Education." *America* (April 7, 1990):347.

Origen. "Prologue to the Commentary on the Song of Songs."In *Origen.* Translated by Rowan Greer. New York: Paulist Press, 1979.

Paley, William. *Natural Theology.* Oxford: Oxford University Press, 2006.

Pick, John "Editorial: Here and Now," *Renascence: A Critical Journal of Letters,* Vol 1 (1948–1949), 2.

———. "The Renascence in American Catholic Letters."In *The Catholic Renascence in a Disintegrating World.* Edited by Norman Weyand, S.J. (Chicago, IL: Loyola University Press, 1951),

Piderit, John J., S. J., and Melanie M. Morey, eds., *Teaching the Tradition: Catholic Themes in Academic Disciplines* (New York: Oxford University Press, 2012).

Pieper, Joseph. *Leisure: The Basis of Culture.* Indianapolis: Liberty Fund, n. d.

Pinkard, Terry. *Hegel: A Biography.* Cambridge: Cambridge University Press, 2000.

Pius X. *Pascendi Dominici Gregis* (1907). Boston: Pauline Books & Media, n.d.

Pius XI. *Divini Illius Magistri*(1929). Washington, DC: National Catholic Welfare Conference, 1936.

Pius XII. *Humani Generis* (1950). Boston: Pauline Books & Media, n.d.

Polkinghorne, John. *Exploring Reality: The Intertwining of Science and Religion.* New Haven, CT: Yale University Press, 2005.

Preville, Joseph R. "Catholic Colleges, the Courts, and the Constitution: A Tale of Two Cases." *Church History* 58, no. 2 (June 1989): 197–210.

———. "Catholic Colleges and the Supreme Court: The Case of Tilton vs. Richardson." *Journal of Church and State* 30 (Spring 1988): 291–307.

Principe, Walter. "Toward Defining Spirituality." *Sciences Religieuses/Studies in Religion* 12 (Spring 1983): 127–41.

Rahner, Karl. "Christian Humanism," *Theological Investigations,* 23 vols.(New York: Seabury, 1976)

———. *Foundations of Christian Faith: An Introduction to the Idea of Christianity.* Translated by William V. Dych. New York: Seabury Press, 1978.

———. "On the Relationship Between Natural Science and Theology." *Theological Investigations,* vol. 19, 16–23. New York: Crossroads, 1983.

———. "On the Situation of the Catholic Intellectual," *Theological Investigations,* vols. (New York: Herder and Herder, 1971)

————. "Revelation." *Sacramentum Mundi: An Encyclopedia of Theology*, vol. 5, 348–55. New York: Herder and Herder, 1970.

————. "Reflections on the *Foundations of Christian Faith*," *Theology Today* 28, no. 3 (Fall 1980).

————. "Theology as Engaged in an Interdisciplinary Dialogue with the Sciences." In *Theological Investigations*, vol. 13, 80–102. New York: Crossroads, 1983.

Rausch, Thomas P. *Educating for Faith and Justice: Catholic Higher Education Today.* Collegeville, MN: Liturgical Press, 2010.

Redden, John D., and Francis A. Ryan. *A Catholic Philosophy of Education.* Milwaukee, WI: Bruce Publishing, 1955.

Reuben, Julie A. *The Making of the Modern University: Intellectual Transformation and the Marginalization of Morality.* Chicago, IL: University of Chicago Press, 1996.

Roche, Mark W. *The Intellectual Appeal of Catholicism and the Idea of a Catholic University.* Notre Dame, IN: University of Notre Dame Press, 2003.

Roemer v. Maryland Board of Public Works, 426 U.S. 736 (1976).

Rooney, Edward B., S.J., "The Philosophy of Academic Freedom." In *A Philosophical Symposium on American Catholic Education*. Edited by Hunter Guthrie, S.J. and Gerald G. Walsh, S.J.(New York: Fordham University Press, 1941)

Ross, Eva J. "Sociology and the Catholic." *American Catholic Sociological Review* 1 (1940): 6–9.

Ryan, John Julian. *The Idea of a Catholic College.* New York: Sheed & Ward, 1945.

————. *Beyond Humanism: Towards a Philosophy of Catholic Education.* New York: Sheed & Ward, 1950.

Schelling, F. W. J. *On University Studies.* Translated by E. S. Morgan. Edited by Norbert Guterman. Athens: Ohio University Press, 1966.

Schiavone, Christopher F. *Rationality and Revelation in Rahner: The Contemplative Dimension.* New York: Peter Lang, 1994.

Schindler, David L. *Heart of the World, Center of the Church: Communio Ecclesiology, Liberalism, and Liberation.* Grand Rapids, MI: Eerdmans; Edinburgh: T & T Clark, 1996.

————. "Religious Freedom, Truth, and American Liberalism: Another Look at John Courtney Murray," *Communio* 21 (Winter 1994).

Schleiermacher, Friedrich. *Occasional Thoughts on Universities in the German Sense, with an Appendix Regarding a University Soon to Be Established.* Translated by Terrence Tice and Edwina Lawler. San Francisco: Edwin Mellen Press, 1991.

————. *On Religion: Speeches to Its Cultured Despisers.* Translated by Richard Crouter. New York; Cambridge University Press, 1988, 1996.

Schineller, Peter, S.J. *A Handbook of Inculturation.* New York: Paulist Press, 1990.

Scholem, Gershom. *On the Kabbalah and Its Symbolism.* Translated by Ralph Manheim. New York: Schocken Books, 1969.

Schubert, Frank. *A Sociological Study of Secularization Trends in American Catholic Higher Education.* Lewiston, ME: Edwin Mellen, 1990.

Sheen, Fulton J. "Organic Fields of Study." *Catholic Educational Review* 28 (1930): 201–7.

———. "Education for a Catholic Renaissance." *NCEA Bulletin* 26 (1929): 45–54.

Shorter, Aylward. *Towards a Theology of Inculturation.* Maryknoll, NY: Orbis Books, 1994.

Society of Jesus. *Documents of the 31st and 32nd General Congregations of the Society of Jesus.* Edited by John W. Padberg, S. J. Saint Louis, MO: The Institute of Jesuit Sources, 1977.

Sparr, Arnold. *To Promote, Defend, and Redeem: The Catholic Literary Revival and the Cultural Transformation of American Catholicism, 1920–1960.* Westport, CT: Greenwood Press, 1990.

———. *Frank O'Malley: Thinker, Critic, Revivalist* (Notre Dame, IN: University of Notre Dame Press, 1983).

Sr. Mary Louise, S.L., ed., *Over the Bent World* (New York: Sheed and Ward, 1939)

St. Augustine. *City of God.* Translated by Henry Bettenson. London: Penguin, 1972.

———. *Confessions.* Translated by Maria Boulding, O.S.B. New York: Vintage, 1998.

———. *Soliloquies* I: 12. Translated by Kim Paffenroth. Hyde Park, New York: New City Press, 2000.

———. *Teaching Christianity: De Doctrina Christiana.* Translated by Edmund Hill, O. P. Hyde Park, New York: New City Press, 1996.

———. *The Trinity XII: 24.*Translated by Edmund Hill, O. P. Brooklyn, New York: New City Press, 1991.

Teilhard de Chardin, Pierre. *The Phenomenon of Man.* London: Collins, 1955.

Thornton, Francis B. ed., *Return to Tradition: A Directive Anthology.* Milwaukee, WI: Bruce Publishing Company, 1948.

Tillich, Paul. *History of Christian Thought: From Its Judaic Origins to Existentialism.* New York: Simon and Schuster, 1967.

———. *Systematic Theology.* Vol. 1. Chicago, IL: University of Chicago Press, 1951.

Tilton v. Richardson, 403 U.S. 672 (1971).

Torrell, Jean-Pierre, O.P. *Spiritual Master.* Vol. 2 of *St. Thomas Aquinas.* Translated by Robert Royal. Washington, DC: Catholic University of America Press, 2003.

Turner, James. *Language, Religion, Knowledge.* Notre Dame, IN: University of Notre Dame Press, 2003.

Roberts,John H., and Turner,James.. *The Sacred & the Secular University.* Princeton, NJ: Princeton University Press, 2000.

Varga, Nicholas. *Baltimore's Loyola, Loyola's Baltimore, 1851–1986.* Baltimore, MD: Maryland Historical Society, 1990.

Waaijman, Kees. *Spirituality: Forms, Foundations, Methods.* Leuven: Peeters, 2002.

Ward, Leo R. *Blueprint for a Catholic University.* St. Louis, MO: B. Herder, 1949.

Ware, Kallistos. "Scholasticism and Orthodoxy: Theological Method as a Factor in the Schism," *Eastern Churches Review* 5 (1973): 23.

White, Alan. *Schelling: An Introduction to the System of Freedom*. New Haven, CT: Yale University Press, 1983.

Williams, Paul L., ed. *Catholic Higher Education: Proceedings of the Eleventh Convention of the Fellowship of Catholic Scholars*. Pittston, PA: Northeast Books, 1989.

Whitehead, A. N. *Science and the Modern World*. New York: Free Press, 1967.

Worgul, George S. Jr. *Issues in Academic Freedom*. Pittsburgh, PA: Duquesne University Press, 1992.

Young, Pamela C., C. S. J. "Theological Education in American Catholic Higher Education, 1939–1973." Ph.D. diss., Marquette University, May 1995.

Index